Educational Research and Innov

MW01016733

Teachers as Designers of Learning Environments

THE IMPORTANCE OF INNOVATIVE PEDAGOGIES

Alejandro Paniagua and David Istance

OECD

BETTER POLICIES FOR BETTER LIVES

This work is published under the responsibility of the Secretary-General of the OECD. The opinions expressed and arguments employed herein do not necessarily reflect the official views of OECD member countries.

This document, as well as any data and any map included herein, are without prejudice to the status of or sovereignty over any territory, to the delimitation of international frontiers and boundaries and to the name of any territory, city or area.

Please cite this publication as:
Paniagua, A. and D. Istance (2018), *Teachers as Designers of Learning Environments: The Importance of Innovative Pedagogies*, Educational Research and Innovation, OECD Publishing, Paris
http://dx.doi.org/10.1787/9789264085374-en

ISBN 978-92-64-08536-7 (print)
ISBN 978-92-64-08537-4 (PDF)

Series: Educational Research and Innovation
ISSN 2076-9660 (print)
ISSN 2076-9679 (online)

The statistical data for Israel are supplied by and under the responsibility of the relevant Israeli authorities. The use of such data by the OECD is without prejudice to the status of the Golan Heights, East Jerusalem and Israeli settlements in the West Bank under the terms of international law.

Photo credits: Cover © Marish/Shutterstock.com.

Foreword

There is growing recognition of the importance of pedagogy in school reform around the world. This is a consequence of the increasing ambition of educational aims and a more expansive view of what young people can achieve. The shift in focus towards learner-centred pedagogies reflects a more inclusive view about who can learn and how, intended to allow everyone to do so to a high level. The strong contemporary focus on competences requires a corresponding strong focus on pedagogy.

There is also growing recognition that for mainstream education to develop the knowledge and skills needed in the 21st century, innovation is needed. The common policy variables of structures, regulation and institutional arrangements, and resourcing are relatively far removed from the classroom where learning gains are achieved. Because pedagogical relations play out at the micro level through the interactions of learners and educators in multiple settings and episodes – which are hard to capture in a single system let alone across many - this has proved to be an elusive area for international exchange and analysis.

Earlier OECD/Centre for Educational Research and Innovation (CERI) work on Innovative Learning Environments developed a framework that placed the "pedagogical core" and seven key learning principles at the heart of innovative, powerful learning environments. This new volume extends this analysis with a systematic examination of the different pedagogies themselves.

Teachers as Designers of Learning Environments explores new approaches to teaching and learning and provides original frameworks and concepts to better understand the conditions through which innovative pedagogies can be developed and scaled. It also brings together examples and experiences from networks of schools from diverse parts of the world. In doing so, it seeks to foster a community of innovators, researchers, and policy-shapers and influence the wider discourse, in systems and the educational work of OECD and return the attention to the heart of modern teaching and learning: innovative pedagogies.

Andreas Schleicher
Director for Education and Skills
Special Advisor on Education Policy to the Secretary-General

Acknowledgements

First and foremost we would like to thank the Jaume Bofill Foundation in Barcelona, in particular Ismael Palacin and Valtencir Mendes, for their continued generous support. The foundation hosted a small expert meeting and a larger seminar in Barcelona in April 2016, and additionally financed two Catalan experts - Marc Lafuente and Alejandro Paniagua - to join the OECD Secretariat as secondees. They have made an invaluable contribution to the research, analysis and the operational side of the work.

We want warmly to thank the expert authors who contributed analyses on different aspects of pedagogy and innovation for this project, published in full in an OECD Education Working Paper, Peterson, A. et al. (2018), and in abridged form in Chapter 3. These are: Hanna Dumont, Marc Lafuente, Nancy Law, and Amelia Peterson. They additionally generously participated in expert meetings and provided feedback on earlier drafts of this report.

They were joined by other expert colleagues to whom we also wish to extend our sincere gratitude: Gaëlle Chapelle, Philippa Cordingley, Jelmer Evers, Valerie Hannon, Anthony Mackay, Valtencir Mendes, Mariana Martinez-Salgado, Monica Nadal, Mike Sharples, and Anne Sliwka. Others have responded to the ideas and analysis presented in this volume at various events around the world over the past couple of years; we want to take this occasion to extend a collective thanks to them.

We would like to acknowledge the key role played by the networks featured in this report (for a full listing, see Chapter 11). They gave generously of their time and expertise in responding to our initial inquiries, then in completing a detailed questionnaire and in reviewing initial draft texts of the chapters analysing their responses. We also thank the schools and practitioners involved in the networks who generously provided their own time and insights in completing the questionnaire.

Marc Lafuente completed initial analyses, reflected in this volume, after his year with the OECD came to end. Alejandro Paniagua has taken a major role in the design, drafting and editing of this volume. After his retirement from the OECD Secretariat mid-2017, David Istance continued to work in on this volume, sharing the drafting and editing. Since mid-2017, this publication also benefited from the guidance and expertise of Tracey Burns, who contributed with the drafting, editing and preparation for the publication.

We wish to thank our colleagues in the Centre for Educational Research and Innovation (CERI) and the EDU Directorate working on related projects for their inputs and advice. Dirk Van Damme and Deborah Roseveare provided oversight, direction and valuable advice during the process. We also wish to thank Matthew Gill, who made an enormous contribution to both editing and the preparation of the publication, and EDU Communications colleagues and the PAC team, especially Rachel Linden and Anne-Lise Prigent, for their helpful editorial advice.

We are grateful for the encouragement and support of the CERI Governing Board in the development of the project and this volume.

Table of contents

Tables

Figures

Boxes

Executive Summary

Pedagogy is at the heart of teaching and learning. Preparing young people to become lifelong learners with a deep knowledge of subject matter and a broad set of social skills requires understanding how pedagogy influences learning. Doing so shifts the perception of teachers from technicians who strive to attain the education goals set by the curriculum to experts in the art and science of teaching. Seen through this lens, innovation in teaching becomes a problem-solving process rooted in teachers' professionalism, a normal response to addressing the daily changes of constantly changing classrooms.

Teachers as Designers of Learning Environments: The Importance of Innovative Pedagogies sets the stage for educators and policy-makers to innovate teaching by looking at what is currently taking place in schools as potential seeds for change. At the heart of these approaches is a sensitivity to the natural inclinations of learners towards play, creativity, collaboration and inquiry. Examples from 27 national and international networks of schools are used to illustrate how teachers use these innovative practices.

The importance of innovative pedagogies

Pedagogy is a complex concept. A better understanding of innovative pedagogies is required in order to address contemporary educational challenges and improve teachers' professional competences. The first part of this volume sets out the three types of dynamic interactions that are related to pedagogy: between knowledge and practice, research sciences and creative implementations, and educational theories and particular practices.

Understanding how and when innovative pedagogies work requires critical reflection on the purpose and combinations of pedagogies and the potentials of adaptive teaching. The influence of content areas and the context of 'new learners' in teaching, and how to frame system-based pedagogical change are also crucial. These are the main components of an organising conceptual framework, the C's framework, which underpins the analysis of the volume.

Clusters of innovative pedagogical approaches

Setting out a pedagogical continuum allows for the identification of six clusters of innovative pedagogies: Blended Learning, Computational Thinking, Experiential Learning, Embodied Learning, Multiliteracies and Discussion Based Teaching, and Gamification. These clusters are created to streamline and group together the hundreds of innovative approaches and promising new practices that currently populate the innovation landscape. Each individual cluster is underpinned by different learning theories and pedagogical approaches.

The second part of this volume explores how to implement these innovations effectively. It offers key elements and challenges that schools and teachers need to address, as well as insights about how to attune these new implementations in relation to particular learners and content domains.

Networks of innovative schools

Networks of innovative schools are an important lever of change, critical for understanding and scaling discrete classroom level innovations. The third part of this volume summarises the work and approaches of 27 national and international networks of innovative schools. The networks featured are diverse and multi-faceted, with some focusing more on the implementation of similar innovations defined by common pedagogical principles, while others work as laboratories for sharing different innovative practices or as a platform to provide professional development to teachers.

This diversity is reflected in the main approaches to teaching and learning reported by the networks, schools and practitioners. Despite this diversity, one key element shared by all networks is their deep engagement with pedagogy and its innovation, and particularly, their endorsement of the OECD Principles of Learning. Another key finding is the role of networks in providing continuous professional development and other forms of teacher support as a way to successfully implement innovative pedagogies.

The main challenge in the analysis of these networks is to understand the impact of the various pedagogical approaches. Improving the measurement of holistic approaches and complex skills is a key area to address in scaling innovative pedagogies.

Key messages

Teachers as Designers of Learning Environments: The Importance of Innovative Pedagogies sets out a series of key messages for research and policy:

- *Innovative pedagogies are a fundamental part of teacher professionalism.* Innovation in teaching is a problem-solving process rooted in teachers' professionalism, rather than an add-on applied by only some teachers in some schools.
- *Mapping the content of innovation is key to advancing a new framework for teaching.* The clusters of pedagogies offer a roadmap that can help teachers and policy-makers navigate the innovation landscape, and a first step to building an international framework for pedagogies.
- *Innovative pedagogies should build on the natural learning inclinations of students.* A key lever for improving the preparation of 21st century skills and the engagement of learners lies in the ability of pedagogies to match the natural inclinations of learners towards play, creativity, collaboration and inquiry.
- *Achieving student-centred focus requires deliberate planning.* In focusing on the role of teachers as creative professionals, the report calls for a highly deliberate form of teaching that promotes student centeredness and active participation.
- *School networks are a crucial source of support for teachers.* Teachers in school networks are continuously in contact with a large community of practice and other resources that are essential support for their professional development.
- *Innovative pedagogies must align with teacher experience and skills.* Innovation in teaching should be understood as a process in which teachers reflect on their own practices, to better align their personal capacities with innovative pedagogies.

- *Domains must be more connected to allow for teaching innovation.* Teachers need to become aware of the way domains organise their teaching and how these domains can be better connected to make innovations more effective.
- *New assessment frameworks are necessary and required to understand and spread innovative pedagogies.* New ways of measuring outcomes that are broad enough to capture 21st century skills and other non-academic outcomes are an imperative for identifying how innovative pedagogies work, and under which conditions.

Part I. The importance of innovative pedagogies

Chapter 1. The importance of innovating pedagogy: Overview and key messages

This chapter sets the stage for this report in arguing the importance of pedagogy for educational policy. It starts by locating the role of pedagogy in the current policy discourse and discusses the need to improve the understanding of innovative pedagogies in order to better address contemporary educational challenges. It then describes the three main strands of this report. First, it introduces the conceptual architecture, the C's framework, which underpins the analysis throughout the volume. Second, it sets out six clusters of innovative pedagogies which are: blended learning, computational thinking, experiential learning, embodied learning, multiliteracies and discussion-based teaching, and gamification. Third, it describes the role of networks of innovative schools in promoting and scaling innovative pedagogies. The chapter ends with a summary of key messages arising from the outputs of these three main strands of work.

1.1. Why pedagogy matters

Pedagogy is at the core of teaching and learning. Indeed many other education policies will only lead to better learning outcomes if they lead to changes in teaching and learning practices through different channels.

Pedagogies are specific configurations of teaching and learning in interaction. They combine theory and practice, ways of thinking and implementing learning designs. There are many different pedagogical approaches in use across education systems today. A clearer understanding of what different pedagogical approaches involve and how teachers can apply them is a key priority for policy-makers wanting to achieve better learning outcomes for all students.

Pedagogy has also become more complex as the aims of education systems have become more ambitious about what young people can achieve. The shift towards learner-centred pedagogies is part of a larger change towards expecting higher levels of educational attainment, in stark contrast to systems a century ago. Countries also now aim to prepare all their young people to become lifelong learners with a deep understanding and a broad set of social skills.

The strong focus on learners acquiring a diverse set of competences requires a correspondingly strong focus on pedagogy. Curriculum policy strategies in many countries now include explicit recognition of what are often called 21st century skills. Yet acquiring competences such as collaboration, persistence, creativity, and innovation depends fundamentally on the modelling of the teaching and learning itself i.e. pedagogy. If the 21st century competences are to be systematically developed, rather than being left to emerge by accident, then pedagogy must be deliberately designed to foster these competences. Innovative pedagogies can play an important role in this.

Learner-centred pedagogies, such as inquiry-based learning or collaborative learning, are particularly suitable in giving the learner an active role and promoting the application of key skills and attitudes. Assessment of such competences demands the use of complex and authentic tasks rather than being excessively focused on discrete knowledge. Teacher modelling, demonstrations and the presentation of information remain highly relevant but framed with the ultimate objective of promoting students' performance and their active role in solving tasks.

New pedagogical approaches are also needed to keep education relevant and engage young people. Moreover, the knowledge and skills being developed need to change in tune with the world of the 21st century, and they need to be taught and learnt deeply so that they can be adapted by young people in rapidly-changing circumstances. This is critical to engaging in and sustaining innovation.

Importantly, it must be understood that emphasising competences does not come at the expense of content knowledge and a deep grasp of substance. Instead, the demanding policy reality is that both 21st century competencies and a deep understanding of content knowledge are needed. Hence, effective pedagogy requires teachers to have expert professional repertoires to support the simultaneous pursuit of the deep learning of content and of ambitious transversal competences that need to be practised to be acquired.

1.2. Pedagogy and teacher professionalism

Pedagogical accomplishment and expertise are at the core of teacher professionalism. A strong focus on pedagogy is needed in order to understand and promote teacher professional competences. However, pedagogy also presents formidable analytical problems to grasp given the sheer number and the dynamism of the relationships involved; there are no widely agreed definitions; and because pedagogy encapsulates a complex interaction of knowledge and practice. Teaching is an art as well as a science. Even teachers often find it difficult to talk about their teaching, compared with discussing the curriculum, learning, or classroom management. Professional expertise is both about the practical complex art of teaching and the design of learning environments to get the most from the teaching and pedagogy.

Pedagogical expertise is exercised through good classroom management, ensuring a supportive climate, and assessment. "Classroom management" is how teachers keep students organised, attentive and focused; "supportive climate" refers to the student-teacher relationship and is high when teachers give positive and constructive feedback; "cognitive activation" means teaching that fosters student cognitive engagement with the subject matter. Expert teachers consistently achieve these tasks. Different pedagogies have developed different ways of balancing these three tasks, and to achieve these three components, expert teachers draw on a combination of pedagogical approaches.

Pedagogy also needs to be combined with expertise in the design of learning environments to get the most out of it. To understand the teaching profession as one in which professionals are steeped in teaching and learning requires the focus on pedagogy, where they connect scientific theories to their daily experiences and particular contexts. The view of teachers is evolving from technicians who implement the educational ideas and procedures of the curriculum to teachers as designers of learning environments and as experts in the art and science of teaching. Making the core pedagogical knowledge that defines teacher professionalism more visible should enhance teachers' status rather than diminish it.

Teacher professionalism depends on collaborative learning, design and networking and is not reducible to a set of individual traits. Concepts of professionalism are often highly individualistic and assumed to reside in the knowledge and capabilities of individual teachers. In fact, this report shows that professionalism depends on collaborative learning and design, and active networking. It is precisely through the idea of teachers as designers of learning that innovation at the level of practice can be seen as a normal side of the teaching profession to solve the daily challenges in a context which is in constant change.

Bringing pedagogy to the fore is to recognise the professional expertise of educators and to bring such expertise into the public policy arena rather than left guarded behind the classroom door.

1.3. Key elements of effective pedagogies: The five C's framework

The "Cs" framework (Figure 1.1) has been developed to provide a powerful set of lenses through which educators, leaders and policy-makers may address the wide range of issues raised by pedagogical development and choices. The framework incorporates a particular philosophy and precepts for action that are holistic, and works as an alternative to the fragmented and disaggregated research and policy perspectives that often prevail in addressing pedagogy.

Figure 1.1. The five C's Framework

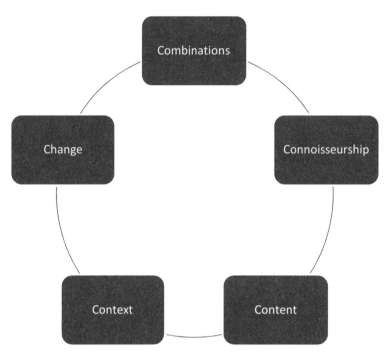

Research on the general principles of good teaching has shown that effectiveness is not determined primarily by the "surface level" of specific teaching methods or ways of organising classrooms, but rather by the "deep level" of instruction, i.e. the quality of interactions between teachers and students around meaningful content. Instead of analysing the effectiveness of specific teaching methods, there is need to further identify and study the underlying principles at work within and across classrooms. The following section goes through each of the Cs in turn.

1.3.1. Combinations (of pedagogies)

A single teacher, let alone teams of educators, never uses one pedagogical method exclusively. A pedagogical approach is made up of several specific methods combined in systematic ways. Pedagogies need to be understood holistically rather than broken down into unconnected practices and techniques - hence the focus on combinations, clusters of pedagogical approaches and networks. Looking beyond the effectiveness of specific teaching methods, there is need to understand the power of these when combined (and done expertly – see connoisseurship below).

Two layers are involved, one about combining discrete practices within a framing pedagogical approach, and one about how combinations of established approaches can meet long-term educational goals; in both cases, a central question is one of balance.

Effective schools and networks often anchor their learning design and teaching within a restricted set of approaches and pedagogies in combination. A school with an overarching pedagogical design has made a collective decision about how to combine several pedagogies to meet multiple educational goals. By doing this the power of each pedagogy is strengthened considerably: individual teacher planning is reinforced at the organisational level as is teacher collaboration, while students more readily transfer the learning approaches developed in one year or subject area to another. Such coherence of pedagogical approach is more the exception than the rule.

1.3.2. Connoisseurship (of expert teachers and learning communities)

The concept of "connoisseurship" captures the idea of expert application of pedagogies. If particular pedagogies are inappropriately applied, it will not be surprising that they have only limited impact on outcomes (assuming such outcomes can be measured). They may be done well or badly, even when well-chosen for the educational challenge in question.

The effectiveness of different pedagogies depends on what they are trying to achieve, their appropriateness for the learners, and whether they are well implemented. Complex, including innovatory, pedagogical designs need expert teachers and teaching strategies – that is, connoisseurship.

This means deep expertise and understanding, not the routine application of techniques. When the pedagogies discussed in this report are applied without such expertise, there is often neglect of teaching and learning content and low levels of student interaction, with teachers more concerned with the logistics of organising the learning activities and classrooms.

As described above, the effectiveness of teaching is less a reflection of the "surface level" of specific teaching methods or classroom organisation, and more the "deep level" quality teacher/student interactions around meaningful content. This means deep level teacher connoisseurship, expertise and understanding, not the routine application of techniques.

An example where connoisseurship matters is the 'flipped classroom' approach. When integrating technology in lesson planning and development, technological pedagogical and content knowledge (TPACK) is required, but so too is expert lesson planning and timing in order to deliver the lesson. Effective teachers in flipped classrooms also need the expertise to organise and orchestrate discussion and collaborative work and to create the procedures for managing the dynamics of work done at home and in the classroom.

1.3.3. Content (inherent in all teaching and learning)

Content is crucial to all teaching and learning. Students and teachers do not learn and teach in a vacuum – they learn and teach something! There is no trade-off to be made between learning knowledge and applying processes of learning, metacognition and the like because both are fundamental. However, particular pedagogies may be more appropriate than others for particular types of knowledge and competence areas. Hence, the report also explores questions about pedagogies for particular subjects or competence sets. Questions about what is worth learning and how best to teach it often lies at the heart of approaches termed "innovative".

However, seeking excellence across the board - knowledge acquisition and deep understanding, general competences and positive attitudes - brings considerable pedagogical challenge. Innovative approaches are inherently nested to content and may even be based on new content such as robotics, dance, design, or computation. Knowledge domains can strongly influence teachers and teaching, even when the aim is to develop transversal knowledge and competences.

While guided by general principles, innovations in specific subjects may identify their own pedagogical interpretations, combinations, and specific methods. For example, in *mathematics*, innovation needs to increase student engagement and learning outcomes, pointing towards pedagogies using more open, complex and authentic tasks, such as problem-based, project-based, and inquiry-based learning. In *non-native language learning*, pedagogy should provide both input to the learner and the opportunity to create output, including through task-based and project-based learning, and connecting teaching to other contexts within the school, district or wider world. In the *socio-emotional domain,* pedagogies include active and performance-based approaches that engage students' personal feelings and their relationships through role-playing, collaborative-based pedagogies, gaming, case study work, and social problem-solving.

1.3.4. (The reach of) context

Context influences pedagogical appropriateness and effectiveness, but context also shapes who is learning and what is relevant to the students. Obvious though it may seem, some of the most important contextual factors are represented by *schools and education systems themselves*. An important dimension of school context is the organisational routines or patterns of collective behaviour. When directed at changing pedagogy, such as through teacher peer observation and sharing practice, such organisational routines positively impact on teacher learning and outcomes.

Social and cultural backgrounds are key contextual factors and pedagogical choices and expertise are critical for addressing equity. Educators must have sophisticated pedagogical repertoires in addressing diversity and the expertise to deploy pedagogies differently within the same class. The research reviewed in this report suggests that those with lower abilities and less cultural capital need more scaffolding and teaching support than higher achievers. Innovative pedagogy is thus not about the removal of scaffolding in favour of discovery, as it is sometimes portrayed. In fact, such removal is often counter-productive for the very students it seeks to favour.

The digital environment is a further key contextual factor. A popular assumption that young learners are "tech-savvy" in all contexts can result in omitting digital literacy from the curriculum, and/or leaving students to work with technology on their own ("because they already know how to use it"). However, using technology well for pedagogical purposes is no easy task. ICT itself does not enhance learning nor does the sophistication of the technology applied. One of the pitfalls of ICT integration is when teachers adopt traditional pedagogical strategies. Another risk is that teachers become more concerned about how they use ICT, than about the benefits of technology for their students.

1.3.5. Making change happen

Teacher learning – collaborative, action-oriented, and co-designed - is fundamental to change. It is underpinned by the same learning principles that determine effective student learning - collaborative, inquiry-focused, and addressing authentic professional problems. Pedagogical innovations require deep changes in teachers' practices and roles in which they are co-designers. Innovations in teaching and learning are not so much assimilated as adopted progressively and creatively by teachers who know how to use their own experiences as "anchors" for implementation and innovation.

Training models focusing on imparting knowledge and skills are generally not effective in bringing about change in pedagogical practice, as compared with providing experiential, iterative, action-oriented learning with teachers collaborating in well-targeted communities of practice. Networks are critical in this process, emphasising the transformation of culture and practice. They emphasise trust and partnerships with families, employers and the wider community in support of change and in this underline the need for a strong focus on implementation, and maintaining focus with all on board.

Successful change can be understood as a process of learning, with change at one level being promoted by the alignment and mutual reinforcement of the other levels. Scale matters and stakeholders at different levels need to be engaged in a process of learning for the innovation to be scaled. Scalable adaptations have often evolved from the original model inspiration and may well not be high-fidelity replications.

1.4. Identifying clusters of pedagogical approaches

For both policy and practice, it is useful to consider pedagogy in the space that lies between broad principles and specific teaching methods and practices. Pedagogical approaches populate the middle ground on this spectrum. They are more practically-oriented than the theoretical models at one end of the spectrum, while yielding insights that are more easily generalised than the discrete practices that lie at the other end of the spectrum.

Six broad clusters of pedagogical approaches were developed for this volume through literature searches and consultations with diverse experts. They are: blended learning, gamification, computational thinking, experiential learning, embodied learning, and multiliteracies and discussion-based teaching.

These clusters are not stand-alone approaches, since these pedagogies share key features. They are all strongly focused on learner engagement and collaboration; they foster critical thinking and are grounded in what is relevant to learners; and they all can exploit the potential of digital technologies. The clusters can be organised and combined in different ways to enhance their effectiveness and to create unique approaches to teaching and learning. Combining the approaches means moving beyond the fragmented focus on specific pedagogical innovations to highlight the importance of the creative work of teachers and schools when adjusting, adapting, mixing and updating the clusters of innovative pedagogies. These commonalities notwithstanding, each of the pedagogical clusters identifies a distinct focus:

- The organisation of the teaching and learning, in and out-of-school (blended).
- The relevance of play (games).
- The individual as cognitive problem-solver (computational).
- The wider environment and ways to experience and study it (experiential).
- The whole individual, including the social, emotional, artistic and physical (embodied).
- The diverse and contested nature of literacy (multiliteracies).

Blended learning rethinks established routines to get more from teaching. This pedagogical approach blends student work and teaching for understanding, adapts their sequencing and draws heavily on digital learning resources. The aim is to be both more engaging and coherent for learners and to free teachers from routine practice in favour of interactive and intensive classroom activities. There are three main forms within this cluster of pedagogies:

- *The inverted/flipped classroom*, in which students work on material first and only then access the teacher(s) to practice, clarify and deepen understanding.

- *The lab-based model* in which a group of students rotates between a school lab and the classroom with the application of content through face-to-face interactions with teachers.
- '*In-Class*' blending, in which individual students follow a customised schedule rotating between online and face-to-face instruction.

To be successful, blended learning requires profound re-thinking of teacher and student roles and the willingness to adapt teaching, requiring innovation and professional engagement. When it relies on digital resources, it assumes teachers have the skill to operate technologies and an understanding of content, technology, and pedagogy in interaction. Blended learning can also be demanding of pedagogical (including digital) infrastructure and software design.

Gamification builds on how games can capture student interest and facilitate learning. Play occupies an important place in children's learning, and supports intellectual, emotional and social well-being. It opens up potential learning experiences, driven by self-motivation and interest. Gaming in education takes different forms (e.g. gamification, game-based learning, serious games), but in this report "gamification" encompasses the pedagogical core of gaming and the benefits of playful environments for engagement and well-being.

There are two main pedagogical components: mechanical elements (rapid feedback, badges and goals, participation, and progressive challenge) and emotional elements (narratives and identities, collaboration and competition).

Gamification has been used successfully in a range of subjects, such as science, maths, languages, physical education, history, and art and design. Gamification can foster self-regulated learning, collaboration, exploration and creativity. It can also teach complex rules to players, introduce them to unfamiliar worlds, and engage them in unfamiliar tasks and logics. How to exploit the pedagogic structure of games while maintaining the element of play is a key challenge.

Computational thinking develops problem-solving through computer science. This looks at problems in ways that computers do and then uses them to solve those problems. Its techniques include approximate solutions, parallel processing, model checking, debugging, and search strategies. Its basic elements are:

- *Logical reasoning*: analyse and deduce outcomes.
- *Decomposition*: break down a complex problem into smaller ones.
- *Algorithms*: describe routines and create step-by-step instructions.
- *Abstraction*: capture the essence of a problem, removing unnecessary detail.
- *Patterns*: identify common solutions to common problems.

Instead of emphasising the improvement of generic ICT skills, computational thinking takes programming and coding as a new form of literacy and as a new approach to ICTs. With computers and computer science providing interfaces between student experiences of the world and their abstract knowledge and skills, computational thinking becomes a comprehensive scientific approach and 21st century competences. It brings together a language (coding), process (problem-solving), tools (programs), and uses experimentation and learning-by-doing to produce discrete outputs. Inquiry skills are developed through logical reasoning, algorithm framing and decomposition, while programming and coding foster writing abilities.

Experiential learning takes place through active experience, inquiry and reflection. This approach mixes content and process; reduces guidance; promotes engagement; enables connections to be made between learning and the wider environment; and generates insights from experience.

Its four main components are:

- *Concrete experience* of a task potentially disruptive of students' existing understanding.
- *Reflective observation,* moving between hypotheses and values, and addressing conflicting ideas.
- *Abstract conceptualisation,* making sense of experiences and reflections and building abstract ideas.
- *Active experimentation,* putting learning into action in a way relevant to the student.

Well-known innovative pedagogical approaches in this cluster include inquiry-based learning and service-learning. It also includes more recent approaches such as education for sustainable development and outdoor learning. Guidance and scaffolding play pivotal roles. Decisions need to be made about which areas can best use experiential learning and to identify potential activities that fit course objectives. Experiential learning thus needs to build platforms for active learning experiences and explicitly encourage reflection.

Embodied learning connects the physical, artistic, emotional and social. This entails a significant shift in many education systems that have traditionally favoured abstract thinking, the individual and passive content acquisition. Embodied pedagogies develop and exploit two natural dispositions in the young - creativity and expression – and consciously use creative experiences and active student involvement to promote knowledge acquisition. Three main approaches are discussed in this report:

- *School-based physical culture*: focusing on the role of physical education as an encompassing resource to enhance personal qualities and thinking skills.
- *Arts-integrated learning:* promoting student engagement through connecting arts with other subjects.
- *Maker culture:* tinkering and the construction of tools and artefacts.

Embodied learning is particularly suited to develop curiosity, sensitivity, multiple perspective-taking, risk-taking, and metaphorical thinking, and other metacognitive and executive skills fostering learner achievement. It develops socio-emotional skills and other fundamental interdisciplinary content e.g. gender issues, diversity. It is therefore highly relevant to 21st century competences.

Multiliteracies and discussion-based teaching aims at developing cultural distance and critical capacities and refers to a range of practices and principles rather than a single pedagogical approach. Literacy lies at the heart of student learning and critical literacies situate knowledge in its political, cultural and authorial context, deconstructing narratives through interchange and collaboration. While class discussion is valuable no matter what the pedagogical approach, it becomes central in the questioning of received ideas and dislocating the centrality of any dominant language. The four main principles of this pedagogical cluster are:

- *Situated practice* uses students' life experiences to create meaningful classroom activities within a community of learners.

- *Active teacher interventions* scaffolds learning through collaborations between teachers and learners in complex tasks.
- *Critical framing* encourages constructive critique and distance from what has been learnt, so that students can apply and extend it.
- *Transformed practice* encourages students to extend their learning to other situations and cultural contexts.

This pedagogical approach work best when teachers know about the lives and interests of the students, their communities, and the wider historical forces impacting on them. Teachers must ensure proper scaffolding to let learners reflect during complex tasks, and they also need to learn about power issues, and be skilled in discussion techniques.

1.5. The role of networks in promoting innovative pedagogies

Networks play a key role in the development of coherent pedagogical approaches, support materials, professional sharing and learning and leadership. The focus on networks in developing innovative pedagogies for powerful learning built on the insights of recent OECD/CERI analyses of innovative learning environments that identified the "meso-level" as critical for understanding and scaling innovations (OECD, 2013; 2015).

This report illustrates a rich diversity of ways in which networks promote innovation, organised around three distinct forms: "Pedagogical Approach Networks", "Innovation Promotion Networks", and "Professional Learning Networks". Each are presented in this report focusing, respectively, on the promotion of particular pedagogical approaches, platforms for innovation exchange (including pedagogical innovation), and networks for professional learning.

Professional learning is given central importance by the networks and is the core mission and activity of many of them. Some of the learning is school-based within the single institution, but much is clustered in the network or organised at a higher level. The professional learning is often for building capacity and expertise in the approaches being promoted. The networks provide learning leadership within systems, organising events and forums for shared professional work.

The networks studied recognise as important all the OECD Seven Principles of Learning (see Box 1.1), while giving special priority to enhancing student engagement and the social nature of learning. Formative assessment features prominently and many are seeking learning that extends beyond the measures that are conventionally covered by summative assessments and certification.

Box 1.1. The OECD Seven Principles of Learning

1. Make learning central, and encourage engagement and awareness in students of their own learning strategies.
2. Ensure that learning is social and often collaborative.
3. Be highly attuned to motivations and the emotions involved in learning.
4. Be acutely sensitive to individual differences, including in prior knowledge.
5. Be demanding for each learner but without excessive overload.
6. Use assessments consistent with the main goals for learning, with a strong emphasis on formative feedback.
7. Promote horizontal connection across learning activities, across subjects, and across in- and out-of-school learning.

Source: Dumont, H., D. Istance and F. Benavides (eds.) (2010), *The Nature of Learning: Using Research to Inspire Practice*, OECD Publishing, Paris, http://dx.doi.org/10.1787/9789264086487-en.

1.6. Reshaping the policy discourse: Key messages

This report, while emerging out of a research project, can provide important information to help shape policy development and enrich its discourse. Its value lies in both identifying helpful ways of framing discourse and offering new frameworks to underpin more constructive and effective discourse.

The following section sets out the key messages of this volume. They emerge from the analysis of the conceptualisation and framework of pedagogy, the selection and analysis of the compilation of clusters of innovative pedagogies and the work carried out with networks of innovative schools.

1.6.1. The importance of innovative pedagogies for teacher professionalism

The focus on pedagogies is critical to understanding the teaching profession as one in which professionals think about teaching and learning by connecting scientific theories to their daily experiences and particular contexts. This shifts the view of teachers from technicians who implement the educational ideas and procedures of the curriculum to professionals who approach teaching as a process that deals with substance and judgement. This in turn promotes the view of teachers as designers of learning environments.

Using this lens, innovation at the level of practice is thus a normal response to addressing the daily challenges of the constantly changing classroom. Innovation thus becomes a problem-solving process rooted in teachers' professionalism, rather than an add-on applied by only some teachers in some schools.

1.6.2. Mapping the content of innovation is key to advancing a new framework for teaching

The clusters of pedagogies offer a roadmap that can help teachers and policy-makers navigate the innovation landscape, currently populated by hundreds of innovative approaches and promising new practices. It is also a first step to building a necessary international framework for pedagogies, understood as developing a broad international consensus across the teaching profession.

This framework takes as a starting point the argument that teachers are high-level professionals whose professionalism revolves around collaborative pedagogical expertise. It is common in policy discourse to advocate "autonomy" and "collaborative professionalism" while leaving undefined what this means or how the autonomy or collaboration will actually improve outcomes. In offering a clear set of pedagogical approaches, this report offers teachers an effective baseline from which to innovate autonomously. It also provides a framework and a language to inform collective decisions about the innovation of their practices.

1.6.3. Innovative pedagogies should build on the natural learning inclinations of students

A key lever for improving the teaching of 21st century skills and the engagement of learners lies in the ability of pedagogies to match the natural inclinations of learners to play, create, express, collaborate and discover. All the innovative approaches identified and described in this report exploit one or more of these learning inclinations.

Further, these natural learning inclinations go hand in hand with the promotion of scientific methods, creativity and cooperation. A promising way to promote innovative pedagogies for teachers is to address current contemporary challenges within the classroom (e.g. social media or environmental risks). This can potentially allow these learning inclinations to flourish.

1.6.4. Achieving student-centred focus requires deliberate planning

Recognising the key role of pedagogy is not about policy dictating the best teaching methods. Rather, it is a matter of widening the skills of teachers to promote more interactive, horizontal and caring relationships with students. In focusing on the role of teachers as creative professionals, the report calls for teaching that retains a deliberate form of lesson planning promoting student centeredness and active participation.

1.6.5. School networks are a vital source of teacher support

The process of pedagogical innovation entails a process of learning for teachers. They need to be provided with an appropriate system of scaffolding to address several challenges -insecurity, wrong assumptions about innovation, or the weight of professional routines, among others- that hinders their capacity to innovate. Teachers in school networks are continuously in contact with a large community of practice and structures that support their professional development.

Strategic partnerships with universities and rigorous continuous professional development programmes provide teachers with opportunities to learn and reflect with their colleagues, and also to coordinate and improve their innovative practices.

1.6.6. Innovative pedagogies must align with teacher experience and skills

Innovation in teaching should be understood as a process in which teachers engage in creative and deep reflection, rather than as the simple application of techniques. Pedagogical approaches should be integrated progressively as teachers review their own practices, in order to identify and better align their creative, intuitive and personal capacities with innovative pedagogies. Some teachers might incorporate the principles of embodied learning more naturally, for example. Others may feel more confident with arts, design, or gamification as a result of having positive personal experiences.

All teaching designs are based on multiple skills, practices and different relationships of teaching and learning, and often already contain some of the elements that characterise innovative approaches. Alignment is thus key to the re-arrangement of existing practices which accommodate the innovative features described in this report.

1.6.7. Domains must be further connected to allow for teaching innovation

Pedagogies are influenced by content areas, which in turn are permeated by beliefs and 'teaching traditions' that impose a particular view of pedagogies in each domain. Innovative pedagogies may seek to foster new content and skills that are inherently cross-cutting and therefore it is necessary to find a pedagogical space that is not subject specific. In order for this to work, teachers and schools must become aware of the way domains organise their teaching designs and how these domains can be better connected and combined to make innovations more effective.

1.6.8. **New assessment frameworks are necessary to understand and spread innovative pedagogies**

Systems need to continue identifying innovative practices and teachers and school leaders need a better understanding of their effectiveness and impact. New assessment frameworks based on new technologies and non-traditional psychometric models are needed that are broad enough to capture 21st century skills and other non-academic outcomes.

On an individual level, teachers need to improve their capacity to self-report their own experiences in the form of valuable, research-like outputs. On a system level, continued improvement of innovative pedagogies should be based on a competent assessment of their strengths and weaknesses. Understanding how innovative pedagogies work, and under which conditions, is a priority for policy, research, and practice.

1.7. A final note

This volume sets out the case for the importance of pedagogy. Continued innovation in teaching and learning requires a careful understanding of pedagogies and the conditions under which they flourish. As discussed in this report, pedagogy is a fundamental part of teacher general pedagogical knowledge and a key lever to improve teachers' professional competences.

Updating and expanding teachers' professional competences are especially important in order to achieve the ambitious of education systems. Preparing young people to become lifelong learners with a deep understanding and a broad set of social skills requires a deep understanding of the role of pedagogy and the professionalism of teachers.

Lasting system change will avoid excessive expectations about policies directed at areas that are simpler to measure and standardise but further away from an impact on learning. This extends to assessment frameworks that should support contemporary curricula and ambitious pedagogical designs, and not be limited to a few key skills and knowledge domains.

A primary policy role for shaping these areas will often be in establishing fertile conditions and climates, providing support and building capacity. All levels need to be involved, and not only the classroom, where teaching and learning actually takes place. This is about fostering conditions and support (for example, platforms for professional learning, encouragement of networks of schools) and the removal of barriers, such as restrictive assessment and accountability requirements: it will call for review of inherited teaching practices and beliefs about learning and learners.

These are not easy topics. Although innovation has become a common priority in educational systems, schools are largely still seen as resistant to innovation. This is partly a consequence of innovation still being defined as something 'exceptional', as a process in which only well-suited schools or highly motivated or skilled teachers engage. A message arising from this report is that innovation must be seen as a fundamental element of the teaching profession. Teachers work in a complex, evolving environment where the outcomes of their actions are often uncertain. Second, pedagogies are not technical tools that can navigate easily through different environments, but ideas and strategies used by professionals able to adopt and adapt them to accommodate the needs of leaners.

It is now generally acknowledged that the quality of an educational system cannot exceed the quality of its teachers. This volume goes a step further to argue that a teacher cannot help students meet new educational challenges by continuing to draw on a familiar and perhaps even inherited set of pedagogies: here lies the importance of pedagogical innovation.

References

Dumont, H., D. Istance and F. Benavides (eds.) (2010), *The Nature of Learning: Using Research to Inspire Practice*, OECD Publishing, Paris, http://dx.doi.org/10.1787/9789264086487-en.

OECD (2015), *Schooling Redesigned: Towards Innovative Learning Systems*, OECD Publishing, Paris, http://dx.doi.org/10.1787/9789264245914-en.

OECD (2013), *Innovative Learning Environments*, OECD Publishing, Paris, http://dx.doi.org/10.1787/9789264203488-en.

Chapter 2. The complex interaction of teaching and learning: Understanding innovative pedagogies

This chapter starts by locating the work on pedagogy in the wider literature, and identifies some shortcomings surrounding the concept of pedagogy. It then discusses the concept of pedagogy as located in the dynamic interactions of knowledge and practice, of research sciences and creative implementation, and of educational theories and particular practices. The pedagogical continuum is presented as a conceptual tool to identify clusters of innovative pedagogies. The second part of the chapter expands the conceptual framework by including critical reflections about the purpose, effective practice and combinations of pedagogies, the influence of content areas and context, and how to frame system-based pedagogical change. In the last section the building of the compilation is briefly explained, as well as the work with the innovative networks of schools, and the role of these networks to balance the conceptual work of the report, with examples coming from the field.

This chapter looks at pedagogy in relation to knowledge and practice; to the science of learning and the intuitive, creative ways in which teacher practices take place; and to theories of learning and discrete and highly contextualised implementation. These reflections lead to an operational definition of pedagogy is presented.

The chapter then goes on to flesh out the organising framework briefly presented in the previous chapter (the five C's framework). This is followed by a description of two other elements of this work: the compilation of clusters of innovative pedagogies and the consultation with networks of innovative schools.

2.1. Background and wider literature

This study of innovative pedagogy aims to inform teachers and others engaged in education with materials to advise their professional judgements and choices. By widening their awareness of approaches to teaching and learning, they can become more creative in designing learning environments that address new competences and skills, challenges and educational goals.

There has been a longstanding drive to identify effective principles and practices which address education's challenges. Such challenges include student disengagement, improving inclusion and equity, developing deep learning and understanding, and promoting the so-called 21st century skills such as creativity, critical thinking and problem-solving, financial and economic literacy, health and digital literacy, global awareness and citizenship (OECD, 2015a).

Important contributions to this endeavour include:

- the synthesis of 800 meta-analyses in "Visible Learning" (Hattie, 2009);
- the generative framework for technology-enhanced learning and the subsequent *Innovative Pedagogy* series developed by Mike Sharples and his colleagues (Sharples et al., 2009; Sharples et al., 2012-2016);
- the framework created by the global initiative "New Pedagogies for Deep Learning" (Fullan and Langworthy, 2014);
- the subscales offered in "Productive Pedagogies", with its focus on equitable outcomes for marginalised students (Lingard et al., 2003);
- recent reviews in the school effectiveness and school improvement literature (e.g. Reynolds et al., 2014; Muijs, et al. 2014); and
- reports from national (e.g. Pollard, 2010) and international agencies and organisations (e.g. European Agency for Special Needs and Inclusive Education, 2015; Luna Scott, 2015; Dumont, Istance and Benavides, 2010).

Alexander (2004) identified how difficult it is for teachers to talk about their teaching, compared with getting them to discuss curriculum, learning, or classroom management. Similarly, it is difficult in these studies and reports to identify a clear idea of pedagogy and its implications for the organisation of teaching and learning. Much of the work done revolves around setting fundamental learning principles embedded in psycho-cultural and holistic approaches, combining the experiences of alternative education with research conceptualising learning as a complex process in which cognitive, metacognitive and socio-emotional processes interact (Sliwka and Yee, 2015). However, as important as the setting of aspirational goals may be, it does not reveal the operational procedures teachers need to realise such goals at the classroom level.

Another approach has been to review the existing evidence base on 'good teaching', presenting pedagogies as sets of disconnected tools and practices to improve achievement. Yet others seek to balance descriptions of innovative teaching methods with the presentation of certain skills, learning goals and organisational and pedagogical variables (e.g. leadership, curriculum, or assessment). However, by mixing together pedagogy with learning principles, and other school variables, the implications for pedagogy are diffused and there is a lack of clear connection with what happens in the classroom.

Addressing pedagogy in precise terms can help to better understand the complex interactions of teaching and learning in the classroom, and provide teachers with guidelines for reaching desired learning outcomes, rather than offering simple prescriptions (Watkins and Mortimore, 1999). Despite its importance, pedagogy has been increasingly 'thinned out' by the relentless widespread policy focus on curriculum, high-stake testing and assessment (Lingard et al., 2003). It is much easier to model and measure the latter as opposed to the messy complexities of pedagogical interactions.

Our point of departure and overarching question is simple: what do the Principles of Learning (Dumont, Istance and Benavides, 2010; see Table 2.1) look like in terms of pedagogies? By building a more precise understanding of pedagogy and the role of teachers as creative professionals, the goal has been to identify and describe new pedagogical approaches that can help teachers to put these principles in motion when designing learning environments.

Table 2.1. Features of learner and teacher practice consistent with the OECD Principles

Principles	Learners	Teaching
1. Learner centredness	Active learner engagement skilled at self-regulation	Learning at the centre Educators are knowledgeable and collaborative Clarity of vision quality assurance
2. Social nature of learning	Co-operative learning	Social rich pedagogy Collegial activity Flexible learning settings
3. Responsiveness to motivations and emotions	Positive challenge for every learner low disengagement bonds of attachment and trust education of the emotions	Understanding emotions Approaches that motivate
4. Sensitivity to individual differences	Individualised approaches louder learner voice	Rich pedagogical mix Collaborative leadership
5. Graded challenges	Formative assessment wide and deep learning matrices inclusive challenge	High expectations Personalised evidence Growth mind-sets
6. Assessment for learning	Shared expectations deep learning	Clarity of expectations Detailed of feedback
7. Horizontal connectedness	Connectedness to the community	Connecting across subjects and topics

Source: Based on OECD (2013), Innovative Learning Environments, OECD Publishing, Paris, http://dx.doi.org/10.1787/9789264203488-en.

2.2. The concept of pedagogy

2.2.1. Pedagogy in the interactions of teaching and learning in classroom practice

Putting pedagogy to the fore is thus to ask about how teaching and learning are organised, how differentiated teaching may be achieved, and how these decisions have important consequences for classroom management and assessment, all of which are open to improvement. A good starting point in conceptualising pedagogy is Loughran's definition (2013). This takes pedagogies as ways of looking at the interactions of teaching and learning in the real time of classroom practice. Pedagogy is thus both knowledge (ways of looking at) and action (the decision-making and designs shaping the interactions of teaching and learning in classroom practice). Figure 2.1 illustrates this duality of pedagogy and the way decisions about instruction are informed by knowledge about the relations of teaching and learning. At the same time, the figure illustrates how these repertoires for designing learning environments and practice build on previous instruction and thus it represents a dynamic model connecting knowledge and action.

Figure 2.1. Pedagogies as knowledge and as practices

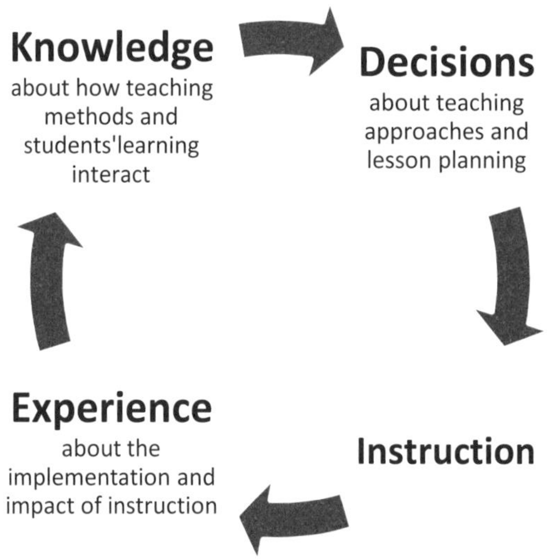

Knowledge
about how teaching methods and students'learning interact

Decisions
about teaching approaches and lesson planning

Instruction

Experience
about the implementation and impact of instruction

Source: Guerriero, S. (ed.) (2017), *Pedagogical Knowledge and the Changing Nature of the Teaching Profession*, OECD Publishing, Paris, http://dx.doi.org/10.1787/9789264270695-en.

Knowledge about pedagogies can be seen as part of what is commonly known as 'general pedagogical knowledge' (GPK) - inclusive of knowledge about classroom management, assessment, and awareness of student differences (Voss et al., 2011). Putting pedagogy to the fore highlights that the way in which teaching and learning are framed has important consequences for classroom management and assessment, which constantly impact on the relationships between teaching and learning (see Figure 2.2). Any improvement in classroom management impacts not only on student outcomes but also on the implementation of any particular pedagogical approach (Korpershoek et al., 2014). Similarly, as teaching and learning interact through pedagogy, teachers need to know about their pupils' progress just as learners do: recognition of the desired goal, evidence about achievement, and strategies for closing the gap between these two are all integral to improving learner attainment and to teacher judgements about the use of pedagogies (Black and Wiliam, 1998).

Figure 2.2. Pedagogy and general pedagogical knowledge (GPK)

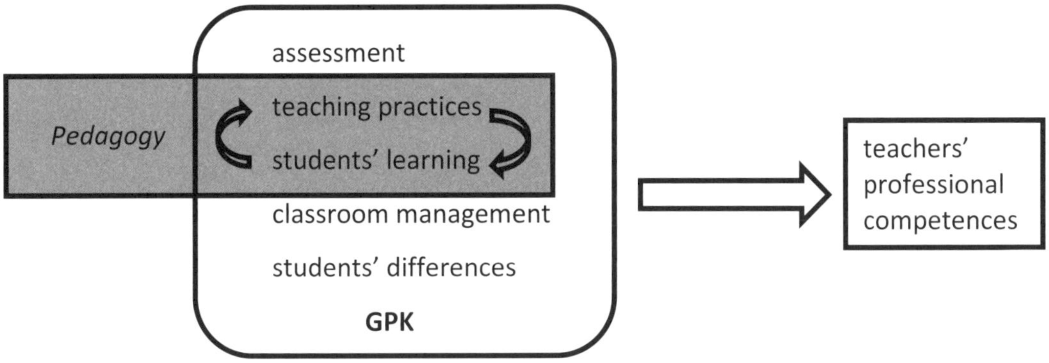

Pedagogy as craft combining teaching and learning as science and as art

To deepen the concept of pedagogy understood as the dynamic interaction of knowledge and practice about teaching and learning, it is useful to refer to Pollard's definition of 'pedagogic expertise' (2010) and his conceptualisation of pedagogy as simultaneously a form of science, craft, and art (Figure 2.3).

Pedagogy as science is the knowledge and as art is in the practice. Pedagogy as science refers to how forms of instruction are made explicit, coherent and generalisable through the learning sciences. Pedagogy as art refers to how teachers implement pedagogical approaches, strategies and tools intuitively and creatively, through contextualised personal responses and capacities. The interaction between these two ends comes together in the notion of 'craft', as a mastery of a repertoire of skills and practices - knowledge about practice and putting knowledge into practice. Pedagogy as craft stands in the interface between the learning sciences and idiosyncratic, contextualised teacher classroom practices; it encapsulates scientific knowledge in application and intuitive practice, informing professional judgements about approaches to teaching.

Figure 2.3. Pedagogy in the interplay of science, craft and art

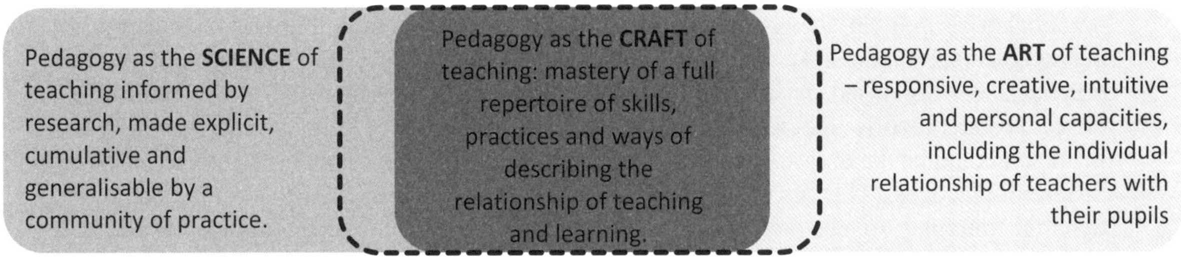

Source: Adapted from Pollard, A. (ed.) (2010), *Professionalism as Pedagogy: A Contemporary Opportunity: A Commentary by TLRP and GTCE*, TLRP, London.

Craft, then, lies in the dynamic intersection of science and art (dark blue zone), but is wider with boundaries as indicated by the dashed line. Craft includes scientific knowledge that is not yet fully validated as implementation into practice or is still permeating teaching practices; it also incorporates practices that are well-established but with only limited scientific evidence about their impact.

Theoretical models and discrete practices - the pedagogical continuum

Pedagogy is thus by its nature hybrid: it is knowledge and it is practice (Figure 2.1), and it is scientific knowledge that is commonly implemented in the form of an art (Figure 2.3). Pedagogies are not simply rational mechanisms or 'how-to-fix' methodologies informed by science; they are practices charged with powerful cultural meanings, personal experiences and beliefs (Fuller and Clarke, 1994; Thomas and Loxley, 2002).

Figure 2.4. The pedagogical continuum

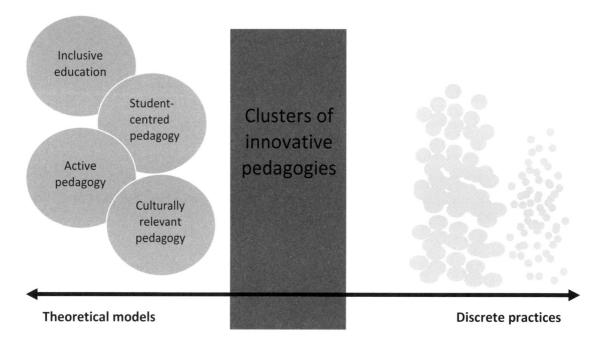

Note: The labels in the bubbles are illustrative examples, not exhaustive categories.

Building on these reflections, we developed the notion of a 'pedagogical continuum' as a practical tool to help locate the different levels of abstraction that are attached to pedagogies (see Figure 2.4). One end of the continuum shows a high dispersion of good practices, not organised or streamlined into coherent approaches. At the other end are broad, abstract theories that are far from the classroom. With pedagogy as craft, the focus is on shared understandings of teaching and learning, and the relationships between these different practices. This gives clusters of pedagogical approaches that embrace this dynamic interplay of abstraction and detail, of declarative and procedural knowledge, inherent in the notion of craft. It gives a comprehensive landscape of innovative pedagogies, connected to theoretical constructs but respecting the freedom and creativity of teaching.

This methodology required making strategic decisions about how to group practices and their connection to teaching and learning frameworks. This was done using an iterative process: the review of journals and reports on teaching innovation, identification of the theoretical models of teaching and learning in each cluster, and discussion of the main practices consistent with that cluster. The pedagogical continuum is not about learning theories vs teacher practices, but about how pedagogies bring these two levels together.

The position of the different clusters in the middle of the spectrum, and the way in which the practices and theories are filtered on either side, follows from the prominence we gave to the ways that teaching and learning accord with the OECD Principles of Learning (Dumont, Istance and Benavides, 2010). The aim was to arrive at a set of pedagogical clusters that are representative and address the development of 21st century skills, technology, student agency and domains. We built on the importance of combination and connoisseurship in the C's framework, drawing us to coherent bundles of practices that capitalise on the natural learning inclinations of students.

The chosen clusters are not stand-alone approaches as there are strong links between them. They seek to see through the 'noise' commonly surrounding innovation and teaching and begin to draw a roadmap for teachers and policy-makers in thinking about classroom teaching and learning. Some of these clusters are relatively well known and longstanding, such as experiential learning, while others, for instance multiliteracies and discussion-based teaching, are less familiar. The labels are interpreted broadly: for example, gamification is viewed as more than using games in classrooms but also as an approach that harnesses the pedagogical potential of games and transfers it to formal teaching.

2.3. Framing the study – the "Cs"

In order to provide a lens through which to interrogate the innovative pedagogies compiled, the "Cs" framework was developed. It is a conceptual organiser and it is offered as an output in its own right as a set of lenses that others may adopt. It incorporates a particular philosophy and precepts for action - holistic and oriented towards practice and change - as an alternative to the fragmentation of many research methodologies. The Cs focus attention on the following five dimensions:

Figure 2.5. The C's framework

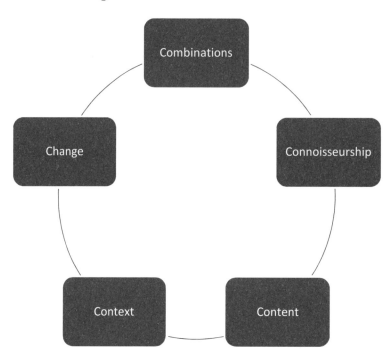

2.3.1. The Cs elaborated

This section elaborates what each of these dimensions means and how it relates to the overall analysis of this volume.

Combinations

Mixes and combinations of pedagogies are integral characteristics of any educational situation. A single teacher, let alone teams of educators, never uses one pedagogical method exclusively. A pedagogical approach is made up of several specific methods combined in systematic ways for specific purposes. Innovation may lie as much in the way in which those pedagogies are combined or applied as in any specific methods or practices. That is, pedagogies need to be understood holistically rather than only as unconnected practices and techniques. Examples of associations among pedagogical approaches can be found in Chapter 4.

As suggested by Peterson (Chapter 3), effective schools and networks tend to anchor their learning design and teaching within a restricted set of combined pedagogical approaches. Clarity and coherence are enhanced through having a limited set of framing pedagogical approaches, which provide a framework for activities, address dilemmas of organisation, and familiarise students with the sequences for more self-directed learning within the overall teaching strategy. Each approach contains discrete pedagogies to achieve more specific teaching and learning goals.

A school with an overarching pedagogical design has made a collective decision about how to combine several pedagogies to meet multiple educational goals. The power of each pedagogy is thereby strengthened considerably: individual teacher planning is reinforced at the organisational level as is teacher collaboration, while students more readily transfer the learning approaches developed in one year or subject area to another.

Such coherence of pedagogical approach remains, however, more the exception than the rule.

Box 2.1. Examples of 'anchors' in school networks

The *Amara Berri* network (Spain) emphasises that real life should be immersed in the daily life of classroom activities. Through cross-cutting themes and project-based designs, the classroom becomes a space where children discuss, practice and acquire those skills and competences that promote their well-being. The pedagogical approach revolves around game activities and students' vital interests.

Better Movers and Thinkers (Scotland) is an approach to learning and teaching in physical education used in a local network of schools. It is designed to develop the ability of all children and young people to move and think in a more cohesive way. It focuses on developing the executive function skills essential to guide cognitive processes towards intended outcome.

The *Escuela Nueva* network (Colombia and international) promotes reflexive learning centred on the students, where they can collaborate, and which privileges the role of the community and assessment. Key practices are: working through learning guidelines which students use on their own or in groups; learning corners, focused on particular projects where students can experiment and interact; the classroom library; the student council; mail for suggestions and friendship; and student self-control of school attendance.

Pedagogical combinations, as noted by Peterson in Chapter 3, are a ripe area for further research as there is limited knowledge about them and a lack of research on the relationships between pedagogical combinations and a variety of educational outcomes. Going further, studying common combinations of pedagogies could identity those practices which are common to several pedagogies, such as presentations of learning or student self-assessment. Building teacher and student familiarity with these practices could facilitate the development of greater diversity of pedagogical combinations across a school or system.

Connoisseurship

The concept of "connoisseurship" captures the idea of expert application of specific pedagogies; clarifying connoisseurship is about contributing to understanding the conditions and meta-principles behind "powerful learning". An example can illustrate this concept, taken from the OECD *Nature of Learning*, 2010 report:

> Inquiry approaches… are highly dependent on the knowledge and skills of the teachers engaged in trying to implement them. When these approaches are poorly understood, teachers often think of them as "unstructured," rather than appreciating that they require extensive scaffolding and constant assessment and redirection as they unfold. Teachers need time and a community to support their capacity to organise sustained project work. It takes significant pedagogical sophistication to manage extended projects in classrooms so as to maintain a focus on "doing with understanding" rather than "doing for the sake of doing" (Barron and Darling-Hammond, 2010: 202).

If particular pedagogies are inappropriately applied, it will not be surprising that they have only limited impact on outcomes (assuming such outcomes can be measured). More generally, particular pedagogies may be done with different degrees of expertise, even when well-chosen for the educational challenge in question. Evaluative studies of practices done in the name of a specific approach understate its potential when they include the poorly-implemented as well as expert applications.

Context

Pedagogical innovation should be sensitive to context. Some of the most relevant contextual factors are the impact (or not) of being surrounded by digital media; the influence of different socio-cultural backgrounds; and the role of values, even religion.

LaFuente (Chapter 3) focuses on the nature of "new learners" as context, and how that shapes the possibilities and challenges facing pedagogical design. He identifies five broad trends in the use of technologies, multimedia materials, multi-tasking and non-linear and interactive environments, games, and collaborative activities using Web 2.0 learning. In the same chapter, discussing about how to address the always diverse needs of learners in the classroom, Dumont describes how individualised instruction is a promising pedagogical approach to sensitise teachers to student differences that arise from their different context and needs. She goes on to discuss that too often teachers are more concerned with organising the learning activities of individual students than with engaging in meaningful interactions with students about the learning content, with low levels of student group interaction. It underlines the close links of pedagogy with classroom management, and emphasises the importance of professional learning and collaboration.

Context itself needs to be contextualised: findings about the influence of, say, social background on pedagogical strategies from one culture or system may well not hold elsewhere. Hence, though it is difficult to generalise about the impact of context, this volume will illuminate how particular pedagogical approaches and innovations respond to particular contextual circumstances.

Content

Knowledge domains can strongly influence teaching, teachers and organisation, even when transversal knowledge and competences are needed. Domains have their own epistemic structures which may define specific pedagogical requirements. Teaching in a domain reflects historical traditions which can be very powerful and hard to change. Subjects filter teacher practice, and often structure their work and professional collaboration, with separate policy initiatives. Subject teachers tend to form sub-cultures with their own beliefs, norms and teaching practices. All these may influence teaching and pedagogical choices.

Lafuente, in his reflection on the content domains of mathematics, non-native language and socio-emotional learning, describes how each domain has its own particular combination of epistemic structure, its relation to knowledge and skills, the beliefs of teachers, and the routines imposed by how these subjects have been taught traditionally by a community of practice. The focus on competences, new skills and OECD's Learning Principles offers a vantage point to analyse the weight of domains and the relationships between innovative practices, cross-cutting competences and content, and the traditional school subjects.

Change

It is further important to ask how different pedagogies can best be introduced, developed and sustained in different learning contexts, especially schools, as well as the role played by the networks and learning communities. The focus on change includes policies, strategies and initiatives aimed at promoting certain pedagogical approaches. Professional learning will feature prominently in any strategy to introduce and sustain change.

Pedagogical "anchors" are designs that serve as coherent frames for change and implementation. Approaches as sets of practices are designs or 'anchor points' to help align and implement pedagogical innovations. Innovations in teaching and learning are not so much assimilated by teachers as adopted progressively through the 'anchor points' and the creative adaptation by teachers. The focus on clusters of pedagogical approaches signals the value of coherent, accessible options for teaching and learning rather than educators being constantly faced by a bewildering array of unconnected choices about teaching methods and their impact on learning and outcomes.

Teacher learning – collaborative, action-oriented, and co-designed – is fundamental to change. The literature on teacher learning for implementation suggests that training models based on imparting knowledge and skills are not the most effective means of bringing about change in pedagogical practice as compared with experiential, action-oriented learning with teachers collaborating in communities of practice. The collaborative design of curricular materials enhances teacher professional development in contextualising the learning, reinforcing teacher agency, and providing for iterative, continuous improvement.

As discussed by Law (Chapter 3), change should be conceptualised as learning. The conditions and factors influencing student learning, and the changes identified to improve these, can usefully be conceptualised as learning outcomes of those levels. Even when the ultimate location of change is in classrooms, supportive change is needed at each level, calling for alignment and mutual reinforcement.

2.4. The methodology behind the volume

The project methodology has involved putting together the compilation of innovative pedagogies; identifying networks promoting different pedagogical approaches and engaging them through a questionnaire; and commissioning a set of complementary expert papers on relevant themes. The main initial work focused on the conceptualisation of the C's framework, followed by building the compilation. Next came the identification and work with networks of innovative schools. This process was iterative, in which later work on the concepts and framework was further strengthened by the compilation, and informed by the questionnaires received from the networks (see Box 2.2).

Box 2.2. A brief history of the OECD/CERI work

This volume is the main output of the OECD/CERI Innovative Pedagogies for Powerful Learning project. It emerged out of earlier work on Innovative Learning Environments, which placed the pedagogical core and the learning principles at the heart of innovative, powerful learning environments. The new work extends this through a systematic examination of the different pedagogies themselves.

Initial scoping began in 2015 with the preparation of different reviews regarding pedagogy, innovation and teaching practices. The C's framework was outlined in an international meeting in April 2016, along with the main structure of the project. During the second half of 2016 the focus was around strengthening conceptualisation, while identifying innovative approaches and networks of innovative schools. By the end of 2016, a first selection of networks was made and a questionnaire elaborated.

Further refinement of the conceptual architecture and the development of the compilation of innovative pedagogies took place in 2017, as well as the further selection and contact with networks. A small expert meeting mid-2017 reviewed the initial draft report, which subsequently has been revised and extended for this publication.

For more information on the project, please see:
www.oecd.org/education/ceri/innovative-pedagogies-for-powerful-learning.htm.

2.4.1. The compilation of clusters of innovative pedagogies

The aim of the compilation is to offer a map of innovative pedagogies, as bundles of practices and coherent patterns. In its creation, the first criterion was to look for approaches which have targeted 21st century skills, student engagement and agency, equity, technology, and which address the OECD Principles of Learning. A further criterion for choosing these approaches is that they have an implementation track record that extends beyond anecdote, even in the absence of a robust evidence base of their impact. The clusters were identified through different sources: international reports, repositories of journals (e.g. ERIC) and specialised journals; different experts and identified networks of innovative schools, which in turn led to further reviews of research and policy papers.

Table 2.2 summarises the criteria for selecting the six clusters in the Compilation. It includes the main challenges which arose for each pedagogical approach. The table highlights those learning principles and 21st century skills that are particularly targeted in each case. It also indicates the main sources used - analysis of innovative networks, feedback from stakeholders, literature review, or the searches for matching skills.

Table 2.2. Criteria for selecting pedagogical approaches

Pattern	Criteria Selection		
	Source	Learning Principles	21st century Skills
Blended learning	Networks	2. Social nature of learning 4. Sensitivity to Individual differences 5. Graded challenges 6. Assessment for learning	Problem solving-digital literacy
Gamification	Networks	2. Social Nature of learning 3. Motivations and emotions 5. Graded challenges 6. Assessment for learning	Digital literacy
Computational thinking	Review of research	3. Motivations and emotions 5. Graded challenges	Problem solving-digital literacy-creativity
Experiential learning	Networks and review of research	2. Social nature of learning 3. Motivations and emotions	Problem solving-global awareness-citizenship-critical thinking
Embodied learning	Feedback and 21st century skills	2. Social nature of learning 3. Motivations and emotions .4. Sensitivity to individual differences	Creativity-health literacy
Multi/Critical literacies and discussion-based teaching	21st century skills	2. Social Nature of Learning 3. Motivations and emotions	Digital literacy-citizenship-critical thinking

2.4.2. Approaching the networks

Networks were targeted as opposed to single schools in order to take examples that had already spread and been replicated in other settings, i.e. with some proof of scalability. The focus on networks of schools built on previous work identifying the meso-level as a privileged arena from where to understand and scale up innovations (OECD, 2015b). Networks are not the only organisational form of interest in making educational change - but they are critical. "Network" has been interpreted very broadly to allow for coverage of different kinds of groupings.

The initial universe of cases revolved around networks of innovative schools advancing a common pedagogy, called "Pedagogical Approach Networks". To these, two more categories were added:

- Networks that share the broad aim of innovating teaching and learning (including pedagogy), and which facilitate mutual exchange and development; these are termed "Innovation Promotion Networks".
- Networks primarily oriented towards providing the professional learning to enable pedagogical and related innovation, focused especially on teachers and leaders; these are called "Professional Learning Networks".

The questionnaire (see Annex 2.A) asked about the main pedagogical approaches followed by the networks, including alignment with the OECD Learning Principles and the role of learner voice and agency. It asked about specific features such as whether any particular groups or communities have been targeted (context), any subjects or domains for which the approach has been especially applied (content), the approach to 21st century competences, assessment, technology and whether any aspects must be practised for the approach to be effective (connoisseurship). Organisational questions included demands on schools and teachers, how the network itself functions, as well as whether the network/organisation had been evaluated. As well as the main network organisers, it was requested that the questionnaire be also completed by practitioners and schools in order to gain additional insights from the ground.

References

Alexander, R. (2004), "Still no pedagogy? Principle, pragmatism and compliance in primary education", *Cambridge Journal of Education*, Vol. 34/1, pp.7-33.

Barron, B. and L. Darling-Hammond (2010), "Prospects and challenges for inquiry-based approaches to learning", in *The Nature of Learning: Using Research to Inspire Practice,* OECD Publishing, Paris, http://dx.doi.org/10.1787/9789264086487-en.

Black, P. and D. Wiliam (1998), "Assessment and classroom learning", *Assessment in Education: Principles, Policy & Practice*, Vol. 5/1, pp. 7-74.

Dumont, H., D. Istance and F. Benavides (eds.) (2010), *The Nature of Learning: Using Research to Inspire Practice*, OECD Publishing, Paris, http://dx.doi.org/10.1787/9789264086487-en.

European Agency for Special Needs and Inclusive Education (2015), *Empowering Teachers to Promote Inclusive Education. Conceptual Framework and Methodology*, European Agency for Special Needs and Inclusive Education, Odense, Denmark.

Fullan, M. and M. Langworthy (2014), *A Rich Seam: How New Pedagogies Find Deep Learning*, Pearson, London.

Fuller, B. and P. Clarke (1994), "Raising school effects while ignoring culture? Local conditions and the influence of classroom tools, rules, and pedagogy", *Review of Educational Research*, Vol. 64/1, pp. 119-157.

Guerriero, S. (ed.) (2017), *Pedagogical Knowledge and the Changing Nature of the Teaching Profession*, OECD Publishing, Paris, http://dx.doi.org/10.1787/9789264270695-en.

Hattie, J. (2009), *Visible Learning: A Synthesis of Over 800 Meta-Analyses Relating to Achievement*, Routledge, London.

Korpershoek, H., et al. (2014), *Effective Classroom Management Strategies and Classroom Management Programs for Educational Practice*, RUG/GION, Groningen.

Lingard, B., D. Hayes and M. Mills (2003), "Teachers and Productive Pedagogies: contextualising, conceptualising, utilising", *Pedagogy, Culture & Society*, Vol. 11/3, pp. 399-424.

Loughran, J. (2013), "Pedagogy: Making sense of the complex relationship between teaching and learning", *Curriculum Inquiry*, Vol. 43/1, pp. 118-141.

Luna Scott, C. (2015), "The Futures of Learning 3: What kind of pedagogies for the 21st century?", *ERF Working Papers Series*, No. 15, UNESCO, Paris.

OECD (2015a), *OECD Education 2030*, First Informal working group meeting, internal working paper.

OECD (2015b), *Schooling Redesigned: Towards Innovative Learning Systems*, OECD Publishing, Paris, http://dx.doi.org/10.1787/9789264245914-en.

OECD (2013), *Innovative Learning Environments*, OECD Publishing, Paris. http://dx.doi.org/10.1787/9789264203488-en.

Pollard, A. (ed.) (2010), *Professionalism as Pedagogy: A Contemporary Opportunity: A Commentary By TLRP And GTCE*, TLRP, London.

Sharples, M., et al. (2016), *Innovating Pedagogy 2016: Open University Innovation Report 5*, The Open University, Milton Keynes.

Sharples, M., et al. (2009), New Modes of Technology-enhanced Learning: Opportunities and challenges, Research Report, Becta, https://www.researchgate.net/publication/255633078_New_Modes_of_Technology-enhanced_Learning_Opportunities_and_challenges.

Skrtic, T. (1991), "The special education paradox: Equity as the way to excellence", *Harvard Educational Review*, Vol. 61/2, pp. 148-207.

Sliwka, A. and B. Yee (2015), "From alternative education to the mainstream: Approaches in Canada and Germany to preparing learners to live in a changing world", *European Journal of Education*, Vol. 50/2, pp. 175-183.

Sonmark, K., et al. (2017), "Understanding teachers' pedagogical knowledge: report on an international pilot study", *OECD Education Working Papers*, No. 159, OECD Publishing, Paris, http://dx.doi.org/10.1787/43332ebd-en.

Thomas, G. and A. Loxley (2002), *Deconstructing Special Education and Constructing Inclusion*, Open University Press, Berkshire.

Voss, T., M. Kunter and J. Baumert (2011), "Assessing teacher candidates' general pedagogical/psychological knowledge: Test construction and validation", *Journal of In-Service Education*, Vol. 103/4, pp. 952-969.

Annex 2.A. Questionnaire to networks

Annex Box 2.A.1. Questionnaire to networks on innovative pedagogies

Questionnaire sent to network leaders and teachers

A. Overview

A.1. Please describe in a paragraph the background and history of your organisation/network. (To avoid a lengthy description, please include a source to which we can refer for more details if needed.)

A.2. Please describe the key pedagogical practices in the schools in your organisation/network.

A.3. OECD/CERI has developed a set of principles to help guide teaching and learning (see Box 2.A.2.): please select the 2-3 of these principles that apply especially in your approach and describe how they get put into practice.

Annex Table 2.A.1. The OECD seven principles of learning

1	Make learning central, and encourage engagement and awareness in students of their own learning strategies.
2	Ensure that learning is social and often collaborative.
3	Be highly attuned to motivations and the emotions involved in learning.
4	Be acutely sensitive to individual differences, including in prior knowledge.
5	Be demanding for each learner but without excessive overload.
6	Use assessments consistent with the main goals for learning, with a strong emphasis on formative feedback.
7	Promote horizontal connection across learning activities, across subjects, and across in- and out-of-school learning.

A.4. Please summarise the nature of learner voice and learner agency in your main pedagogical approach, including the relationship of students with teachers and peers and their room to take decisions in the teaching and learning process.

B. Specific Features of your Pedagogical Approach

B.1. Are there particular groups of learners or communities for which your approach has been mainly applied? If there has been a specific focus, what are the reasons for it?

B.2. Are there particular subjects, content areas or domains for which your approach has been mainly applied? If there has been a specific focus, what are the reasons for it?

B.3. How adapted is your approach to the so-called 21st century competences like creativity, critical thinking, problem-solving, collaboration, and digital literacy? Do they feature explicitly and is your approach especially effective in developing one or more of them?

B.4. Does technology play a central role in your main pedagogical approach and if so how? Or is it more technology-neutral?

B.5 How is assessment used in combination with teaching? Who uses the assessment information and for what purpose?

B.6. How demanding is your approach on teachers? What kinds of professional learning do they need and how readily available is it?

B.7. What are the organisational demands of widespread adoption of your pedagogical approach on schools and institutions? How have those demands been met?

B.8. Are there specific aspects that must be practised for the approach to be effective? Is there an evidence base that shows why these aspects are so pivotal?

C. The Operation of your Organisation/Network

C.1. In what way do the membership schools work with the organisation/network as regards the pedagogical approach they use in classrooms etc.? How, if at all, is fidelity to the approach assured?

C.2. Has the work of the schools in your organisation/network been or is it being evaluated, how has this been done, and what does the evaluative evidence show about learning change?

C.3. Has your organisation/network grown in recent years and what are the main factors facilitating or hindering this?

Chapter 3. Building the C's framework: Insights and reflections

This chapter presents an abridged summary of a series of papers that provide a complementary analysis to underpin the project's conceptual work. The original contributions can be found in full in an OECD Education Working Paper, Peterson, A. et al. (2018). Amelia Peterson's first contribution on pedagogy and purpose, and Hanna Dumont's contribution on adaptive teaching, are wide-ranging in scope and cover a broad range of pedagogical approaches. These are followed by Amelia Peterson's analyses of combinations of pedagogies, where it is discussed the role of networks promoting particular innovative approaches. Marc Lafuente looks first at content domains (mathematics, non-native languages, and socio-emotional learning) and how they relate to pedagogies. He then contributes to the thinking on "new learners" and technology, as important context influencing pedagogical choices and implementation. The final section by Nancy Law is focused on change, through the particular prism of technology-enhanced pedagogical innovations.

3.1. The purpose of pedagogy (Amelia Peterson, Harvard University)

Pedagogies provide frameworks for the multitude of decisions teachers have to make about how they teach. Innovation in pedagogy, like any kind of innovation, takes existing ideas, tools or practices and brings them together in new ways to solve problems when current practice is not adequately meeting needs. To now, the choice of pedagogy has often been made ad hoc or based on whatever a teacher had encountered in their teacher education or their own schooling (Lortie, 2002). But where teachers are supported by high quality teacher education and strong professional infrastructures, they are enabled to make concerted decisions about pedagogy, acting as designers of learning by selecting approaches with a clear sense of their intended impact (Jensen et al., 2015).

Certain strands of education research are aimed at providing teachers with the evidence to make informed decisions about pedagogy (Higgins et al., 2015). But, developing and selecting pedagogies involves more than working out what is "effective" as indicated by impact on diverse measures of learning. Different pedagogies are based on different theories of learning and what is regarded as most important; the full power of a pedagogy – and of pedagogical innovation – can only be evaluated in taking into account all the things the pedagogies are trying to achieve.

3.1.1. Pedagogies aim at multiple purposes

The goal of teaching is more than just the transfer of content from one person to another. The way that people are taught affects how and what students learn. Particular pedagogical approaches have been developed and refined to promote a variety of different kinds of learning: for example, learning of explicit content, learning of particular ways of doing things, or the learning of values and habits. This variety increases the decisions that teachers must make.

Choices about pedagogy may be determined by assumptions about the way different approaches produce certain outcomes. Table 3.1 makes explicit some of these assumptions, though it is not meant to be exhaustive. It illustrates how established pedagogical approaches have developed in line with different kinds of intentions, and therefore why comparisons of approaches come down to more than just the question about which pedagogy is "most effective".

Table 3.1. Different approaches have different purposes

	We use this approach so that students can...	...with the intention of promoting...
Mastery-based	build knowledge and skills sequentially with practice	fluency, automaticity
Spaced learning	memorise core knowledge, practice recall	fluency, automaticity
Problem-based	apply skills or knowledge to a situation	meaning-making, skill transfer
Place-based	connect knowledge with their context	meaning-making, identity building
Discussion-based	practice articulation, take in other perspectives	communication, perspective-taking
Flipped learning	self-pace when meeting new content	metacognition, self-management
Inquiry	make connections, make their own learning path	metacognition, self-management
Product-oriented	be motivated, produce high quality work	engagement, perseverance

3.1.3. Pedagogies organise people and time

Teaching is a highly complex task. Over the course of each day, week and year, a teacher has to make thousands of decisions. To make these choices effectively teachers may draw on what is sometimes called pedagogical content knowledge. Then there are choices about how to initiate, organise and maintain momentum in periods of learning.

Many popular pedagogical approaches have been developed as ways to organise a teaching and learning process in support of three key organisational tasks: i) choosing a focus for the learning; ii) managing the learning process; and iii) determining the length and shape of an "arc of learning" (an individual lesson, a series of tasks over some days, or a sequence or project stretching over weeks, months or more). Similarly, pedagogical approaches imply different decisions about how topics are chosen and scoped, and how the actual process of learning is managed.

Table 3.2. Different approaches promote different ways of organising learning

	...chooses focus		...manages learning process			...ends the learning arc		
	Teacher	Student	Teacher	Student	Groups	Assessment	Product	Time
Mastery-based	x		x	x		x		
Spaced learning	x			x				x
Problem-based	x			x	x	x		
Place-based	x	x			x		x	
Discussion	x		x					x
Flipped learning	x			x		x		x
Inquiry		x		x	x	x	x	
Product-oriented	x	x		x	x		x	

3.1.4. Pedagogies bundle practices

The final advantage to thinking in terms of established pedagogical approaches is that an approach typically groups together sets of discrete research-based practices, thus aiding communication across contexts, where different labels may well be attached to similar bundles of practices. By focusing on specific practices, teachers can move beyond the buzz words to really understand the how and the why of a particular pedagogical approach. Breaking down approaches into practices with specific aims – or even into the mechanisms which explain how a practice achieves its effect (Peterson, 2016) – may be an important precursor to understanding the potential of new innovations in pedagogy.

3.2. Adaptive teaching: Students' differences and productive learning (Hanna Dumont, German Institute for International Educational Research, Berlin)

Students enter school with a vast range of differences, which together determine how well and how fast they will learn at school. School systems around the world are thus faced with the challenge of how to organise learning for large numbers of students while at the same time responding to the diverse needs of each one of them. This is about ensuring that each student receives an optimal learning experience, while also tackling well-documented educational inequalities. "Adaptive teaching" is a promising approach to address the challenge of student heterogeneity in the classroom.

3.2.1. Adaptive teaching as a general pedagogical approach

The idea of adapting classroom instruction to individual students has a long tradition. Research in earlier decades aimed to find the best instructional method for each student or groups of students with similar characteristics in order to develop formalised adaptive educational programmes (Cronbach & Snow, 1977). The key finding was that students' general cognitive abilities interact with the level of structure provided by the teacher: students who score lower on measures of general ability do better in teacher-controlled learning environments, in which teachers maintain a high level of control, lessons are broken down into small units, with direct instruction and frequent feedback. The contrary holds for students with higher general ability, who benefit from so-called discovery or learner-centred learning environments.

However, students differ on so many more dimensions and instructional methods function so differently depending on context, that it is extremely difficult to guide instruction through generalisations about which treatments best serve which learners. The concept of "adaptive teaching" was a response to this realisation in which teachers are seen as best able to make moment-to-moment decisions about what works for each of their students. As defined by Corno and Snow it is:

> *"...teaching that arranges environmental conditions to fit learner individual differences. As learners gain in aptitude through experience with respect to the instructional goals at hand, such teaching adapts by becoming less intrusive. Less intrusion, less teacher or instructional mediation, increases the learner's information processing and/or behavioural burdens, and with this the need for more learner self-regulation" (1986; 621).*

The goal is that each learner, beginning or advanced, will be equally challenged by the instruction. This not only applies to differences between students, it also applies to differences within students; that is, adaptive teaching takes into account that students develop capabilities over time, making a continuous adaptation of instruction necessary as students become more competent learners. In addition to the dynamic nature of adaptation, key features as proposed by Corno (2008) are:

- *Student differences*: Student differences (regarding their cognitive abilities, prior knowledge, interests, motivations, personality) are seen as opportunities not as obstacles for teaching and learning.
- *Self-regulated learning*: Teachers adapt to students while fostering self-regulated learning so that the learner is also expected to adapt to the instruction.
- *Macro- and micro-adaptations*: While macro-adaptions, i.e. instructional programmes shaped by formal assessments, may sometimes occur, micro-adaptions as moment-to-moment adjustments in response to individual student differences, informally assessed, lie at the heart of adaptive teaching.
- *Group context*: The goal of adaptive teaching is that all students can fully participate in classroom learning opportunities.

Adaptive teaching is an overarching pedagogical approach into which related concepts such as *differentiation, individualised instruction, personalised learning, open instruction, formative assessment* and *self-regulated learning* can be integrated. It does not favour a specific instructional method, and incorporates many pedagogies such as direct instruction, specific interventions, motivational enhancements, cooperative learning, modelling guided practice, peer tutoring, independent study, and discovery learning (Randi and Corno, 2005). Which of those pedagogies should best come into play will depend on the specific characteristics and needs of each learner. By viewing student differences as opportunities for teaching and learning, it stands in stark contrast to pedagogical approaches in which instruction is directed at the most typical or average student in a class, which remains the norm in many schools around the world (Dumont, Istance and Benavides, 2010).

3.2.2. Empirical evidence on the effectiveness of adaptive teaching

The call to deal with student heterogeneity by adapting to individual differences within a heterogeneous classroom typically is made on the assumption that this should lead to increased student performance and deeper learning. However, while there are theoretical accounts and examples of what adaptive teaching can look like in practice (e.g. Randi and Corno, 2005), there is little empirical evidence on the effectiveness of adaptive teaching to promote student learning. One reason for the scarcity of empirical evidence may be that adaptive teaching is not widespread, making it difficult to study, especially through randomised and representative samples. Complicating the empirical study of adaptive teaching further, teachers who do adaptive teaching use different methods to accomplish this, so adaptive teaching looks different between classrooms. However, related research may be used as indirect evidence for its potential to increase student performance when certain conditions are met:

- Studies comparing homogeneous with heterogeneous ability groupings come to the conclusion that grouping practices by themselves have no or only very small effects on student performance (e.g. Schofield, 2010; Slavin, 1987, 1990). What matters seems to be the instruction and not so much the grouping of students.
- Research on individualised instruction and instructional quality shows that differentiation and individualisation practices, which are often applied in adaptive teaching, are only effective when students engage with the learning content in depth and are stimulated cognitively. Such cognitive engagement by students depends on the quality of interactions between teachers and students around meaningful content and the quality of teacher explanations (e.g. Clarke, Resnick and Rosé, 2015; Patrick, Mantzicopoulos and Sears, 2012).
- Research on discovery learning shows that minimal teacher guidance is ineffective for most student learning (e.g. Alfieri, Brooks and Aldrich, 2011). However, guided discovery learning, in which teachers provide feedback, assist learners and elicit explanations, is effective for larger numbers of students (Alfieri et al., 2011; Hardy, 2006). Therefore, teachers always need to guide students, even throughout instructional phases when students have more freedom and responsibility for their own learning activities.
- Micro-level research from the learning sciences on understanding how students learn (Dumont, Istance and Benavides, 2010; Sawyer, 2015) suggests that in order for learning to be effective, the teacher is to provide just the right amount of instructional support so that each learner makes sense of the content by connecting it to their prior knowledge.

3.2.3. Adaptive teaching and equality of opportunity

Not only is the idea of adapting teaching to individual differences associated with the aim of raising student performance, it has also been expected to ensure equal learning opportunities for students. Corno (2008) argues that through micro-adaptations, teachers create a "middle ground" in the classroom, which brings students of different levels closer together. Unfortunately, there is even less empirical evidence about the relationship between adaptive and equality of opportunity than on the effectiveness of adaptive teaching.

However, promising insights come from two well-evaluated U.S school reform programmes that were designed for disadvantaged students —*Success for All* created by Robert Slavin and colleagues, and the *University of Chicago Charter School* founded by Anthony Bryk, Stephen Raudenbush and others. They have shown that high quality instruction can reduce inequalities (Borman et al., 2007; McGhee Hassrick, Raudenbush and Rosen, 2017). They did not call it adaptive teaching but in both teachers "skilfully 'assess and instruct' moment by moment" (McGhee Hassrick et al., 2017: 11); this evidently mirrors the micro-adaptations at the heart of adaptive teaching. In a similar vein, Yeh (2017) also suggested that achievement gaps can be closed through what he calls "rapid performance feedback": an individualised and structured model of instruction, in which each student is presented with tasks that are challenging but not too difficult, so that they have a high likelihood of receiving positive performance feedback on a daily basis.

As awareness grows that the creation of homogenous groups through practices of tracking and classroom instruction aimed at a typical student is not the ideal way to deal with student differences, there is a clear need for pedagogies that can productively address heterogeneity in the classroom and student differences. Interestingly, there are schools around the world that already teach micro-adaptively (e.g. OECD, 2013). These schools are often located in areas with a particularly diverse student body or have even increased the level of student heterogeneity by creating mixed-aged groups or including students with special needs. They are ahead of the current debate in policy and research: they can inspire us to cross the bridge between research and practice from the other side by translating practice into research.

3.3. Combinations of pedagogies, innovative and established (Amelia Peterson, Harvard University)

As education has multiple goals, the design of learning will always require a variety of practices and pedagogical approaches. There are two layers to address combinations, one about discrete practices within a framing pedagogical approach, and one about how combinations of established approaches can meet long-term educational goals. Where schools are thinking carefully about their learning design, they tend to anchor that design in a small number of approaches which are defined by the different ways they arrange time and agency. Each frame involves discrete pedagogies to achieve more specific teaching and learning goals within the sequence. The study of pedagogical combinations offers a fruitful way to understand how established pedagogical approaches can be brought together to create effective learning designs.

3.3.1. The evidence base

The learning sciences and the science of youth development provide a foundation for understanding the range of outcomes which pedagogies seek to achieve (Dumont, Istance and Benavides, 2010). The long traditions of pedagogical theory provide a basis for defining certain approaches and their contribution to outcomes. The ability to describe teaching and its impacts accurately has advanced through large-scale studies of teaching, including video studies and international surveys (e.g. Vieluf et al., 2012). One such sequence of studies concludes that impactful teachers are those who consistently achieve three central tasks: classroom management (structure); classroom climate (support); and cognitive activation (engagement and challenge) (Klieme, Pauli and Reusser, 2009). This is supported by a rich variety of other research which highlights the importance of both the social and emotional conditions created by interaction with teachers and peers, and the cognitive demand of tasks (National Research Council, 2003). Different pedagogies have developed different ways of balancing the three tasks and teachers are likely draw on a combination of pedagogical approaches.

The majority of research on teaching practices takes an evaluative frame and seeks to establish the 'effect' of a practice, using causal inference methods focusing on an individual pedagogy rather than on pedagogical combinations. There is no guarantee that practices studied in isolation have the same effect once combined (and ideally, any combination should equate to more than the sum of its parts). Systematic studies of the impacts of combining pedagogies may be found in studies of 'deeper learning' schools (Zeiser et al., 2014) or of the international baccalaureate programs (Saavedra, 2014), which tend to involve combinations of more discipline-centric and more inquiry or project-based pedagogies.

3.3.2. The context of combinations - expanded goals for education

Schools are expected to fulfil a number of important functions at once, including to prepare young people as future citizens, as well as to help them develop core knowledge and skills to be successful in work and life. If education were all about imparting content knowledge, developing and evaluating pedagogy would be all about establishing the best methods to promote memorisation and understanding of knowledge and concepts. But discipline-centric pedagogies cover only part of what a teacher, school or system might want to develop in students and there has been a concerted shift towards pedagogies which develop higher-level personal and social competences, driven by at least four factors.

First, there has been recognition that developing students' personal and social competences is a foundation for higher learning (Farrington et al., 2012). Second, societies and industries founded on digital technologies require people to manage and use a more complex array of information and increase the value of social skills. Third, societal changes have increased the complexity of choices and tasks young people face as they transition from adolescence to adulthood. Finally, in some quarters there has been a pushback against the intensified focus on standardised assessments of cognitive skills.

The shift in focus towards learner-centred pedagogies is part of a larger change in the way the goals of learning are acknowledged, who can learn and how. The science of learning has changed the way human potential and skill development are approached. There has been an increase in 'mastery-based' approaches to education which are intended to allow everyone to learn to a high level – a stark difference from the systems of a century ago. The shift in the balance of educational purposes from imparting an established body of knowledge to preparing lifelong learners has considerably implications for pedagogy.

3.3.3. The importance of pedagogical combinations

Teaching to develop personal competences cannot be achieved effectively without some teaching for knowledge acquisition, while teaching knowledge alone is futile if students do not have the personal and social competences to put it to use. It is only useful to talk about 'discipline-centric' and 'student-centric' pedagogies for the purpose of clarity about intentions. In actual teaching, teachers find they need to bring these different pedagogies back together to meet the multiple dimensions of learning. Teaching is therefore all about combinations.

Achieving balance

In combining pedagogies, the central question is one of balance. How teachers organise their own time and that of their students has implications for the range of opportunities students have to develop competences, and the depth and breadth of knowledge they acquire. The table below illustrates how different established pedagogies tend to lead to different kinds of learning experiences.

Table 3.3. Different approaches create different learning experiences

		What makes students keep working?			
		Teacher instruction	Self-managed	Group dynamics	
What do students work on?	Teacher choice	Lecture	'Personalised'	Collaborative	Time-based
	Co-constructed	Mastery-based	Blended	Discussion	Continuous assessment
	Student choice	Scaffolded inquiry	Independent inquiry	Project-based	Final product
					When do we move on?

Trade-offs in combining pedagogies: variety vs. familiarity

Each type of pedagogy comes with trade-offs related to the advantages and disadvantages of different set-ups. Combining pedagogies which share common practices can help reduce the trade-offs of using too many pedagogies. For example, in a school where students are practiced in inquiry-based learning, teachers might feel more confident in combining his approach with challenges or complex projects, knowing that students are competent at managing their own learning. Studying common combinations of pedagogies can help to identity those practices which are common to several pedagogies, such as presentations of learning, or student self-assessment.

Combining pedagogies into a school design

When a school has a robust, overarching pedagogical design, it has made a collective decision as a community about how to combine several pedagogies to meet multiple educational goals. The advantage of this is that the power of each pedagogy is strengthened considerably. When teachers are working with the same pedagogical approach, individual teacher planning can be reinforced, and teachers can collaborate more easily, sharing ideas and improving each other's practice. Students in such schools can transfer the learning of one year or subject area to another. The promotion of long-term outcomes is likely to be more successful when carried out across a whole school.

3.3.4. Creating strong combinations

Depth and balance: successful models seem to be those which balance approaches that maximise opportunities for students' personal and social development, with those which prioritise the development of core skills and knowledge.

A strong core, but with variations: each model has a single central approach which typically cuts across different subject areas or disciplines. Teachers view this as a 'core pedagogy' which provides a rhythm to the school day, week and year. Both within this structure and in separately allotted times, teachers also adopt subject-specific pedagogies to propel learning in particular domains. The combinations ensure that knowledge and skill development do not lose out amidst the focus on the core pedagogy.

3.3.5. Outstanding questions for research and practice

Balance – across what arc of learning? Some schools or networks are in a position to create a pedagogical design that covers the whole duration of formal schooling (or even beyond) but not always. Further work on how combinations are created at each stage of education could help inform this question.

Optimising – for what? In seeking to identify innovative combinations of pedagogies, it is necessary to have some way of evaluating what makes one combination better than another. But the combinations of pedagogies likely to lead to optimal knowledge outcomes may not be the same as that which leads to optimal personal and social development.

Less is more, or more is better? With the proliferation of network-specific versions of many pedagogical approaches, it is an open question whether it would be desirable to try to combine several of these together. It might be more desirable for a network to focus on building the best possible capacity around fewer anchors and frames, to create their own 'core pedagogy'.

3.4. Pedagogies and content: Mathematics, non-native languages, and socio-emotional learning (Marc Lafuente, Educational consultant)

3.4.1. Pedagogies – domain-neutral?

How independent are pedagogies from domains? Might a pedagogy be equally effective across domains or are specific pedagogies needed for particular domains and learning goals? The generalist school assumes that human development means to acquire general human capacities such as understanding or speech, which are used in whatever the context. Knowledge, skills and attitudes are transferable from one domain to another and the teacher's task is to "pedagogise" subject matter for students to learn it (Segall, 2004). The specialised school considers human development as the acquisition and accumulation of knowledge within different domains and is commonly associated with knowledge-centric school curricula. Pedagogy is inseparable from what is being taught - teachers identify the pedagogical nature of such materials, and work with and around them. For transfer to occur, it needs to be promoted explicitly through teaching practices (Dochy, 1992). Resolution of the two through a middle position is what may be called a "domain-sensitive" approach: pedagogies are shaped by domain specificities but they also work towards shared underlying aims like enhancing learner engagement, or social interaction and collaboration.

Although knowledge, skills and attitudes present both domain-specific and domain-transcending elements, they vary in the mix: knowledge tends to be more domain-specific than skills, especially when skills rely on heuristic procedures like note-taking or concept-mapping (Pozo and Postigo, 2000), while skills tend to be more domain-specific than attitudes. Mathematics is a subject that typically involves domain-specific competences, and relies on a large body of mathematical knowledge. Socio-emotional education, on the other hand, typically promotes domain-transcending competences, needing attitudes relevant across many learning tasks and contexts, like accepting plurality and difference or identifying and solving conflicts, and norms such as the rejection of violence.

Implications for pedagogy

There has been a growing policy interest in general competences, especially those described as "21st century competences" (Voogt and Roblin, 2012). This has sometimes led to instructional practices "apart from" school subjects and domains whereas fostering them within domains is essential so that students know how to use them in different contexts; indeed, this should be a major objective of instruction (Partnership For 21st Century Skills, 2009). It is complex because general competences impose their own pedagogical requirements which then need to be integrated within the pedagogical particularities of domain-related competences. Fostering general and specific competences at the same time means adopting sequences and combinations of pedagogies that find a balance between teacher-centred and learner-centred approaches and between focusing on students' understanding and their performance.

3.4.2. Pedagogical challenges in mathematics, non-native language and socio-emotional education

In *mathematics*, innovation needs to address the challenge of increasing student engagement and learning outcomes, which often means deploying pedagogies using more open, complex and authentic tasks, such as problem-based, project-based, and inquiry-based learning (e.g. Savelsbergh et al., 2016). Effective pedagogies need to focus on student's mathematical reasoning and sense-making (Boaler, 2012), fostering a conceptual discourse instead of a calculational one (Cobb and Jackson, 2011).

In *non-native language learning*, fluency and accuracy are both necessary which give a clear direction for innovating with pedagogy. It should ensure that the learning of grammatical form and communication are interconnected, and that they are embedded in meaningful and authentic contexts (Dalili, 2011). Common pedagogies to respond to these challenges are task-based learning (Ellis, 2003), and project-based learning (Chang and Tung, 2009), and may mean connecting teaching to other contexts.

Pedagogical innovations in the *socio-emotional domain* include, for instance, active and performance-based pedagogies that work on students' personal feelings and their relationships like role-playing, collaborative-based pedagogies, gaming, case study work, and social problem-solving (e.g. Rimm-Kaufman and Hulleman, 2015). Collaborative approaches like small group learning, and socially interactive pedagogies involving discussion, are especially important for promoting communication and emotional skills, as well as pro-social attitudes (e.g. Sprung et al., 2015).

3.4.3. Pedagogies, domains and the OECD Learning Principles

Pedagogies for learner engagement

Increased engagement, in mathematics and other domains, often means adoption of problem-solving, project-based, and inquiry-based approaches (e.g. Savelsbergh et al., 2016). Pedagogies based on metacognition have been used for increasing student engagement and improve self-regulation (e.g. Mevarech and Kramarski, 2014). For non-native language teaching, pedagogies engage students when they foster both mental representation of the language, and the ability to use it functionally (Van Patten and Benati, 2010). Pedagogies should both structure well-designed input and engage them in generating meaningful output (Wong, 2013). Teaching for socio-emotional learning tends to emphasise active and performance-based pedagogies (Durlak et al., 2011).

Pedagogies for social learning

In mathematics instruction, strong effects are associated with cooperative learning (e.g. Slavin, Lake and Groff, 2009), when all in the groups contribute (Cobb and Jackson, 2011) and when teachers guide and resolve doubts only when necessary. Developing instructional conversation is important for integrating communication and grammar, with teachers or more expert peers scaffolding learners through meaningful interaction while bringing out grammatical forms (Dalili, 2011). Language-minority children can especially benefit from cooperative learning (Cheung and Slavin, 2012). When socio-emotional education crosses subjects, there is common value in collaborative learning pedagogies with students working towards collective goals (Yoder, 2014).

Pedagogies sensitive to motivations and emotions

Regarding mathematics, addressing emotions is translated into encouraging every student to advance and foster self-awareness of progress, treating mistakes as opportunities for learning (Ingram, Pitt and Baldry, 2015), and shifting from appraising "the final answer" to evaluating student's comprehension (Näslund-Hadley, Cabrol and Ibarraran, 2009). Innovation in non-native language instruction has also focused on preventing language anxiety (Hashemi and Abbasi, 2013), which is more prevalent in listening and speaking tasks (Horwitz and Young, 1991). Education for socio-emotional development generally yields positive outcomes regarding self-perception and attachment to school and less distress and disruptive behaviour (Rimm-Kaufman and Hulleman, 2015), which in turn have a positive impact on other learning outcomes (Durlak et al., 2011).

Pedagogies to recognise individual differences

Gender and socio-cultural background are the differences that have attracted most attention regarding mathematics learning (Pais, 2012). Some propose contextualising learning as an opportunity to improve understanding of mathematical content (González, McIntyre and Rosebery, 2001), or to de-track grouping (e.g. Boaler, 2008). With non-native language teaching, pedagogies have been focused on taking into account the background and the conventions of the student's socio-cultural group (García et al., 2010), and reducing language anxiety levels (Woodrow and Chapman, 2002). Teaching for socio-emotional learning is also about developing understanding of individual differences and how to respond to different student profiles, especially related to gender and socio-cultural background.

Pedagogies to challenge students

In mathematics, difficulty should adjust to the learner and should challenge them through multiple resources like graphics or puzzles (Boaler, 2012). The sequence of learning tasks should present increasing difficulty, furthering understanding and performance (Cobb et al., 2011). Making tasks progressively more demanding is important in non-native language teaching (Barcroft, 2012) as well, with pedagogies constantly challenging the learner to understand more difficult input, and produce more complex output. Challenging students and providing support structures help develop socio-emotional competences, which demands time and attention, and using diverse learning tasks (Durlak et al., 2011).

Pedagogies for formative assessment and feedback

Research in mathematics education suggests that assessment practices should align with open-ended, complex and authentic mathematics tasks (Jones and Inglis, 2015), with a focus on students' intentions and approaches to solving the task, not only "corrective feedback". The same applies to non-native language teaching, where tasks should not be artificially separated by one skill such as a listening or speaking test but should involve a mix as in real-life (e.g. Bachman and Palmer, 2010). Performance-based tasks may be appropriate to promote socio-emotional learning, with teachers setting tasks that activate students' skills and attitudes such as collaboration or role-playing.

Pedagogies for horizontal connectedness

In mathematics, innovative pedagogies often aim to avoid excessively closed, repetitive and highly de-contextualised tasks without any connection to other domains or real-life contexts, often through problem-, inquiry-, and project-based approaches. Many researcher studies conclude that language-minority children benefit more from bilingual education than from non-native language monolingual instruction (Cummins, 2012). Research suggests the relevance of community-based approaches in socio-emotional learning (Durlak et al., 2011), in particular those linking the school to its community (Elias, 2014).

3.5. Attuning pedagogies to the context of 'new learners' and technology (Marc Lafuente, Educational consultant)

Some have asserted that there is a new type of young person who learns in new ways: digital natives (Prensky, 2001), the netGeneration (Tapscott, 2009), the iGeneration (Rosen, Carrier and Cheever, 2010), New Millennials (Howe and Strauss, 2000), and many others. They all assume that young people growing up with technology have acquired distinctive ways of learning. Empirical studies suggest, however, that the reality is more complex than this. Younger generations are heterogeneous in technology use and cannot be assumed to be digitally competent (e.g. Margaryan, Littlejohn and Vojt, 2011). Reshaping pedagogies to better meet new learning needs and interests requires a validated picture of what young people and their needs really are.

3.5.1. Technology use

Information and Communication Technology (ICT) is ever more pervasive and young people access it ever earlier and spend more time using it (OECD, 2015a). Teenagers spend on average two hours daily using computers for leisure, especially browsing the Internet for fun and participating in social networks. There is, however, no easy transition between the informal uses of technology and those commonly proposed in formal schooling. Meta-studies have generally yielded modest positive results in favour of using technology in classrooms (e.g. Sung, Chang and Liu, 2016; Cheung and Slavin, 2012). PISA analyses suggest that learning outcomes have not improved in countries that have heavily invested in technology (OECD, 2015a), and ICT may even be detrimental to learning if it is not appropriately integrated into the educational setting.

Table 3.4. Pedagogical implications of technology use

Advantages		Challenges	
Technology can improve learning outcomes.	Technology can improve learning engagement and motivation.	Young learners may not be technology savvy.	Technology may reproduce traditional pedagogies.
How pedagogies can help			
Pedagogies use technology as a complement of teaching and not as a substitute of it. Pedagogies give learners an active role and promote collaboration, while teachers use information to adjust support.	Pedagogies motivate learners "through technology" and not "to use technology". Pedagogies promote intrinsic motivation and avoid reliance on "novelty".	Pedagogies promote digital literacy. Pedagogies assess that students have the prior competences to engage with digital environments.	Pedagogies avoid transmission practices with teachers monopolising the technology. Pedagogies push students towards active strategies in using technology.

3.5.2. Multimedia

Children spend more time than ever in on-screen activities such as watching television, surfing the web and playing games on computers, tablets and cell phones (e.g. Bus, Takacs and Kegel, 2015). A common feature of those activities is how verbal and non-verbal information are combined in the same environment. In particular, children's books are adopting electronic formats that enable listening to the story, looking at animated pictures, listening to background sounds and music, and so forth. This creates a challenge for schools in which teaching has traditionally been dominated by text.

Research has shown that the different media may enhance learning, but under certain conditions. Takacs, Swart and Bus (2015) conducted a meta-analysis of technology-enhanced storybooks to find a small but positive effect of the multimedia on story comprehension and expressive vocabulary learning.

Table 3.5. Pedagogical implications of multimedia materials

Advantages		Challenges	
Multimedia materials can improve learning outcomes.	Students can engage in multimedia authoring.	Multimedia materials can create distraction.	Multimedia materials can create overload.
How pedagogies can help			
Pedagogies use sound instructional designs and adequately integrate them. Pedagogies take advantage of their power to represent narratives.	Pedagogies focus on promoting multimedia literacy especially in the construction of artefacts.	Pedagogies accompany the learner and scaffold their use of the materials. Pedagogies focus on relevant contents and productively integrate multimedia extra-features.	Practitioners make sure that multimedia contents can be understood by learners. Practitioners clarify the use of multimedia features and ensure that learners are able to use them.

3.5.3. Multi-tasking

Research shows that the average number of online activities per user has increased in OECD countries, especially in younger people (OECD, 2016a). Young people are thus regular multi-taskers, constantly switching or performing different tasks at the same time. Laboratory experimental research shows that multi-tasking is less efficient than single-task performance whether in time invested or accuracy achieved (Cardoso-Leite, Green and Bavelier, 2015). The daily use of technology inside and outside the classroom thus typically involves multi-tasking and yet it generally adds little to learning, unless it is carried out for very specific instructional purposes.

Table 3.6. Pedagogical implications of multi-tasking and interactive environments

Advantages		Challenges	
Teaching can prepare students for a world of distractions.	Interactive and non-linear environments can support learning.	Multi-tasking can be detrimental to learning.	Interactive and non-linear environments can encourage the "butterfly defect".
What pedagogies can do			
Pedagogies promote awareness of multi-tasking and its consequences.	Environments are designed and implemented according to sound pedagogical approaches.	Pedagogies actively address harmful multi-tasking.	Pedagogies promote use of knowledge frameworks by learners.
Pedagogies foster self-control and judicious use of multi-tasking in the classroom.	Designers and practitioners ensure that environments are suitable for learners.	Pedagogies are especially careful about multi-tasking regarding younger learners.	Pedagogies ensure that learners have sufficient competences to navigate the environment.

3.5.4. Active learning and gaming environments

Popular claims about young learners generally have them preferring active roles, needing constant rewards and positive feedback if they are to persist; preferring hands-on activities rather than listening to teachers; and preferring to play games, especially video games. The pedagogical challenge is to take advantage of the appeal of gaming for learning purposes (Lenhart et al., 2015). Evidence suggests that video games may be educationally valuable, provided that other key factors are met. The most important element is an adequate pedagogical integration of the game into the instructional context (Arnab et al., 2012).

Table 3.7. Pedagogical implications of gaming environments

Advantages		Challenges	
Gaming can yield positive learning outcomes.	Gaming can promote authentic learning.	Gaming can promote extrinsic motivation.	Gaming can cause overload and frustration.
What pedagogy can do			
Pedagogies ensure sound integration of video games into the instructional context.	Pedagogies ensure exploration and manipulation of realistic scenarios.	Practitioners focus students' attention on essential elements of learning.	Pedagogies provide useful feedback to the learner.
Pedagogies promote complementary structured activities to maximise the gaming experience.	Designers and practitioners ensure access to high quality digital games.	Pedagogies rely on simpler video games.	Pedagogies match the learner profile with the gaming experience.

3.5.5. Collaboration and social activities

Young learners are often assumed to need constant connectivity with peers and some studies have identified a preference for collaboration and technology-rich environments (e.g. Bekebrede, Warmelink and Mayer, 2011). Although evidence is still not extensive, research suggests that for Web 2.0 tools to be effective in schools is not so much about integrating Web 2.0 tools in the classroom, but about implementing the underpinning principles of Web 2.0 activities through pedagogy. So, it is the "Web 2.0 pedagogy" that is important, with blogs, podcasts, social networking sites and virtual worlds as tools to realise this approach. Such pedagogical approaches demand that teachers mentor and foster competences for self-regulated learning, compatible with learners as (pro-) active and collaborative.

Table 3.8. Pedagogical implications of collaborative and Web 2.0 environments

Advantages		Challenges	
Web 2.0 tools need to be implemented through adequate pedagogies.	Common Web 2.0 tools can be harnessed to improve collaboration competences.	Web 2.0 tools used with traditional pedagogies give rise to issues and tensions.	Web 2.0 tools can cause distraction.
What pedagogy can do			
Implement the "Web 2.0 principles". Practitioners adopt a mentor role and support self-regulated learning (e.g. orchestration).	Pedagogies use "real" tools to show new venues and ways of collaboration. Learning goes outside the classroom and students gain competences for lifelong learning.	Avoid transmission approaches and the automatisation of routines. Avoid the omnipresence of text and traditional conception of authorship.	Practitioners promote abilities to self-regulate the learning activity and stay on task. Practitioners and students work together to prevent and avoid common distractions.

3.6. Change and technology-enhanced innovative pedagogies (Nancy Law, University of Hong Kong)

Socio-political and education systems differ, and strategies for change should pay attention to the local ecological contexts to build "architectures for multi-level multi-scale (MLMS) learning". Learning outcomes extend beyond beliefs, knowledge and skills, to include organisational structures, decision-making processes, rules and regulations. Artefacts, social, physical and digital infrastructure and organisational routines are important learning outcomes at the different levels. This conception of learning outcomes lies at the core of the MLMS learning model. Structures and mechanisms for interactions and decision-making can be intentionally designed to foster self-organised learning towards the overarching vision and goals for student learning. This model can help guide pedagogical and assessment design, feedback and evaluation of MLMS learning for scalable technology-enhanced innovative pedagogies (TEPI) and serve as a framework to guide policy-makers, practitioners and researchers towards implementing TEPIs at scale.

3.6.1. Scaling technology-enhanced innovative pedagogy: the challenge

Since the 1990s, many countries have launched Technology-Enhanced Learning (TEL) initiatives, involving major investments to furnish schools with computing devices, Internet connectivity, extensive training and professional development of teachers. The rationale is often based on the expectation that learning through ICT will transform the learning process (Pelgrum and Law, 2003) to achieve 21st century outcomes such as collaboration, communication, creativity and critical thinking (Partnership for 21st Century Skills, 2009). However, principals indicating that ICT is very important for achieving pedagogical goals remain few in number, particularly so in economically developed countries with high computer/student ratios and levels of Internet access. More worrying, it is well documented that digital technology *per se* does not bring enhanced learning outcomes, as so much depends on the pedagogy adopted (Fisher, 2006). E-Learning needs to be an integral part of a deep pedagogical transformation in order to bring about the 21st century outcomes often mentioned in policy documents (Law, 2008a).

Using the international comparative SITES-M2 study, Law, Yuen and Fox (2011) identified six dimensions of innovativeness; of those, the roles of teachers and students in learning were the most highly correlated with the innovativeness - the non-traditional nature - of the learning outcomes achieved. Further, the pedagogical innovativeness of the case studies had no correlation with the sophistication of the learning technologies adopted. In fact, Law et al. found that the innovations implemented at larger scale tend to have less ambitious educational goals as a common strategic basis for participation, requiring lower levels of innovativeness in the pedagogical practices (Law, Kampylis and Punie, 2013).

3.6.2. Mechanisms of change at multiple levels for scalability

The most often cited approach for scaling innovations is Roger's diffusion model (Rogers, 2003). This model highlights the importance of communication and the need to attend to the social context and connections of the targeted audience for adoption. However, it takes innovations as ready solutions that only need to be implemented whereas technological tools and resources are just the media for realising TEPIs. A model for understanding the scalability of TEPIs needs to include mechanisms for change in the innovation adoption process by teachers and schools.

Design-based research: teachers as co-designers in TEPIs

TEPIs require deep changes in teachers' practices and roles in the classroom, thus requiring new knowledge, skills as well as beliefs about the goals and processes of learning (Law, 2008a). Training models focusing on imparting knowledge and skills are not effective in bringing about change in pedagogical practice. Models that report successful change provide experiential, action-oriented learning with teachers collaborating in communities of practice (Looi, Lim and Chen, 2008). Engaging teachers as co-designers in the implementation of technology-enhanced learning activities results in the greatest integration of technology-rich activities in teachers' practices compared with them being re-designers or simply executors of designed activities (Cviko, McKenney and Voogt, 2014).

Co-design is an effective form of teacher professional learning activity for change as it is underpinned by the same learning science principles as have been identified for effective student learning: collaborative, inquiry-focused, and addressing authentic real-life problems (OECD, 2008; 2010). This gives agency to teachers as learners and fosters the development of professional learning communities (Lieberman, Campbell and Yashkina, 2015).

However, classrooms are nested within schools, districts, state and national education systems and are influenced by wider commercial, political, bureaucratic, and professional organisations (Davis, 2008). In order to understand how TEPIs develop, the SITES-M2 study collected information about wider school, regional and national level contexts (Kozma, 2003). The study showed that school level factors such as leadership involvement and school culture had an important influence on the initiation and development of the TEPIs. Law (2008b) found school leadership engagement to be a strong contributing factor to the sustainability of the innovations. Cases where the school leadership supported teacher collaboration and the establishment of teacher communities of practice showed higher sustainability, as these provided mechanisms for sustained teacher learning.

Building multi-level learning architectures to support pedagogical innovation

Unlike the contexts studied in design-based research, where the participating teachers are generally innovators or early adopters, systemic change requires buy-in and new practices from the majority of teachers. Hence, understanding scaling pedagogical innovations can be enriched by literature on the implementation of pedagogical change through leadership at school and district levels.

In a study of how school leadership in four demographically different schools mediated teacher implementation of curriculum policy, Spillane, Parise and Sherer (2011) identify the importance of organisational routines as "coupling mechanisms" to change teachers' practices. Organisational routines as defined by Feldman and Pentland (2003) refer to "a repetitive, recognisable pattern of interdependent actions, involving multiple actors" (p. 95). These routines connect specific elements of the policy regulation to the formal structure and administrative practice of the school to achieve greater alignment with teachers' practices. By creating mechanisms and expectations for teachers to regularly share such important aspects of their practice as content coverage and grading student work, the organisational routines make these practices more transparent and open to monitoring.

Stein and Coburn (2008) discuss how successful implementations require effective channels of influence across community boundaries, extending interaction beyond teachers in the same school to include other communities within and outside their own school. They clarified this using Wenger's (1998) concept of "architectures for learning" - the organisational environments that foster teacher learning through communities of practice.

3.6.3. A multi-level multi-scale (MLMS) model of learning for scalable TEPIs

Here, a model for studying interdependencies using a parsimonious learning framework is proposed. As a dynamic model it includes changes at each of the levels, which all require learning and those learnings within and across levels are interdependent.

1. *Changes at each level are conceptualised as learning*: the conditions or factors at different levels influencing student learning should be conceptualised as learning outcomes of those levels, including: teachers' TPCK and assessment skills; the organisational structures, curricula, assessment and appraisal systems of schools; and national education policies, e-Learning strategies, teacher certification requirements and school inspection criteria.
2. *Tangible and conceptual artefacts as learning outcomes*: the main learning outcomes at the student level are seen as 21st century abilities such as critical thinking, collaboration and communication. Likewise at the other levels, the outcomes are policy and implementation decisions, ideally arising from collaborative problem-solving. There are feedback loops connecting the constructs within each level and connecting constructs across the different system levels.
3. *Scale matters*: stakeholders at each level have to generate the learning outcomes through a process of authentic problem-solving – they also have to engage in 21st

century learning. Collaborative inquiry and idea diversity are important knowledge-building principles.

4. *Architectures for multi-level stakeholder engagement*: conditions for learning at the different levels such as classroom and school routines, staff appraisal criteria, national curriculum and assessment methods, are interdependent. For the innovation to develop at scale, these conditions need to evolve organically and interdependently over time through self-organising learning interactions across the different levels.

References

Alfieri, L., P.J. Brooks and N.J. Aldrich (2011), "Does discovery-based instruction enhance learning?" *Journal of Educational Psychology*, Vol. 103/1, pp. 1–18.

Arnab, S., et al. (2012), "Framing the adoption of serious games in formal education", *Electronic Journal of e-Learning*, Vol. 10/2, pp. 159-171.

Bachman, L.F. and A.S. Palmer (2010), "Language assessment in practice: Developing language assessments and justifying their use in the real world", Oxford University Press, Oxford, UK.

Barcroft, J. (2012), *Input-Based Incremental Vocabulary Instruction, TESOL International Association*, Alexandria, VA.

Bekebrede, G., H.J.G. Warmelink and I.S. Mayer (2011), "Reviewing the need for gaming in education to accommodate the net generation", *Computers and Education*, Vol. 57/2, pp. 1521-1529.

Boaler, J. (2012), "From psychological imprisonment to intellectual freedom – The different roles that school mathematics can take in students' lives", in *Proceedings of the 12th International Congress on Mathematics Education*.

Boaler, J. (2008), "Promoting 'relational equity' and high mathematics achievement through an innovative mixed-ability approach", *British Educational Research Journal*, Vol. 34/2, pp. 167-194.

Borman, G.D., et al. (2007), "Final reading outcomes of the national randomized field trial of success for all", *American Educational Research Journal*, Vol. 44/3, pp. 701–731.

Bus, A.G., Z.K. Takacs and C.A.T. Kegel (2015), "Affordances and limitations of electronic storybooks for young children's emergent literacy", *Developmental Review*, Vol. 35, pp. 79-97.

Cardoso-Leite, P., C.S. Green and D. Bavelier (2015), "On the impact of new technologies on multi-tasking", *Developmental Review*, Vol. 35, pp. 98-112.

Chang, S.Y. and C.A. Tung (2009), "Incorporating 21st century skills into business English instruction", *Feng Chia Journal of Humanities and Social Sciences,* Vol. 19, pp. 255-286.

Cheung, A.C.K. and R.E. Slavin (2012), "Effective reading programs for Spanish-dominant English language learners (ELLs) in the elementary grades: A synthesis of research", *Review of Educational Research,* Vol. 82/4, pp. 351–395.

Clarke, S.N., L.B. Resnick and C.P. Rosé (2015), "Dialogic instruction: A new frontier", in L. Corno and E. Anderman (eds.), *Handbook of Educational Psychology (3rd edition)*, pp. 378-389.

Cobb, P. and K. Jackson (2011), "Towards an empirically grounded theory of action for improving the quality of mathematics teaching at scale", *Mathematics Teacher Education and Development*, Vol. 13/1, pp. 6-33.

Corno, L. (2008), "On teaching adaptively", *Educational Psychologist*, Vol. 43/3, pp. 161-173.

Corno, L. and R.E. Snow (1986), "Adapting teaching to individual differences among learners", in M.C. Wittrock (ed.), *Handbook of Research on Teaching*, pp. 605-629), Mac-Millan, London.

Cronbach, L.J. and R.E. Snow (1977), Aptitudes and Instructional Methods: A Handbook for Research on Interactions, Irvington, New York.

Cummins, J. (2012), "The intersection of cognitive and sociocultural factors in the development of reading comprehension among immigrant students", *Reading and Writing*, Vol. 25/8, pp. 1973-1990.

Cviko, A., S. McKenney and J. Voogt (2014), "Teacher roles in designing technology-rich learning activities for early literacy: A cross-case analysis", *Computers and Education*, Vol. 72, pp. 68-79.

Dalili, M.V. (2011), "On the integration of form and meaning in English Language Teaching (ELT): An overview of current pedagogical options", *Procedia-Social and Behavioral Sciences*, Vol. 15.

Dochy, F. (1992), *Assessment of Prior Knowledge as a Determinant for Future Learning*, Jessica Kingsley Publishers, Utrecht, London.

Dumont, H., D. Istance and F. Benavides (eds.) (2010), *The Nature of Learning: Using Research to Inspire Practice*, OECD Publishing, Paris, http://dx.doi.org/10.1787/9789264 086487-en.

Durlak, J.A., et al. (2011), "The impact of enhancing students' social and emotional learning: A meta-analysis of school-based universal interventions", *Child development*, Vol. 82/1, pp. 405-432.

Elias, M.J. (2014), "The future of character education and social-emotional learning: The need for whole school and community-linked approaches", *Journal of Research in Character Education*, Vol. 10/1, pp. 37-42.

Ellis, R. (2003), *Task-Based Language Learning and Teaching,* Oxford University Press, Oxford.

Farrington, C.A., et al. (2012), *Teaching Adolescents to Become Learners. The Role of Non-cognitive Factors in Shaping School Performance: A Critical Literature Review*, University of Chicago Consortium on Chicago School Research, Chicago.

Feldman, M. S. and B.T. Pentland (2003), "Reconceptualising organizational routines as a source of flexibility and change", *Administrative Science Quarterly*, Vol. 48, pp. 94–118.

Fisher, T. (2006), "Educational transformation: Is it, like beauty? In the eye of the beholder, or will we know it when we see it?", *Education and Information Technologies*, Vol. 11.3, pp. 293-303.

García, E., et al. (2010), "Developing responsive teachers: A challenge for a demographic reality", *Journal of Teacher Education*, Vol. 61/1-2, pp. 132-142.

González, N., E. McIntyre and A.S. Rosebery (2001), *Classroom Diversity: Connecting Curriculum to Students' Lives,* Heinemann, Portsmouth, NH.

Guerriero, S. and N. Révai (2017), "Knowledge-based teaching and the evolution of a profession", in S. Guerriero (ed.), *Pedagogical Knowledge and the Changing Nature of the Teaching Profession*, OECD Publishing, Paris.

Hardy, I. (2006), "Effects of instructional support within constructivist learning environments for elementary school students' understanding of "floating and sinking", *Journal of Educational Psychology*, Vol. 98/2, pp. 307–326.

Hashemi, M. and M. Abbasi (2013), "The role of the teacher in alleviating anxiety in language classes", *International Research Journal of Applied and Basic Sciences*, Vol. 4/3, pp. 640-646.

Higgins, S., et al. (2015), *The Sutton Trust-Education Endowment Foundation Teaching and Learning Toolkit*, Education Endowment Foundation, London.

Horwitz, E.K. and D.J. Young (1991), *Language Anxiety: From Theory and Research to Classroom Implications,* Prentice-Hall, Englewood Cliffs, NJ.

Howe, N. and W. Strauss (2000), *Millennials Rising: The Next Great Generation*, Vintage Books, New York.

Ingram, J., A. Pitt and F. Baldry (2015), "Handling errors as they arise in whole-class interactions", *Research in Mathematics Education*, Vol. 17/3, pp. 183-197.

Jones, I. and M. Inglis (2015), "The problem of assessing problem-solving: Can comparative judgement help?", *Educational Studies in Mathematics*, Vol. 89/3, pp. 337-355.

Klieme, E., C. Pauli and K. Reusser (2009), "The Pythagoras study: Investigating the effects of teaching and learning in Swiss and German mathematics classrooms", in J. Tomáš and T. Seidel (eds.), *The Power of Video Studies in Investigating Teaching and Learning in the Classroom*, Waxmann, Munster.

Law, N. (2008a), "Teacher learning beyond knowledge for pedagogical innovations with ICT", in J.M. Voogt and G.A. Knezek (eds.), *International Handbook of Information Technology in Primary and Secondary Education*, pp. 425-434, Springer, New York.

Law, N. (2008b), "Technology-supported pedagogical innovations: The challenge of sustainability and transferability in the information age", in C.-H. Ng and P. Renshaw (eds.), *Reforming Learning: Issues, Concepts and Practices in the Asian-Pacific Region*, pp. 319-343, Springer, New York.

Law, N., P. Kampylis and Y. Punie (2013), "Towards a policy framework for understanding and upscaling ICT-enabled learning innovations: Synthesis and Conclusions", in P. Kampylis, N. Law, and Y. Punie (eds.), *ICT-enabled innovation for learning in Europe and Asia: Exploring conditions for sustainability, scalability and impact at system level*, pp. 115-135, Publications Office of the European Union, Luxembourg.

Law, N., W.J Pelgrum and T. Plomp (eds.) (2008), *Pedagogy and ICT in Schools around the World: Findings from the SITES 2006 Study*, CERC and Springer, Hong Kong.

Law, N., A.Yuen and B. Fox (2011), *Educational Innovations beyond Technology: Nurturing Leadership and Establishing Learning Organizations*, Springer, New York.

Lenhart, A. et al. (2015), "Teens, technology and friendships", *Pew Research Centre*, www.pewinternet.org/2015/08/06/teens-technology-and-friendships/ (accessed 9 October 2016).

Lieberman, A., C. Campbell and A. Yashkina (2015), "Teachers at the centre: Learning and leading", *The New Educator*, Vol. 11/2, pp. 121-129.

Looi, C.K., W.Y. Lim and W. Chen (2008, "Communities of practice for continuing professional development in the 21st century", in J.M. Voogt and G.A. Knezek (eds.), *International Handbook of Information Technology in Primary and Secondary Education*, pp. 489-505, Springer, New York.

Lortie, D.C. (2002), *Schoolteacher: A Sociological Study (2nd edition)*, University of Chicago Press, Chicago.

Margaryan, A., A. Littlejohn and G. Vojt (2011), "Are digital natives a myth or reality? University students' use of digital technologies", *Computers and Education*, Vol. 56/2, pp. 429-440.

Mevarech, Z. and B. Kramarski (2014), *Critical Maths for Innovative Societies: The Role of Metacognitive Pedagogies*, OECD Publishing, Paris. http://dx.doi.org/10.1787/9789264223561-en.

McGhee Hassrick, E., S.W. Raudenbush and L. Rosen (2017), *The Ambitious Elementary School. Its Conception, Design, and Implications for Educational Equality*, The University of Chicago Press, Chicago.

Näslund-Hadley, E., M. Cabrol and P. Ibarraran (2009), *Beyond Chalk and Talk: Experimental Math and Science Education in Argentina*, Inter-American Development Bank, Washington, DC.

National Research Council and the Institute of Medicine (2003), "Engaging schools: Fostering high school students' motivation to learn", *Committee on Increasing High School Students' Engagement and Motivation to Learn. Board on Children, Youth, and Families*, Division of Behavioral and Social Sciences and Education, The National Academies Press, Washington, DC.

OECD (2016), *Trends Shaping Education 2016*, OECD Publishing, Paris, http://dx.doi.org/10.1787/trends_edu-2016-en.

OECD (2015), *Students, Computers and Learning: Making the Connection*, OECD Publishing, Paris, http://dx.doi.org/10.1787/9789264239555-en.

OECD (2013), *Innovative Learning Environments*, OECD Publishing, Paris, http://dx.doi.org/10.1787/9789264203488-en.

OECD (2008), *Innovating to Learn, Learning to Innovate*, OECD Publishing, Paris, http://dx.doi.org/10.1787/9789264047983-en.

Pais, A. (2012), "A critical approach to equity in mathematics education", in O. Skovsmose and B. Greer (eds.), *Opening the Cage: Critique and Politics of Mathematics Education*, Sense Publishers, Rotterdam.

Partnership For 21st Century Skills (2009), *The MILE Guide. Milestones for improving Learning and Education,* www.p21.org/storage/documents/MILE_Guide_091101.pdf (accessed 27 September 2016).

Patrick, H., P. Mantzicopoulos and D. Sears (2012), "Effective classrooms", in K.R. Harris, S. Graham and T. Urdan (eds.), *APA Educational Psychology Handbook. Volume 2: Individual Differences and Cultural and Contextual Factors*, pp. 443-369), American Psychological Association, Washington, D.C.

Pelgrum, W.J. and N. Law (2003), ICT in Education around the World: Trends, Problems and Prospects, UNESCO, Paris.

Peterson, A. et al. (2018) "Understanding innovative pedagogies: Key themes to analyse new approaches to teaching and learning", *OE CD Education Working Papers*, No. 172, OECD Publishing, https://doi.org/10.1787/9f843a6e-en.

Peterson, A. (2016), "Getting "what works" working: building blocks for the integration of experimental and improvement science", *International Journal of Research and Method in Education*, Vol. 39/3, pp. 299–313, http://doi.org/10.1080/1743727X.2016.1170114.

Pozo, J.I. and Y. Postigo (2000), *Los Procedimientos Como Contenidos Escolares: El Uso Estratégico de la Información* [Procedures as School Contents: Strategic Use of Information], Edebé, Barcelona.

Prensky, M. (2001), "Digital natives, digital immigrants", *On the Horizon*, Vol. 9/5, pp. 1-12.

Randi, J. and L. Corno (2005), "Teaching and learner variation. Pedagogy - Learning for Teaching", *British Journal of Educational Psychology*, Monograph Series II, Vol. 3, pp. 47-69.

Rimm-Kaufman, S.E. and C.S. Hulleman (2015), "Social and emotional learning in elementary school settings: Identifying mechanisms that matter", in J. Durlak and R. Weissberg (eds.), *The Handbook of Social and Emotional Learning,* Guilford, New York, NY.

Saavedra, A.R. (2014), "The academic impact of enrolment in international baccalaureate diploma programs: A case study of Chicago public schools", *Teachers College Record*, Vol. 116/4.

Savelsbergh, E.R. et al. (2016), "Effects of innovative science and mathematics teaching on student attitudes and achievement: A meta-analytic study", *Educational Research Review*, Vol. 19, pp. 158-172.

Sawyer, R. K. (2015), *The Cambridge Handbook of the Learning Sciences (2nd edition),* Cambridge Univ. Press, Cambridge.

Segall, A. (2004), "Revisiting pedagogical content knowledge: The pedagogy of content/the content of pedagogy", *Teaching and Teacher Education*, Vol. 20/5, pp. 489-504.

Schofield, J.W. (2010), "International evidence on ability grouping with curriculum differentiation and the achievement gap in secondary schools", *Teachers College Record*, Vol. 112/5, pp. 1492-1528.

Slavin, R.E., C. Lake and C. Groff (2009), "Effective programs in middle and high school mathematics: A best-evidence synthesis", *Review of Educational Research*, http://dx.doi.org/10.3102/0034654308330968.

Slavin, R.E. (1990), "Achievement effects of ability grouping in secondary schools: A best-evidence synthesis", Review of Educational Research, Vol. 60/3, pp. 471-499, http://dx.doi.org/10.3102/00346543060003471.

Slavin, R.E. (1987), "Ability grouping and student achievement in elementary schools: A best-evidence synthesis", Review of Educational Research, Vol. 57/3, pp. 293-336.

Spillane, J.P., L.M. Parise and J.Z. Sherer (2011), "Organizational routines as coupling mechanisms policy, school administration, and the technical core", *American Educational Research Journal*, Vol. 48/3, pp. 586-619.

Sprung, M. et al. (2015), "Children's emotion understanding: A meta-analysis of training studies", *Developmental Review*, Vol. 37, pp. 41-65.

Stein, M.K. and C.E. Coburn (2008), "Architectures for learning: A comparative analysis of two urban school districts", *American Journal of Education*, Vol. 114/4, pp. 583-626.

Sung, Y.T., K.E. Chang and T.C. Liu (2016), "The effects of integrating mobile devices with teaching and learning on students' learning performance: A meta-analysis and research synthesis", *Computers and Education*, Vol. 94, pp. 252-275.

Takacs, Z.K., E.K. Swart and A.G. Bus (2015), "Benefits and pitfalls of multimedia and interactive features in technology-enhanced storybooks- A meta-analysis", *Review of Educational Research*, Vol. 85/4, pp. 698-739.

Tapscott, D. (2009), *Grown up Digital: How the Net Generation is Changing Your World*, McGraw-Hill, New York.

Van Patten, B. and A. Benati (2010), *Key Terms in Second Language Acquisition*, Continuum, London.

Vieluf, S., et al. (2012), *Teaching Practices and Pedagogical Innovations: Evidence from TALIS*, OECD Publishing, Paris, http://dx.doi.org/10.1787/9789264123540-en.

Voogt, J. and N.P. Roblin (2012), "A comparative analysis of international frameworks for 21st century competences: Implications for national curriculum policies", *Journal of Curriculum Studies*, Vol. 44/3, pp. 299-321.

Wenger, E. (1998). "Communities of practice: Learning as a social system", *Systems Thinker*, Vol. 9/5, pp. 1-5.

Wong, W. (2013), "Input and output in SLA. Applying theories of mental representation and skill", in J. Schwieter (ed.), *Innovative Research and Practices in Second Language Acquisition and Bilingualism,* Benjamins, Amsterdam, The Netherlands/Philadelphia, PA.

Woodrow, L. and E. Chapman (2002) (1-5 December 2002), *"Second language speaking anxiety of learners of English for academic purposes in Australia"*, paper presented at the AARE 2002 Annual Conference, Brisbane, Australia, www.aare.edu.au (accessed 16 August 2016).

Yeh, S. (2017), *Solving the Achievement Gap. Overcoming the Structure of School Inequality*, Palgrave Macmillan, New York.

Yoder, N. (2014), *Teaching the Whole Child: Instructional Practices that Support Social-emotional Learning in Three Teacher Evaluation Frameworks*, Revised Edition, American Institutes for Research, Washington, D.C.

Zeiser, K., et al. (2014), *Evidence of Deeper Learning Outcomes (3 of 3)*, American Institutes for Research, Washington, D.C., www.air.org/resource/evidence-deeper-learning-outcomes-3-3.

Part II. A compilation of innovative pedagogical approaches

Chapter 4. Six clusters of innovative pedagogies

Work on innovative pedagogy needs to be grounded in concrete examples of what this covers. The first part of this chapter describes the criteria and process followed to identify, select and build six discrete clusters of innovative pedagogies. A key criteria is the particular operationalisation of pedagogy as a dynamic interaction between different educational theories and the discrete implementations of teaching practices in the classroom. Then it is briefly explained the way in which the different dimensions of the C's framework are used to describe and analyse the clusters of innovations. It argues that these clusters are not necessarily stand-alone approaches, and proposes ways in which these clusters of innovative pedagogies can be combined to further reinforce each other. The chapter ends with an overview of the six following chapters in this part of the publication, each of which covers a specific cluster of innovative pedagogies in more detail.

4.1. Identifying and selecting innovative pedagogies

Work on innovative pedagogy needs to be grounded in concrete examples. In this volume, pedagogies are defined as the designed interactions of teaching and learning, and the ways of looking at these interactions. Pedagogy is thus both knowledge (ways of looking at) and action (the decision-making and designs shaping the interactions of teaching and learning in classroom practice). Compiling examples of innovative pedagogies has called for decisions about granularity and generality: the aim has been to compile clusters or families of innovative pedagogical approaches rather than to list numerous teaching methods that can be subsumed within the main pedagogical approaches.

Innovation is considered as alternative or fresh solutions to outstanding challenges, whether particular action or more abstract strategies. The innovation may lie as much in the way it is being tried or with whom rather than in specific practices. To be innovative in this sense does not depend on being "new": some of the approaches in the compilation have been around for a long time. At a system level, the innovation may lie in mainstreaming approaches that have hitherto been marginal. In fact, Alternative Education has long been a source of inspiration for how teaching and learning can be re-imagined, some aspects which have been widely implemented (e.g. co-education) while others may still be largely confined to 'innovative' schools (e.g. project-based learning). The relationships have been strengthened by the growing body of educational research confirming many of the alternative education learning and teaching principles (Sliwka, 2008). Most of the innovative approaches, indeed, coming from research-based practices are significantly rooted in the designs of socio-constructivist models and the experiences of alternative education schools (Bereiter and Scardamalia, 2008).

In identifying the pedagogical approaches for the Compilation, innovative content or skills as defining criteria was not used. For instance, education for sustainable development (ESD), entrepreneurship, citizenship or arts-based education were not included as examples of innovative approaches, although some of these topics were subsumed into a wider approach. Certain of the clusters, such as Multiple/Critical Literacies and Computational Thinking, are strongly associated with content areas/skills but represent innovative ways to frame teaching and learning more widely. Embodied learning is one cluster in the Compilation that is defined in terms of the importance of arts, design and physical education, areas which offer particular ways of framing teaching and learning overall, and which show potential for realising the targeted learning goals.

Some well-established educational approaches as cooperative and socio-emotional learning, or multi-disciplinary teaching have not been included as separate clusters because these are rather considered as key pillars of the foundations of the 'new science of learning', not pedagogies *per se* (Huffaker and Calvert, 2003; Dumont, Istance and Benevides, 2010). Therefore, the compilation set out clusters of practices that are intentionally based on those new learning principles and for that reason it approaches cooperative learning, for example, as a sort of starting point, a paramount learning goal that any learning design must set. Not surprisingly, the networks presented and discussed in Part III of this report significantly stated that principle two - the social nature of learning - of those described in the nature of learning (Dumont, Istance and Benevides, 2010) was explicitly addressed by their pedagogical approach. Similarly, from the six clusters of pedagogies, Experiential Learning, which is one of the approaches most directly connected with cooperative learning, is the approach that is shared by most of the innovative networks that were contacted.

4.2. The clusters of innovative pedagogies

Figure 4.1. Clusters of innovative pedagogies

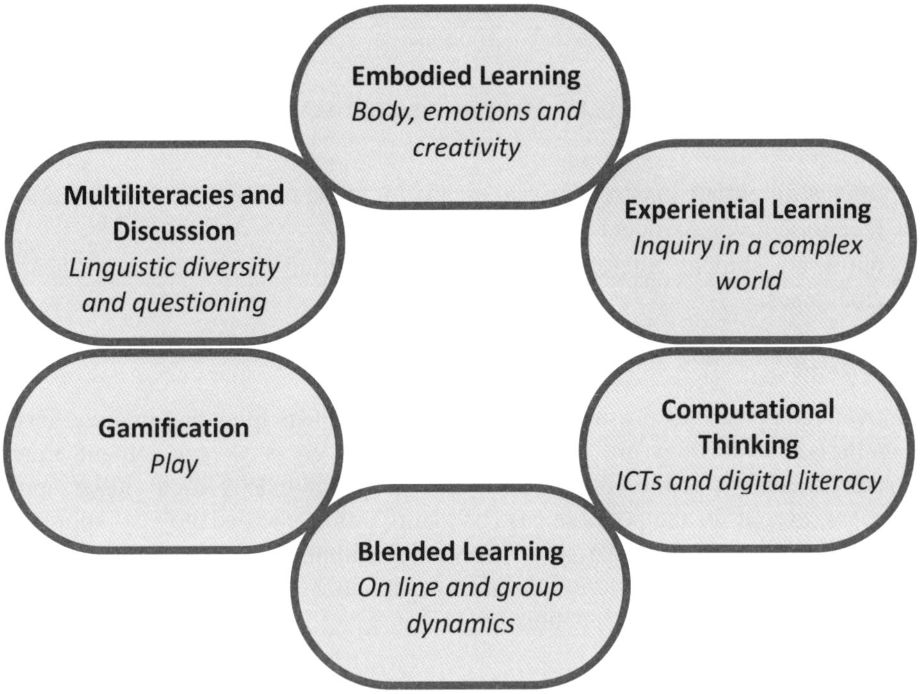

The description and discussion of the six clusters of innovative pedagogies is organised below, through lenses provided by the C's framework.

4.3. Understanding the clusters of innovative pedagogies through the C's framework

4.3.1. Combinations

By addressing pedagogies as clusters of practices that share a common understanding of teaching and learning, each pedagogical approach combines different theoretical models and practices. Explicitly highlighting combinations helps connect theories of teaching and learning with specific pedagogical approaches. Hence, the compilation chapters show either: how practices and approaches are combined to define the particular grouping of that chapter or how the pedagogical cluster is linked to other approaches and teacher practices.

4.3.2. Connoisseurship

The critical dimension of connoisseurship in the compilation is discussed by providing evaluative examples on how best to implement each approach, including an example of expert implementation. The criteria supporting this selection look beyond only academic outcomes to include when possible new principles of learning and 21st century skills. The focus on experiences does not mean that these are valued for 'doing for the sake of doing' but for the extent in which these can show track record and how approaches are being understood and implemented. In multiliteracies and embodied learning, for instance, these experiences show a 'collateral' impact on learning in the benefits of, for example, bilingual or arts-based education. In other cases, the approaches and content are too new to have generated a robust impact evidence base (e.g. computational thinking), though academic outcomes are reported whenever possible.

4.3.3. Context

This dimension in the compilation is used to address how the innovative pedagogies offer more opportunities to learn. Context framing innovative pedagogies is discussed, with regards to how these clusters:

- offer differentiated instruction and means for students to participate in learning;
- recognise diverse student backgrounds;
- build on student interests and connect teaching with real and meaningful challenges.

4.3.4. Content

The innovative approaches pursue the OECD Learning Principles that include horizontal connectedness, and so they are not strongly anchored in particular content areas, and rather refer to content as the competences that are promoted by each cluster approach. Nevertheless, except for the possible case of gamification, the pedagogical approaches in the compilation are not 'subject free'. There are the implicit connections and influences related to the epistemic structure of different domains, and historical traditions and teachers beliefs around subject domains.

4.3.5. Change

Change in the compilation was focused primarily at the classroom level and its immediate surroundings. Scale also underpins all the approaches presented in the compilation, for teachers and schools need to engage in a steady process of integrating these innovations in their practices and pedagogical knowledge. Change is conceptualised as learning and teachers need scaffolding to improve their pedagogical knowledge and successfully adopt an innovation.

4.4. Insights for combining the clusters of innovative pedagogies

Following Peterson (Chapter 3), school designs can benefit enormously from combining different approaches to meet multiple educational goals, finding a balance between domains, skills, and grades of integration of different innovations. This section offers different ways in which the idea of Combinations can be applied to the clusters of innovative pedagogies presented in the compilation. It argues for the need to not view these clusters as stand-alone approaches, since there are strong connections between them. Rather, the nature and the theories underlying these approaches cover common areas and show ways in which these can reinforce each other. In this section the aim is to describe how these six clusters may fit together, overlap and be combined.

The three examples of combinations described in this section do not aim to be exhaustive, and are based on a possible interpretation of the implications of each cluster, rather than on actual experiences coming from school experiences. This is why the first two examples do not include vignettes of the way they might work in a real scenario. However, the third example builds on one real implementation identified in the Italian network Amico Robot. The case of robotics provides with some evidence about the potential impact of combining some of the clusters of innovative pedagogies.

Figure 4.2. The six clusters of innovative pedagogies

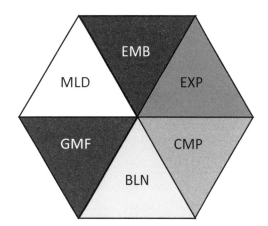

EMB = Embodied learning
EXP = Experiential learning
CMP = Computational thinking
BLN = Blended learning
GMF = Gamification
MLD = Multiliteracies and discussion

4.4.1. Combination 1: Embodied learning and multiliteracies and discussion-based teaching

In this combination, the core link between these two clusters is the fact that language is an inherent form of expression; or similarly, any genuine channel to express ourselves constitutes a form of language. In this sense, arts are a form of communication, one in which codes used for express emotions and ideas need to be mastered or at least traceable – that is, rules of language. On the other hand, is truly difficult to imagine any form of language or serious reflection –or discussion- that is not connected with our identity, feelings, which frame the way people talk, interpret or raise arguments. In this regard, art related tasks can benefit enormously from developing language competences, and vice versa.

Figure 4.3. Combining embodied learning and multiliteracies

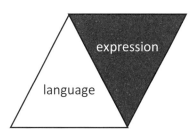

4.4.2. Combination 2: Gamification, embodied learning and computational thinking

These three clusters can be easily combined given the strong links between ICTs and design in the current days. An illustrative example comes from those activities consisting of the use of basic coding languages to design videogames that students can then play – and learn - with. This creates a powerful artefact with creativity and design at its core, whilst using a more restrictive use of computational thinking (coding) and gamification (gaming) as a result.

Figure 4.4. Combining gamification, embodied learning and computational thinking

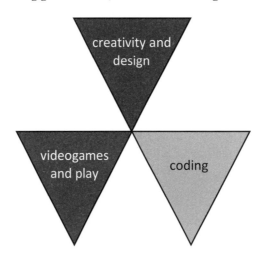

4.4.3. Combination 3: Robotics

This combination is based on one genuine approach coming from one of the networks discussed in Part III of this publication, Amico robot. In the implementation of their pedagogical approach, this network looks at robotics not only as an innovative content, but as a platform to meet three common goals:

- Implement innovative pedagogies, with a great emphasis of the active role of learners.
- Have a new approach to ICTs.
- Develop 21st century skills, such as creativity, team work and metacognition.

In terms of clusters, robotics illustrates the way in which experiential learning, computational thinking and embodied learning are combined, as students need to learn how to design and programme these robots, and also to collaborate and investigate with their peers to improve their creations –there is an annual competition in which schools from the network compete.

Figure 4.5. Suggested combination of clusters representing robotics

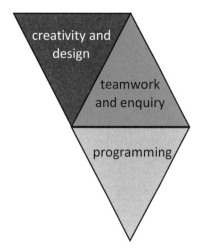

Through presenting how the idea of combinations are not only related to discrete teaching practices, but also to wider pedagogical innovations, it is possible to imagine the diverse ways in which the clusters proposed can potentially describe any given pedagogical innovation. In this sense, the compilation of clusters of innovative pedagogies also works as a tool to organise the current landscape of innovations.

4.5. Overview of the six clusters

The chapters that make up Part II of this volume are each organised around one of the six clusters of innovative pedagogies. More specifically, they are:

Chapter 5: Blended learning *rethinks established routines to get more from teaching.* This pedagogical approach blends student work and teaching for understanding, re-thinking their sequencing and drawing heavily on digital learning resources. The aim is to be both more engaging and coherent for learners, and to free teachers from more routine practice in favour of interactive and intensive classroom activities.

Chapter 6: Gamification *builds on how games can capture student interest and facilitate learning.* "Gamification" encompasses the pedagogical core of gaming and the benefits of playful environments for engagement and well-being. There are two main pedagogical components: mechanical elements (rapid feedback, badges and goals, participation, and progressive challenge) and emotional elements (narratives and identities, collaboration and competition).

Chapter 7: Computational thinking*, developing problem-solving through computer science.* Computational thinking (CT) looks at problems in ways that can be solved by computers. Its basic elements are logical reasoning, decomposition, algorithms, abstraction and patterns. It offers a comprehensive scientific approach, bringing together a language (coding), a process (problem-solving), tools (programmes), and uses experimentation and learning-by-doing.

Chapter 8: Experiential learning *through active experience, inquiry and reflection.* Experiential learning (EL) connects learners with the realities being studied by focusing evidence and strengthening inquiry, while learning about complexity and uncertainty. Innovative pedagogical approaches, such as inquiry-based learning, education for sustainable development, learning-by-doing, outdoor learning, and service-learning, build on or intertwine with EL.

Chapter 9: Embodied learning *connecting with the physical, the emotional and the social.* It revolves around pedagogies using creative experiences and active student involvement to promote knowledge acquisition. There are three main approaches: school-based physical culture; arts education and arts-integrated learning; and maker culture. Embodied Learning entails a significant shift in education systems that have prioritised the abstract, the individual, and content acquisition.

Chapter 10: Multiliteracies and discussion-based teaching *developing cultural distance and critical capacities.* This range of approaches recognises multiple literacies in the contexts of cultural diversity and ubiquitous technology. They include critical literacies which situate knowledge in its political, cultural and authorial contexts. Discussion is central in questioning received ideas and dislocating the hegemony of any dominant language.

References

Bereiter, C. and M. Scardamalia (2008), "Toward Research-based Innovation", in *Innovating to Learn, Learning to Innovate*, OECD Publishing, Paris, http://dx.doi.org/10.1787/9789264047983-5-en.

Dumont, H., D. Istance and F. Benavides (eds.) (2010), *The Nature of Learning: Using Research to Inspire Practice*, OECD Publishing, Paris, http://dx.doi.org/10.1787/9789264086487-en.

Huffaker, D.A. and S.L. Calvert (2003), "The New Science of Learning: Active Learning, Metacognition, and Transfer of Knowledge in E-Learning Applications", *Journal of Educational Computing Research*, Vol. 29/3, pp. 325-334.

Sliwka, A. (2008), "The Contribution of Alternative Education", *Innovating to Learn, Learning to Innovate*, OECD Publishing, Paris, http://dx.doi.org/10.1787/9789264047983-6-en.

Chapter 5. Blended learning

Blended learning seeks to use the potential of new technology to offer more individualised teaching and direct instruction. It is one the main global trends shaping education environments and it has become increasingly important in higher education. This chapter describes the various forms of blended learning, all of which aim to optimise face-to-face interactions and class time. Examples include flipped classrooms and specific forms of e-Learning. The chapter then explores key elements required to effectively implement this approach, including the identification of particular challenges that need to be addressed. This is followed by a reflection on the ways blended learning can be implemented beyond higher education, as well as the suitability of this approach for different content areas. The chapter ends by outlining key conditions for introducing blended learning in schools, such as the need for teachers to enhance their technological pedagogical and content knowledge.

5.1. Definition

The main goal of blended learning is to maximise the benefits of technology and digital resources, to improve the differentiation of instruction according to students' needs, as well as fostering classroom interaction. This pedagogical approach is built on the foundation that the active involvement of students can best be achieved through group dynamics and intense face-to-face interactions. Computer technology can offer direct instruction through individual, highly planned and structured sequences of skills. When computers provide the relevant information, teachers can be freed of more routine practices and have more time for concept application, using more interactive and complex classroom activities or providing 1-on-1 instruction. Figure 5.1 reproduces the idea of Blended Learning, which is commonly simplified as being online courses. The idea is that technology automates and improves certain teaching and learning processes, thus freeing more time for other more interactive classroom activities and scaffolding for those children with more difficulties.

Figure 5.1. The model of blended learning

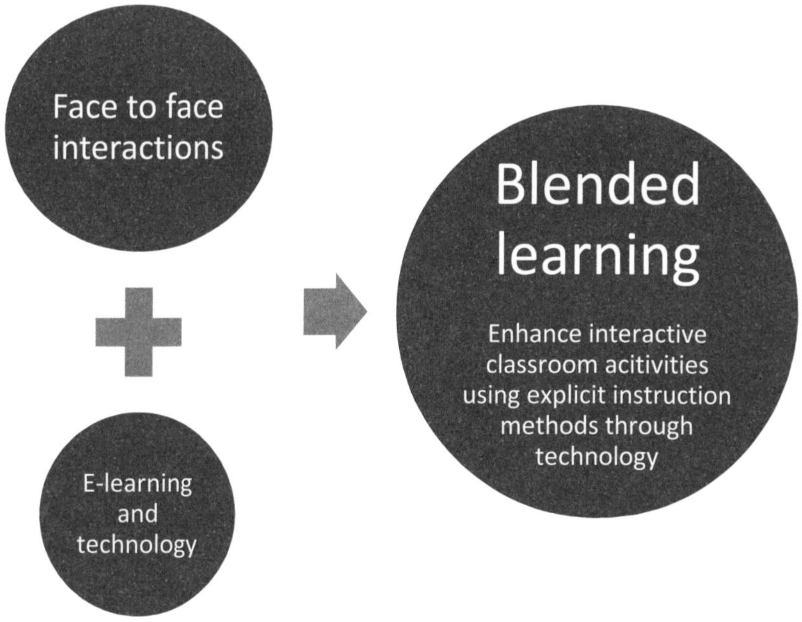

The relations of teachers and students is importantly impacted by blended learning, for it entails changing the main role of the teacher from giving lectures to mentoring; it means to shift direct learning out of the large group and into the individual space.

Blended learning exists on a continuum depending on how the online instruction and face-to-face learning take place. There are three main forms:

- *The inverted/flipped classroom*, in which students are assigned the homework relevant to the next session and then practice this content in the classroom.
- *The Lab-based model of blended learning*, in which a group of students rotate between a school lab or classroom to receive/reinforce/enhance content with the content applied through face-to-face interactions with the teacher.
- *'In-Class' blended learning*, in which individual students follow a customised schedule rotating between online and face-to-face instruction.

These three approaches can be adapted according to the needs of students, the capacities of teachers and the resources available in the school. For example, Ingram et al. (2014) describe the case of five teachers using the flipped classroom model in which students were asked to work on homework assignments based on content-related videos and quizzes. During the next session, after a whole group lecture, each teacher engaged in three different approaches to class time. In approach A students worked individually within a time frame. In approach B students also worked individually, but at their own pace. Thirdly, in approach C, students worked in groups, with computers, moving through various 'stations'. Teacher interactions also differed, ranging from pulling out groups of students and randomly monitoring students (in approaches A and B), to providing particular support in one of the stations (in approach C).

5.2. Combinations

Blended learning combines two sets of pedagogies, one for each phase in which this approach is structured. When students engage in individual, self-directed activity, direct instruction and cognitive tutors are the main pedagogical forms leading the engagement of students in their own learning. Using instructional videos, recorded lectures and other Internet-based items, students can decide whether to pause and rewind the content or to expand and look for more information.

As the majority of the role of the teacher is centred on conceptual application, blended learning is often combined with inquiry-based and collaborative approaches promoting the active and meaningful participation of students. Therefore, the goals of face-to-face interactions are to offer more demanding and complex problem-solving tasks, promote deeper conceptual coverage and fuel peer interactions.

5.3. Connoisseurship

Box 5.1. Improving the effectiveness of flipped classrooms

- Prepare motivating, in-class activities so students can use content information in real-life situations.
- Organise content ahead of time, record videos as though talking to students and repeat as many times as needed.
- Videos should be short and simple and connect directly to assignments.
- Educators should prepare students by discussing the benefits, making a list of what and why students need to know the content from the video; setting deadlines for students; offering a time for them to watch the video, and preparing worksheets, quizzes, and questions to answer after watching the video.
- Feedback must be given as immediately as possible while assessing which steps in the process are working well for students and which less well.
- Do not assume students are comfortable with the technology.

Source: Logan, B. (2015), "Deep exploration of the flipped classroom before implementing", *Journal of Instructional Pedagogies*, Vol. 16, pp. 1-12, www.msdf.org/wp-content/uploads/2016/01/MSDF-Blended-Learning-Report-May-2014.pdf.

Blended learning, including flipped classrooms, is still a relatively new approach and therefore information is scarce about impact (Murphy et al., 2014). Studies that exist report increases in student learning and satisfaction as well as an enhanced sense of purpose in their at-home activities, for these are done to prepare classes rather than to as follow-up to explanations. The interaction and the challenging assignments prepared in class are reported as being more engaging for students, who in turn are also more active.

According to ClassroomWindow and the Flipped Learning Network (2012), two-thirds of the 450 teachers who flipped their classrooms reported increased test scores, with particular benefits for students in advanced placement classes and students with special needs; 80 percent reported improved student attitudes; and 99 percent said they would flip their classrooms again next year. Hamdan et al. (2013) report how a high school transformed itself by flipping the learning after witnessing a strong improvement in student discipline and failure rates.

Box 5.2. Key challenges to be addressed for implementing blended learning

- Focus on struggling students, as they tend to lack the autonomy, motivation and skills to work individually or in high demanding skills in groups thereby risking being marginalised in group interactions.
- Avoid over-reliance on blended learning, which need to be combined with other approaches and lesson plans that have been successful previously.
- Avoid putting too much emphasis on the homework/autonomy required at home or when students are on their own.
- Blended learning should be seen as a way to open up the classroom, innovate and introduce inquiry-based, student-centred pedagogies; it is thus a way to re-think traditional models of teaching and learning.

Source Neilsen, L. (2012), "Five reasons I'm not flipping over the clipped classroom", *Technology & Learning*, Vol. 32/10, pp. 46.

5.3.1. *Example of practice: flipping the unit on 'The Great Gatsby' in a High School*

Shaffer (2015) discusses how the adoption of a flipped approach can have important consequences for teaching practices. In his description of how one English tutor used flipped learning to work on 'The Great Gatsby', Shaffer highlights four areas that characterise 'flipping'.

First, planning and time are the most important factors underpinning this process. During the weeks preceding the unit, the teacher had to decide the activities to 'flip' and reframe them accordingly. A WebQuest for background information, a Google Docs quiz, a blog response and a Vodcast about the main theme covered in the book were selected to guide concept acquisition at home. While at home, students could use available links in the WebQuest, hold discussions on line, or pause or rewind the Vodcast as needed.

Second, technological knowledge and access is an important challenge especially when there is lack of teacher technological skills or issues around student access to the content at home. Technological pedagogical and content knowledge (TPACK) plays a pivotal role when integrating technology as a routine in lesson planning and development.

Pedagogy and classroom discourse is the third. As students complete the web search at home they have already begun the lesson, thus allowing the teacher to work more on challenging discussions and deeper analysis and the process of writing about literature. Therefore, discussion and work in small groups were favoured in the class. The teacher pushed the students to be more critical and to move beyond simple recall questions through requesting comparisons, analysis, connections and deep reflection.

The final characteristic is classroom management. Shaffer identified the need to familiarise students with the accountability arising in the use of technology at home for educational purposes. The teacher created a procedure to control who did the activities proposed at home and to manage the collaborative work of those doing the quiz or the Vodcast together. In conclusion, the teacher found that students were more motivated and understood more challenging questions related to The Great Gatsby because of the time opened up for discussion in the flipped classroom.

5.4. Context

Blended learning in higher education or K-12 classrooms has been mainly implemented through flipped classrooms, acquiring new, more complex skills and improving student engagement. Students are requested to work on their own, as well as to have a good Internet connection at home. In elementary grades and in high schools, flipping and blending learning have gained growing attention (Sharples et al., 2014). Blending learning in the presence of the teacher also helps those children experiencing difficulties or the less motivated. The additional time saved from class lectures allows for the adaptation to different learning styles and pace of students, and for more differentiated instruction. As teachers can invest more time to help students apply the content, they can offer both struggling and advantaged learners greater opportunities to learn.

5.5. Content

Given the varying nature of pedagogical content knowledge and the particularities of each teacher and school, not all subjects and units are equally "flippable". Blended learning and flipped classrooms may work best when the content is more linear, and thus can be broken down to simpler processes, such as maths and sciences as they have traditionally been taught; they have been most in evidence in classrooms being flipped. But it is by no way the only areas in which blended learning can be implemented, as this example shows.

A first challenge arising in using the blended learning approach are students who are less independent, who need the teacher guidance and support in order to read, understand and review the material intended for concept acquisition. Instruction must provide those students with the scaffolding and feedback to help them navigate the computer-based lectures, take advantage of peer collaboration and participate effectively in inquiry-based activities. A second challenge is the degree of complexity of a task or concept: the level of skills and knowledge learners need to acquire or apply the new information and the ability to build creatively on existing knowledge, and adapt it to new learning tasks and contexts. Teachers can meet this challenge by designing activities that directly relate to the skills and knowledge that learners need to mobilise, thus breaking down holistic processes into linear procedures.

5.6. Change

Blended learning can be implemented on a continuum from minimal online activities to minimal face-to-face interactions and take several forms depending on where and when the online activities take place. Further, as the example given reveals, blended learning allows for its implementation in whole units of subjects. This suggests that the extent of change depends on the particular forms and scale in which this flipping/blending occurs in any school.

Three conditions are paramount for implementing and sustaining the blended learning approach:

- *Technological pedagogical and content knowledge (TPACK) skills*. Online and computer-based activities require teachers to operate ICT-based tools. TPACK goes beyond the skills required to operate technologies to include the interaction between knowledge of content, technology, and pedagogy.
- *Appropriate infrastructure and software design*. It is necessary to integrate and often improve ICT resources and their pedagogical use in the classroom or school. Likewise, ICT tools require specific programs and applications that meet the pedagogical needs of the lessons and ease the preparation of online activities.
- *Time and pedagogies*. To "flip" teaching and learning involves re-thinking deeply both the role of the teacher and the students in the classroom, and especially to adapt face-to-face teaching appropriately. Blended learning frequently involves the use of other approaches and new skills in parallel – e.g. inquiry-based activities and facilitating student cooperation. This all requires time and development.

5.7. In summary

- Blended Learning opens the possibility for personalisation of learning through self-paced programs, adaptive online instructional content and small group instruction.
- Students in flipped classrooms may feel more responsible for their learning and recognise that they have multiple options available, in particular scaffolding resources in case they face challenges when acquiring or applying new content.
- Blended Learning allows teachers to experiment with active learning by using ICTs to boost faculty freedom.

References

ClassroomWindow and Flipped Learning Network. (2012). Flipped Classrooms: Improved test scores and teacher satisfaction, https://flippedlearning.org/wp-content/uploads/2016/07/classroomwindowinfographic7-12.pdf.

Hamdan, N., et al. (2013), A White Paper Based on the Literature Review titled 'A Review of Flipped Learning', *Flipped Learning Network & George Mason University*, https://flippedlearning.org/wp-content/uploads/2016/07/WhitePaper_FlippedLearning.pdf.

Ingram, D., et al. (2014), *A Study of the Flipped Math Classroom in the Elementary Grades*, University of Minnesota, Saint Paul, MN.

Logan, B. (2015), "Deep exploration of the flipped classroom before implementing", *Journal of Instructional Pedagogies*, Vol. 16, pp. 1-12. www.msdf.org/wp-content/uploads/2016/01/MSDF-Blended-Learning-Report-May-2014.pdf.

Murphy, R., et al. (2014), *Blended Learning Report*, Michael & Susan Dell Foundation.

Neilsen, L. (2012), "Five reasons I'm not flipping over the clipped classroom", *Technology & Learning*, Vol. 32/10, pp. 46.

Sharples, M., A. Adams, R. Ferguson, M. Gaved, P. McAndrew, B. Rienties, M. Weller and D. Whitelock (2014), "Innovating pedagogy 2014", *Open University Innovation Report 3*, The Open University, Milton Keynes.

Shaffer, S. (2015), "One High School English Teacher on his way to a flipped classroom", *Journal of Adolescent & Adult Literacy*, Vol. 59/5, pp. 563-573.

Chapter 6. Gamification

The use of videogames in innovation and teaching is a major new trend. Part of this importance lies in the attractiveness of making learning as fun and engaging as videogames. The challenge of using gamification as pedagogy comes from the generalised idea that it is rather a pure 'motivational' resource to make lessons more appealing, but not a new way of thinking about teaching and learning. This chapter covers the concept of gamification as an approach seeking to transfer the pedagogical mechanisms of games into formal teaching. The discussion then looks at key elements for the effective implementation of gamification, including the identification of particular challenges that need to be addressed, like using gamification as 'chocolate-covered broccoli' to reinforce traditional teaching. A key idea outlined in this chapter is the need to connect gamification with formal pedagogies in a way in which guides students to perform these tasks they cannot yet perform independently.

6.1. Definition

Play holds an important role in children's learning, and supports intellectual, emotional and social well-being. Research has shown how play, among other things, can improve memory and stimulate the growth of the cerebral cortex, provide avenues for learner engagement in academic tasks, contribute to language development, and promote creative problem-solving and reasoning (Deward, 2014). When children are asked about what is important to them, playing and friends are often reported as their top priorities (Lester and Russell, 2008).

Given the importance of play, playful experiences need to be considered as potential learning experiences, driven by self-motivation and interest. Although there are different forms in which gaming is incorporated into formal education (e.g. gamification, game-based learning, serious games), the term "gamification" is used here to include the pedagogical core of gaming and the benefits of playful environments for engagement and well-being. Tulloch (2014) maintains that 'games function through pedagogy', and thus the challenge is to capture and exploit the pedagogic structure of games while maintaining the element of play. The 'Institute of Play' is a non-profit design studio that creates learning experiences and environments based on the principles of game design; it has distilled these into a set of learning principles (Flatt, 2016). These revolve around inclusion, experimentation and embeddedness, in which:

- Everyone is a participant.
- Learning feels like play.
- Everything is interconnected.
- Learning happens by doing.
- Failure is reframed as iteration.
- Feedback is immediate and ongoing.
- Challenge is constant.

Drawing on these principles, gamification goes beyond 'game designing' to emphasise the underlying benefits of play and the ways that games can be integrated into formal learning. Game-based learning is where an activity mimics a game and includes explicitly playful elements. Meanwhile gamification is about integrating the pedagogical principles of play and games.

6.2. Combinations

Although gamification allows for a wide range of activities (depending on the game mechanics being integrated into the classroom), there are four sets of pedagogies at the core of gamified teaching:

- learning through storytelling;
- assessment for learning;
- problem-solving;
- experiential learning.

Games are based on rules and goals which crystallise in the form of narratives. These narratives give learners a sense of purpose, even an identity. As presented in the *Innovating Pedagogies Series* (Sharples et al., 2014), storytelling offers a way of engaging learners over time, structures the activity in which they are immersed, and encourages customised thinking. Narrative pedagogies focus on interpretation and critical thinking, providing a context-sensitive approach to learning, which is paramount for gamification, and requires learners to explore and collaborate.

While narratives provide the space and purpose of game-like learning environments, continuous assessment provides the guiding force. Through assessments, learners interact and are compelled to respond while being informed of progress. As the impact of their decisions happens concurrently with the development of the activity, both the learners and the teacher can constantly (re)calibrate the challenge and be aware of the extent to which learning goals are being met. This constant feedback is key to achieving a state of flow as defined by Csikszentmihalyi (1990), where the learner is in a state of total focus on the task at hand without feeling too bored, relaxed, anxious or thrilled.

Problem-solving and experiential approaches are inherent to gaming. The environments and narratives in which players interact require them to make decisions and solve problems of increasing difficulty and which often include a degree of inquiry. If the effectiveness and interest of gamification lies in its capacity to engage students, the educational value of gamification is to connect the gaming experience to learning principles and relevant content. This is often achieved by incorporating learners' experience and real-life topics into the narratives and challenges of these game-like tasks.

6.3. Connoisseurship

There is growing research revealing the potential of gamification for improving learning experiences and outcomes. However, the evidence suggests that further improvements are needed in order to create clear goals, challenging tasks, and authentic stories that foster collaboration and discussions (Faiella and Ricciardi, 2015). Gamification is not an educational panacea, and teachers need to identify specific elements that work for particular learning goals. Access to and use of technology and the Internet must ensure that all students can participate equally in the game experiences. Although reports vary depending on the kind of experience and the use made by learners, positive outcomes in cognitive, emotional and social areas have been described, along with calls for caution and for further implementation of diverse experiences (Hamari et al., 2014).

Box 6.1. Improving the effectiveness of gamification

- Deep understanding takes time, reflection, and active engagement, which are the strengths of games. Gamification must not be seen as a shortcut to immediate success (Young et al., 2012).
- There is need to create and build on an educational video game repository (Young et al., 2012).
- Pay special attention to the elements of the 'metagame' (e.g. discussions around the game or activity) and 'metacognition' (strategies to control and regulate cognition) that takes place during the activity (Young et al., 2012).
- Gamification should start with a suitable pedagogical approach which will guide the overall design and sequencing of critical learning interactions and game play (Arnab et al., 2012).
- Focus on the freedom to experiment, fail and receive continuous assessment, so that learners can increase their awareness of their competences, their autonomy and collaboration. (Oxford Analytica, 2015).
- Gamification is well-aligned with mixed skill groups, where students can take on the role of teacher and explain issues to the less advanced (Oxford Analytica, 2015).
- Participation is empowering in gamified experiences when the students can choose between gamification and traditional methods (Faiella and Ricciardi, 2015).

Box 6.2. Key challenges to be addressed for implementing gamification

- Most schools trade off extended immersion for curriculum coverage, individual play, and short exposures, which militates against engaging with game-based environments (Young et al., 2012).
- If too much effort is given to the logics of the gamified experience (including how to cheat), then gamification 'wastes' attention that could otherwise be given to the subject matter (Oxford Analytica, 2015).
- If learning is too explicitly related to the pursuit of points, levels and so on, gamification risks diminishing the reward of learning *per se*, hindering the intrinsic motivation to learn (Oxford Analytica, 2015).
- It is problematic to secure the transfer of knowledge from the context of gamification into the non-game context, so it is paramount to build on well-aligned educational goals and gamified experiences (Faiella and Ricciardi, 2015).
- Engagement and motivation tend to decrease over time, especially when the novelty wears off, placing a premium on long-term perspectives and discrete, well-contextualised experiences (Faiella and Ricciardi, 2015).

6.3.1. Example of practice: using Game of Thrones to gamify the teaching of history in a high school

This example is offered by Natxo Maté (2016) whose specific aim was to 'transform history content into a game', building on the fact that not only children but also adults are constantly willing to 'assault' moments for playing. He calls it a 'spirit' for playing, which can be channelled by games. After testing different experiences (e.g. one-day role gaming), Maté created a webpage with narratives and a universe for the gamified experience to transform a history semester. For example, there is a 'battlefield' area instead of 'homework' and there are not grades but 'glory marks', all designed with images from Game of Thrones (GT). The interplay between technology and narratives creates a bridge to students' interest. The Middle Ages are particularly suitable because the fantasy elements surrounding that period makes it easier to bridge with the universe of GT.

The first element Maté describes is collaboration, to show that peer cooperation is needed to transform the poor town into the capital of the kingdom (the game's goal). In creating this experience, the teacher aimed to make the students sensitive to the different privileges that characterised people's lives at that time. Immersion in a detailed story and identification with realistic characters, are important elements in order for the students to comprehend what it meant to be a servant or noble. The third element is experimentation, where 'failure' is framed just as a step to improvement. The last element is task diversification, so customising the gamified experience. Along with the course book, there are tournaments, a manual, craft activities, and diverse routes to success.

Maté describes five game mechanisms he included in the design:

- challenges and missions, not activities (e.g. decorating the classroom like a church from that age);
- points and progress, whereby students can be promoted to nobility if they succeed in the missions and tournaments;
- rewards, based on the collective work (e.g. use the book text for five minutes during an assessment, listen to music while working in the classroom, and so on);
- constant feedback, provided by a hand-made 'tablet' that recreates the information of the website, with tables resuming achievements;
- badges, to award those attitudes and behaviours aligned with the objectives, such as helping others in tasks or missions.

Maté cautions that this experience is not an example of the miracles of gamification but rather of how a gaming design can be satisfactory for everybody and an additional tool, along with blended learning, to enrich teaching and learning.

6.4. Context

Although gamification and game-based learning are rapidly gaining attention from primary and secondary educators, only around 10% of the experiences documented in 2014 were from these educational levels, with almost half from training or extra-activities rather than strictly academic courses (Carponetto et al., 2014). Most of the potentially new gamification initiatives are still recent and relevant information is limited.

Gamification has been justified by its motivational appeal, with a reluctance to evaluate with hard data. Sometimes, gamification is presented as a way to introduce new and complex skills to adolescents and adults, particularly in Computer Science or IT courses in higher education, while others have stressed early childhood and primary education, given the importance of play at these ages and the more holistic approach of these educational levels (Dichev and Dicheva, 2017).

Gamification could be particularly suitable for those students at risk of disengagement and educational under-achievement; and certain forms of gamification (e.g. videogames) could especially appeal to boys at risk (Oxford Analytica, 2015).

6.5. Content

Several reports have indicated the relevance of gamification in a wide range of subjects, such as science, maths, languages, physical education, history, and art and design. Gamification has been used extensively to support learning in training and one-off activities, as well as in pursuit of transversal objectives such as peer collaboration, completion of homework assignments, fostering exploratory approaches and strengthening learner creativity (Carponetto et al., 2014).

The benefits associated with self-regulated learning, metacognition and non-cognitive outcomes make gamification suitable for transversal content and skills. Rather than identifying content areas in which gamification may prove most useful, it is instead the particular configuration of the games design which provides the basis for its application in such areas or for specific skills (e.g. certain game-related pedagogical components may be more interesting for certain learning outcomes and so on).

6.6. Change

The influence of games on teaching can be broken down into two main components: mechanical elements (rapid feedback, badges and goals, participation, and progressive challenge) and emotional elements (narratives and identities, collaboration/competition). These elements can be incorporated explicitly or implicitly into teaching and the design of lessons, following a continuum from minimal and embedded integration (e.g. certain badges, an explicit sense of purpose framed in a narrative, some role playing) to an explicit educational use of games (video games, serious games). Much of the current debate around gamification risks understating the alternative, pedagogic dimension it offers to inform pedagogies in schooling (Tulloch, 2014). If there is a disconnect 'between the possible instructional affordances of games and how they are integrated into classrooms' (Young et al., 2012), the main challenge of gamification is to change classrooms and teaching practices, thus becoming an interface between the underlying pedagogies of gaming and formal pedagogies (see Table 6.1).

Table 6.1. Connecting gaming with formal pedagogies

Gaming elements	Formal pedagogies	Principles of institute of play
Rapid feedback	Formative assessment	Feedback is immediate and ongoing
Participation	Inclusive education	Everyone is a participant, failure as Iteration
Badges, goals	Experiential learning	Learning happens by doing
Progressive challenge	Adaptive teaching	Challenge is constant
Narratives, identities	Narrative pedagogies	Everything is interconnected
Collaboration/Competition	Collaborative learning	Learning feels like play

The main achievement of gaming, and as a result makes it so appealing, lies in how it can teach complex rules to players, introduce them to unfamiliar worlds, and engage them in tasks and logics without prior skill. Not all games succeed in this, but when it happens it is done by creating the delicate balance between challenge and skills, in a feeling of easiness, fun and what psychologists have named 'flow' (Csikszentmihalyi, 1990); learners avoid being excessively bored, relaxed, anxious or thrilled.

If the Vygotskian notion of 'zone of proximal development' has played a pivotal role in understanding the target 'bandwidth of competences' to inform the design of any learning environment, gamification can help to understand more wholly the importance of the activity itself in appealing to learners' voice and agency. In this sense, the activity becomes the missing component in the 'thin line between the ability, motivation, and enjoyment that encourages students to go beyond the requirements to meet extended goals' (Abdul Jabbar and Felicia, 2015). Figure 6.1 shows the importance of the engagement of learners to establish the zone of proximal development, which is not only about fitting learners' skills with the proposed activity, but also to motivate them to fully use their capacities and skills to reach this zone, as represented by the green arrow.

Figure 6.1. Gamification within educational designs using the zone of proximal development

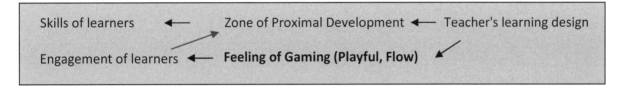

6.7. In summary

- Gamification goes beyond 'game designing' and focuses on the underlying benefits of play and the mechanics of games within the context of formal learning.
- The power of gamification lays in its ability to engage students. The main challenge is how to make game mechanics support learning, avoiding using games as occasional rewards for learning.
- This approach is not an educational panacea - a careful use should focus on identifying specific elements that work for particular learning goals rather than on implementing overarching approaches without enough evidence of effectiveness.

References

Abdul Jabar, A. and P. Felicia (2015), "Gameplay engagement and learning in game-based learning: A systematic review", *Review of Educational Research*, Vol.85/4, pp. 740-779.

Arnab, S., et al. (2012), "Framing the adoption of serious games in formal education", *Electronic Journal of E-Learning*, Vol. 10/2, pp. 159-171.

Csikszentmihalyi, M. (1990), *Flow: The Psychology of Optimal Experience*, Harper & Row, New York.

Dewar, G. (2014), "The cognitive benefits of play; effects on the learning brain", *Parenting Science*, www.parentingscience.com/benefits-of-play.html.

Dichev, C. and D. Dicheva (2017), "Gamifying education: what is known, what is believed and what remains uncertain: a critical review", *International Journal of Educational Technology in Higher Education*, Vol. 14/5, http://dx.doi.org/10.1186/s41239-017-0042-5.

Flatt, R. (2016), "Revolutionising schools with design thinking & game-like learning", *Institute of Play*, www.fbofill.cat/publicacions/presentacio-revolutionizing-schools-design-thinking-game-learning.

Faiella, F. and M. Ricciardi (2015), "Gamification and learning: A review of issues and research", *Journal of e-Learning and Knowledge Society*, Vol. 11/3, pp. 13-21.

Hamari, J., J. Koivisto and H. Sarsa (2014), *Does Gamification Work? A Literature Review of Empirical Studies on Gamification*, Proceedings of the 47th Hawaii International Conference on System Sciences, 6-9 January, Hawaii, USA.

Lester, S. and W. Russell (2008), "Play for a change. Play, policy and practice: A review of contemporary perspectives", *Play England*, http://www.playengland.org.uk/media/120519/play-for-a-change-summary.pdf.

Maté, N. (2016), *Games of Thrones: From Slaves to Kings: A Gamified Experience*, Presentation given at Education Tomorrow, Fundació Jaume Bofill, www.fbofill.cat/videos/joc-de-trons-desclaus-reis-experiencia-de-gamificacion.

Oxford Analytica (2016), "Gamification and the future of education", *World Government Summit*, www.worldgovernmentsummit.org/api/publications/document?id=2b0d6ac4-e97c-6578-b2f8-ff0000a7ddb6.

Sharples, M., et al. (2014), "Innovating Pedagogy 2014: Exploring new forms of teaching, learning and assessment, to guide educators and policy makers", *Open University Innovation Report 3*, The Open University, Milton Keynes.

Tulloch, R. (2014), "Reconceptualising gamification: Play and pedagogy", *Digital Culture & Education,* Vol. 6/4, pp. 317-333.

Young, M., et al. (2012), "Our princess is in another castle: A review of trends in serious gaming for education", *Review of Educational Research*, Vol. 82/1, pp. 61-89.

Chapter 7. Computational thinking

Computational thinking intersects mathematics, ICTs and digital literacy. It aims at addressing maths as a language to coding, and looks at ICTs as a platform for developing a problem-solving reasoning in students. Computational thinking as pedagogy goes beyond simply adding computing science in the curriculum to better understand how scientists use computers to frame and solve real problems. This chapter opens with the pedagogical value of problem-solving skills and computer-based techniques as a necessary form of general pedagogical knowledge. Then the discussion focuses on key areas for the effective implementation of this approach, including the identification of particular challenges that need to be addressed. The value of creativity when integrating computational thinking is also discussed. Special attention is directed to coding as a new competence that is increasingly included in the curriculum. The chapter ends by highlighting the importance of mathematics as cross-cutting competences and the need for professional development for teachers focusing on computational thinking skills.

7.1. Definition

Computational thinking (CT) intersects with mathematics, sciences and digital literacy to offer a unified framework to work a wide range of transversal skills through ICTs. At its core, CT is about looking at a problem in a way that a computer can help us to solve it. This implies having at least a tacit understanding of how a computer works and how to use it to solve real problems and create purposeful products. The starting point is computing but CT does not necessarily mean using computers or mastering programmes or codes. Rather, it is a fresh approach using problem-solving thinking and computer science.

CT is often described as a two-step process: one to imagine the ways to solve a problem and another that to make computers work on the problem. This includes a significant number of discrete techniques, such as approximate solutions, parallel processing, model checking, debugging, and search strategies. There is general agreement around the basic elements of this approach (see Box 7.1.).

Box 7.1. Problem-solving skills and computer-based techniques

- Logical reasoning: analyse, predict and deduce outcomes.
- Decomposition: break down one big, complex problem into many smaller ones.
- Algorithms: identify and describe routines, create step-by-step instructions.
- Abstraction: capture the essential structure of a problem, while removing unnecessary detail.
- Patterns: identify and use common solutions to common problems.

Source: Berry, M. (2014), "Computational thinking in primary schools", *Teach Primary*, http://milesberry.net/2014/03/computational-thinking-in-primary-schools/.

In a technological, research-driven age, skills associated with technological devices give students opportunities to access and navigate the resources of modern society, including in the information technology professions. But whereas much emphasis has been put on improving generic skills regarding ICTs, CT highlights the importance of: 1) developing an understanding of computer science and its relationship with mathematics and sciences; 2) gaining an understanding of computer programming and coding as a new form of literacy (Vee, 2013), thus opening up writing to include images, sound and other modes of composition and communication; and 3) bringing science and mathematics education more in line with current professional practices in these fields.

7.2. Combinations

Coding and computer programming have received significant attention in discussion of CT. CT is sometimes seen as 'algorithmic thinking' and writing codes, but if the goal is to learn how to look to at a problem in new ways, or to find new answers according to a given sets of possibilities - as a computer or programming language might -, then the skills associated with the generation of ideas and openness to develop and explore ideas need to be practised along with CT skills. Consequently, CT is closely connected with approaches to problem-solving, digital literacy, experiential learning and creativity.

Computer science and computers can be thought of as a physical and linguistic interface between students' interactions with the real world and their abstract knowledge and skills. On this view, CT becomes a comprehensive scientific approach, combining a particular language (coding), process (problem-solving) and tools (programs); these produce visible, discrete outputs with an important role given to experimentation, tinkering and learning-by-doing. Logical reasoning, algorithm thinking and decomposition foster the inquiry skills of students, while programming and coding play a supportive role in traditional writing. This all creates fruitful opportunities to combine digital literacy and mathematics to make learners more competent and creative users of information and communication technology.

7.3. Connoisseurship

There is currently a mismatch between the way students engage with computing technologies, such as social networking software or games, and how CT concepts are embedded in K-12 education. Very little research is available on how teachers could be prepared to incorporate CT ideas into their own teaching (Bower et al., 2017). However, there is some promising research showing the positive impact of CT competences on student outcomes in K-12 subject areas, confirming the wider influence of CT beyond students' problem-solving skills. For example, Calao et al. (2015) describe how the development of CT using the Scratch visual programming environment improves student performance in mathematically-related areas such as modelling, reasoning, and problem-solving while providing more engaging learning environments.

Box 7.2. Key areas to secure the effectiveness of computational thinking

- A multidimensional approach for a systematic change is needed to integrate CT at the K-12 level (Yadav et al., 2014).
- Teachers' understanding of CT must build on the subject matter they teach (Yadav et al., 2014).
- There should be an increasing use and sharing of computational vocabulary by both teachers and students regarding the appropriate way to describe problems and solutions (Barr and Stephenson, 2011).
- Recognition that failed solutions is part of the iterative process to reach successful outcomes (Barr and Stephenson, 2011).
- CT tools and environments for children should have low thresholds while the tool should be powerful and extensive enough to lead to satisfactory outcomes: 'low floor, high ceiling' (Grover and Pea, 2013).
- Promote a 'use-modify-create' progression to help learners move from user to modifier to creator of computational artefacts (Grover and Pea, 2013).
- Curricular activities such as game design and robotics have typically proved useful for the iterative exploration of CT and also a good way of introducing computer science to students (Grover and Pea, 2013).
- Combine different computational tools as they vary in their effectiveness to teach the various components of CT (Grover and Pea, 2013).

Another potential impact of CT concerns the opening of opportunities for more student-centred practices and general pedagogical innovation. Teachers working through CT reported that they used either student-centred pedagogies (e.g. problem-solving, project-based, group work, open-ended tasks) or mixed pedagogies in 70% of the cases. After receiving Continuous Professional Development on CT, the proportion of teachers adopting student-centred practices rose to 85% (Yadav et al., 2014). CT has proved to be a fertile way to engage with robotics (Beebots, Lego Robotics) and game-based learning (Repenning et al., 2010).

A central element of CT is programming. It defines a central process for CT that encourages and links all its components. Programming in K-12 goes back to the 1960s when Logo programming was introduced as a way of teaching mathematics. In recent years, the availability of easy-to-use visual programming languages such as Scratch, Toontalk, Stagecast Creator or Alice has renewed this interest alongside the general interest in CT (Lye and Koh, 2014) and its connection with 21st century competences (e.g. creativity, critical thinking and problem-solving). These programs approach programming using the representation of human language, while facilitating CT in K-12 because syntax is reduced to the minimum while producing tangible results (low flow, high ceiling). On-going research suggests that K-12 students using these visual programming languages are able to create digital stories and games as powerful ways to consolidate what they have learnt (Repenning et al., 2010).

Box 7.3. Key challenges to implement CT

- Most teachers are aware of their own lack of understanding of CT concepts, which make them uncomfortable implementing CT activities. Therefore, concept learning is as important as thinking in incorporating CT into pedagogy (Yadav et al., 2014).
- Lack of confidence of teachers in their competence and ability to gain access to resources are major teacher concerns (Bower et al., 2017).
- Although CT does not depend on access to computers or computer science, students need to connect and experiments with computational tools and artefacts; this means it is critical to balance 'plugged' and 'unplugged' activities within a CT approach (Berry, 2017).
- Lack of technological resources, time and advice to incorporate CT to the curriculum (Bower et al., 2017).
- School curriculum is a complex environment with multiple competing priorities: testing pressures on core subjects make it difficult to add such a large concept to an already-busy curriculum (Bower et al., 2017).
- Without guidance on the cognitive aspects of CT, the programming experience may be non-educative as students do not reflect actively on their experience; careful planning is needed to avoid haphazard engagement (Lye and Koh, 2014).

7.3.1. Example of practice: food chain in K-12 education

Computer At School, the Computer Science Teachers Association (CSTA) and the International Society for Technology in Education (ISTE) are some of the leading organisations providing teachers with resources, toolkits, professional development programmes, and a wide range of documentary materials about CT and computer science. This example summarises a learning experience showcased in the CSTA and ISTE's Computational Thinking Teacher Resources Toolkit on ways to integrate CT into education (CSTA & ISTE, 2011). The main goals in this case are to represent data through abstractions, automate solutions through algorithmic thinking, and generalise and transfer problem-solving competences.

It is designed for 9- and 10-year-old students, and introduces Scratch programming as a main outcome. The activity starts with the whole class brainstorming the characteristics of the food chain involving five elements: the sun, grass, a rabbit, a hawk and the decomposition process. The class has to discuss questions around the equilibrium of this particular food chain (e.g. risk conditions or making the chain more complex). Each student then creates a simple Scratch project to show in motion the food chain dynamics and demonstrate their knowledge. The activity concludes with team group work to re-design these projects adding more complexity.

In this activity, several CT components can be identified:

1. In the diagrams and relationships to explain the food chain, students need to create an abstraction that reduces the complexity of the process to highlight the main idea.
2. During the Scratch project, students work with simulations of the food chain, testing models to better demonstrate how the food chain works involving the five elements.
3. The Scratch project also involves a decomposition analysis whereby learners break down their story into manageable parts so that they fit into scratch language. This in turn engages them in using algorithmic thinking to ensure that commands are in line with scratch syntax and that the dynamic representation meets what they expect.
4. The final task allows for team collaboration and further discussion, building on previous brainstorming and animations, extending the activity to reflect more complex contexts and allowing for the transference of previous knowledge.

Box 7.4. Scratch as a programming language for children

Scratch is a visual block based programming language that allows you to programme sprite characters to do specific actions and then watch them happen on the screen. Algorithms are visual set of instructions that, linked, create sequences and repetitions. There are further commands such as selection (actions based on previous decisions), variables (information that changes, such as time or scores), and sensing (which affects the way inputs and outputs are related).

7.4. Context

CT has been coined as a one of the main 21st century skills, a new competence seen to be essential to live in a society heavily influenced by computing, and which needs to be taught and included in the curriculum. All the EU countries surveyed in 2015 included or were planning to include coding in the national curriculum (European Schoolnet, 2015).

Furthermore, CT also offers a new approach to develop transversal skills - a way to foster creativity and meaningful learning. It is a route to learning mathematical thinking in a more experiential way which often involves game-based software in K-8 and lower levels of education. As discussed by Berry (2013), CT is an active, intentionally driven, cooperative pedagogy that can foster the engagement of those more at risk in education. It is a pathway to address gender and social divisions with regard to technologies, and particularly computers and engineering.

7.5. Content

Given the connections between computation, mathematics and engineering, CT tools and skillsets can deepen the learning of mathematics and science, and vice versa. However, most analyses of CT describe a wider landscape (Manila et al. 2014). Organisations such as the Computer Science Teachers Association (CSTA) and the International Society for Technology in Education (ISTE) have defined computational thinking as a 'problem-solving methodology that can be automated and transferred and applied across subjects' (Barr and Stephenson, 2011). CT's core skills and concepts can therefore be embedded in STEM subjects as well as in social studies, language, and arts.

The relationship between CT and any specific content area is shaped by at least two main factors: the age of the learner and the way CT is embedded within the curriculum. It may be taught as an independent subject, building on the mastery of CT-related skills (e.g. learning to code in a specific programming language in higher education), or it may be embedded in contexts without programming or computers (e.g. understanding and representing how honey bees collect nectar, using a panel activity in K-8 education).

7.6. Change

A natural first step for schools to implement CT is to start looking at mathematics and ICTs skills in a more cross-cutting, comprehensive way. Some of the main components of CT (e.g. logical reasoning) have been taught in schools for a long time (Committee for the Workshops on Computational Thinking, 2010); rather than define the adoption of CT as something entirely new, it is more accurate to understand its adoption as generating a shift from strong, subject-based lesson planning to the design of activities based more on transversal competences and skills (Yadav et al., 2016). Weintrop et al. (2015) identified nine core CT competences applicable to K-12: data collection, data analysis, data representation, problem decomposition, abstraction, algorithms, automation, parallelisation, and simulation. In giving more visible importance to logical reasoning, algorithmic thinking and solving (scalable) real-life problems, CT fosters the creation of learning experiences as iterative processes for content to be understood and applied. CT calls for ICT and mathematics to be used as tools for other subjects, such that learners come to acquire CT skills that lead to them building up more complex CT-related skills in programming or information technology.

A second step involves professional development to equip primary and secondary teachers with CT and computing skills. Teachers also need to be familiar with computer systems, networks and the responsible use of ICT. In this regard, the development of a national curriculum (as in the United Kingdom), the availability of rigorous CPD courses and detailed toolkits (e.g. Computing At School resources), and certificates in computer science teaching all contribute to strengthening the expert implementation of CT. If the aim is to strengthen learners' capacity to code and programme then a strong focus on computer languages is needed. This stage might take the form of a competent, qualified teacher leading a specific CT-related subject; it may be a school planning a comprehensive approach to a specific skill, software or computational-related concept (e.g. use of scratch) or to the five CT components through the school year. In terms of change, this step could mean that a school designs CT as the driver to articulate subjects and other concepts and skills through the whole school.

7.7. In summary

- CT can be either understood as a new subject or as a set of transversal competences that go beyond traditional subjects.
- CT implemented means to move from acquiring skills for ICTs to understanding how to frame problems as scientists do, including a flexible approach to coding as a fundamental form of literacy for 21st century learners.
- Teachers need to be supported by CPD and clear step-by-step toolkits that enable a balance between the focus on CT concepts, on teaching practices associated with CT, and on identifying how CT can be embedded in traditional subjects.

References

Barr, V. and C. Stephenson (2011), "Bringing computational thinking to K-12: What is involved and what is the role of the computer science education community?", *ACM Inroads*, Vol. 2/1, pp. 48-54, http://dx.doi.org/10.1145/1929887.1929905.

Berry, M. (2015), QuickStart Primary Handbook. Swindon: BCS. http://primary.quickstartcomputing.org/resources/pdf/qs_handbook.pdf.

Berry, M. (2014), "Computational thinking in primary schools", *Teach Primary*, http://milesberry.net/2014/03/computational-thinking-in-primary-schools/.

Berry, M. (2013), Computing in the national curriculum. A guide for primary teachers, Computer at School. www.computingatschool.org.uk/data/uploads/CASPrimaryComputing.pdf.

Bower, M., et al. (2017), "Improving the computational thinking pedagogical capabilities of school teachers", *Australian Journal of Teacher Education*, Vol. 42/3, pp. 53-72.

Calao, L.A., et al. (2015), "Developing mathematical thinking with scratch. An experiment with 6th grade students", *Proceedings of the EC-TEL 2015, Design for Teaching and Learning in a Networked World, 10th European Conference on Technology Enhanced Learning*, www.springer.com/fr/book/9783319242576.

Committee for the Workshops on Computational Thinking (2010), *Report of a Workshop on the Scope and the Nature of Computational Thinking*, The National Academies Press, Washington, D.C.

CSTA & ISTE (2011), "Computational thinking", *Teachers Resources*, 2nd Edition.

European Schoolnet (2015), *Computing Our Future. Computer Programming and Coding: Priorities, School Curricula and Initiatives across Europe*, http://fcl.eun.org/documents/10180/14689/Computing+our+future_final.pdf/746e36b1-e1a6-4bf1-8105-ea27c0d2bbe0.

Grover, S. and R. Pea (2013), "Computational thinking in K-12: A review of the state of the field", *Educational Researcher*, Vol. 42/1, pp. 38-43.

Lye, S.Y. and J.H.L. Koh (2014), "Review on teaching and learning of computational thinking through programming: What is next for K-12?", *Computers in Human Behaviour*, Vol. 41, pp. 51-61.

Repenning, A., D. Webb and A. Ioannidou (2010), "Scalable Game Design and the Development of a Checklist for Getting Computational Thinking into Public Schools", *Proceedings of the 41st ACM Technical Symposium on Computer Science Education*, pp. 265-269, http://dx.doi.org/10.1145/1734263.1734357.

Vee, A. (2013), "Understanding computer programming as a literacy", *Literacy in Composition Studies*, Vol. 1/2, pp. 42-64.

Weintrop, D., et al. (2016), "Defining computational thinking for mathematics and science classrooms", *Journal of Science Education and Technology*, Vol. 25, pp. 127-147, http://dx.doi.org/10.1007/s10956-015-9581-5.

Yadav, A., et al. (2014), "Computational thinking in elementary and secondary teacher education", *ACM Transactions on Computing Education*, Vol. 14/1, article 5.

Yadav, A., H. Hong and C. Stephenson (2016), "Computational thinking for all: pedagogical approaches to embedding 21st century problem-solving in K-12 classrooms", *Tech Trends*, Vol. 60, pp. 565-568.

Chapter 8. Experiential learning

This cluster includes some approaches that best represent what innovation looks like in schools, for some the approaches included have been around for a significant period of time. In particular, this chapter revolves around three main forms of experiential learning: project-based learning, service-based learning and the teaching of uncertainty competences, as key skills to prepare students to address real, complex challenges. The chapter focuses not only on the importance of the process of discovery and the value of the personal making of meaning, but more widely on the importance of understanding and delivering learning environments as holistic experiences that request the active experimentation of learners with their peers. Then the discussion focuses on key areas to secure the implementation of this approach, including the identification of particular challenges that need to be addressed. In particular it is emphasised how experience does not necessarily take place within the school or a single subject – and therefore the importance of outdoor learning and interdisciplinary planning.

8.1. Definition

Experiential Learning (EL) is defined as approaches where learners are brought directly in contact with the realities being studied. Although its origins can be traced at least as far back to 1938, when Dewey's Experience and Education was published, EL has been continually revisited, as in the modern formulation by Kolb (1984). In short, EL has caught the interest of many educators for its strong focus on the environment, the active involvement of the learner and the role of reflection and addressing conflict. This cluster features addresses two challenges: first, the increasing need to learn from evidence, and for strengthening inquiry skills to address contemporary problems; and second, to ascertain what it means to live in a complex system, where uncertainty and unintended side effects may challenge the understanding of and interventions to problems.

As proposed by Kolb and Kolb (2005), the EL model builds on two learning processes: how students approach new experiences and abstract conceptualisations, and how these experiences are in turn transformed into new learning – that is, reflective observation and active experimentation.

Box 8.1. Main components of experiential learning

- *Concrete Experience*: active involvement (individually or in group) in a discrete task which is potentially disruptive regarding student's beliefs and ideas.
- *Reflective Observation*: the process of resolution of conflict between differences which makes students move back and forth between hypotheses and values.
- *Abstract conceptualisation*: making sense of what has come of the experience and the reflection, by creating, mixing or building on models and ideas.
- *Active experimentation*: putting into action what they have learnt, placing it in a context that is relevant to the student.

Source: Kolb, A.Y. and D.A. Kolb (2005), "Learning styles and learning spaces: Enhancing experiential learning in higher education", *Academy of Management Learning & Education*, Vol. 4/2, pp. 193-212.

EL is based on the idea that human experience is a central source of learning, and therefore the design of learning environments should make use of human experience as part of the learning. Six characteristics define those activities that build on EL (adapted from Chapman et al., 1995):

- mixture of content and process;
- reduced guidance;
- intellectual and emotional engagement in meaningful tasks;
- connections enabled between the task, the wider environment and relationships;
- ensuring critical insights from the experience;
- providing venues for learning outside one's perceived comfort zones.

8.2. Combinations

Although EL can be applied as a stand-alone approach (e.g. the use of manipulatives in mathematics, or the design of experiments in STEM subjects), well known innovative approaches in pedagogy (such as inquiry-based learning, education for sustainable development, learning-by-doing, outdoor learning or service-based learning), either build on the premises of EL or intertwine their own particularities with the pedagogical assumptions of EL. Three of these, given their importance and spread in innovative schools, are good examples of how the principles of EL have been put into practice in different ways.

Project-Based Learning (PBL): the core idea of PBL is that real-world problems capture student interest and invite serious thinking leading to the acquisition and application of new knowledge. Teaching guidance is reduced to give students an active voice and role, which commonly includes the selection of the project and/or the way it is developed. Projects are organised around a driving question or challenge. Students engage iteratively in labs, diverse activities and research; they collaborate, discuss, and learn in a personalised way, engaging in real inquiry.

Service-Based Learning (SBL): service-learning is an approach in which students use knowledge and skills to address genuine community needs. The National Youth Leadership Council (NYLC, 2008) comments how picking up trash from a river is a *service*, whereas studying water samples is *learning*. However, when students collect and analyse water samples to build a case study of local pollution to help a control agency improve water quality, this is an example of *service-learning*. SBL is an approach to foster 21st century skills such as critical thinking, complex reading and writing skills, problem-solving and conflict-resolution. Growing evidence shows a positive impact on personal and social development, civic responsibility, academic learning, motivation to learn, student attendance, career aspirations, school climate and perceptions about their community (Celio, 2011; Billig, 2000).

Teaching uncertainty competences: learning to handle knowledge uncertainty in a complex world requires learning environments that invite uncertainty into the learning process, in order to think critically about the world and be able to make sound decisions. Uncertainty competences, as defined by Tauritz (2016), are about managing uncertain information and situations, and can be divided into three categories: learning to appraise, tolerate and reduce uncertainty. Education for sustainability (EfS) and outdoor/adventure learning are examples of how to teach these competences, drawing on the philosophy, theory and practice of experiential education (including intertwined approaches, such as forest schools). EfS may be seen as a playground of uncertainty. This is due to connecting as it does the local and the global, as well as dealing with complexities, controversies and inequities in the environment, natural heritage, culture, society and the economy. Outdoor/adventure learning demands that individuals confront unfamiliar situations and step outside comfort zones. Both approaches demand collaboration, discussion, reflection and engagement with the wider community.

8.3. Connoisseurship

EL improves the well-being of students, boosting motivation and engagement. A review of outdoor/adventure learning found improvements in self-awareness, self-control, self-responsibility, community integration, teamwork, and general behaviour and school adjustment (Fiennes et al., 2015). Students tend to appreciate the outdoor connection, the hands-on-approach, the relevance of the material and the chance to excel (Scogin et al., 2017). Given the range of approaches associated with EL, effects on standardised tests are mixed and relate to the specific nature of the programme or activity: there is a body of evidence, for instance, suggesting the positive impact of PBL on standardised tests (e.g. Hmelo-Silver et al., 2007).

Regarding the expert implementation of EL, guidance and scaffolding play a pivotal role. These are key variables to make the learning more tractable by making complex and difficult tasks more accessible, manageable, and within the student's zone of proximal development (Hmelo-Silver et al., 2007). EL is neither a simple discovery process, nor aims only to reproduce the epistemology of sciences as the basis for the pedagogy; it is a well-planned learning process building on the meaningful experiences of students engaging in a collaborative, reflexive activity. Scaffolding can play many roles, such as making disciplinary thinking explicit, providing expert guidance, and structuring complex tasks to reduce cognitive requirements. In EL projects, what happens before and after the experience, as well as the secondary activities, are all important and underpin the pedagogical nature of the experience. The emphasis on experiences, engagement, and hands-on activities contributes to a wider model as opposed to the common school focus on abstract cognitive processes, content and linear, unembedded activities.

Box 8.2. Keys to integrating experiential learning into a course

- The selection of a major project or field experience can become the driving force behind the learning and what the students do in the class, ensuring an overarching purpose for what happens in each lesson. In this regard, it is important to discover what the students are interested in, and select how to frame these interests in discrete challenges and problems.
- To ensure the engagement of the students a combination of activities is needed but they should be related to each other and challenging rather than stressful. To keep learners engaged throughout the whole process it is important to match students with appropriate activities.
- Provision of clear assessment criteria and examples from previous courses help guide the learning process and generate the necessary scaffolding.
- Allow students enough time to identify issues, discuss and interchange, and to fail, and provide venues to participate in projects and activities.
- In EL the instructor serves as a guide and a resource to learners, so teachers need to balance scaffolding with providing more freedom to students. The role of the teachers revolves around four main rules (Warren, 1995): provide informed consent, establish a concrete vision, set ground rules that serves as safety nets for students, and provide process tools around team work and problem-solving.
- Experience *per se* does not ensure learning: reflection is the main aspect of EL that connects the experience with the process of abstraction and allows previous knowledge to be applied or challenged.

Source: Adapted from Wurdinger, S.D. (2005), *Using Experiential Learning in the Classroom*, Scarecrow Education, Lanham.

The importance of scaffolding and guidance appears also in one of the main aims of EL - to allow students, regardless of their diverse learning needs, to participate in complex tasks. EL thus shares with gamification the conscious search for a state of 'flow', understood as the right balance between demands and the abilities of students to meet the requested goals. In gamification, doing something 'playful' becomes the catalyst for learning, while in EL the driving force is the connection with the real world and students' interests, that is, the feeling that the activity is 'meaningful'.

Box 8.3. Key challenges to implementing experiential learning

- Testing and accountability driving pedagogical decisions are major hurdles preventing wide-range adoption of experiential-type learning pedagogies. School principals feel that testing policy has a strong impact on teaching (Scogin et al., 2017). And, as standardised tests are more aligned with traditional, fact-based methods, teachers feel more inclined to 'teach-to-the-test' than pursue student interests and incorporate experimentation and student-centred activities into teaching.

- Curriculum and content standards, along with schedules and facilities, are commonly seen as too rigid to accommodate EL-related activities.

- EL teaching practices require more risk-taking in areas in which teachers are often uncomfortable, including: collaboration and co-teaching with other teachers; shifting from directing the instruction to facilitating more group work; managing students groups and projects; and assessing the project to fit the learning goals of the course (Harris, 2015).

8.3.1. Example of practice: Let's make a Garden, a service-based learning program to develop the public space.

The Jaume Bofill Foundation (JBF) in Barcelona is a third-sector organisation that has been leading a programme of SBL-initiatives across Catalonia for more than 15 years. This example comes from a review of an experience that took place in Granollers, as described by Camps (Martín and Rubio, 2006).

The City Council actively collaborated with schools in urbanisation projects, framed through the Educational City Plan and the Council's focus on childhood participation. 'Let's make a Garden' aimed to a) to develop participation in the education community; and b) to reframe perceptions of local projects. It sought to personalise the public space in order to develop learners' civic skills and sense of belonging. Learners participated throughout the project, including the design and technical phases.

The first stage of the project was to gain knowledge about green areas in the city in order to start thinking about and designing the future garden. Learners came to understand the complexity of designing a green area, including variables such as the economic, leisure, aesthetics, sustainability and maintenance. The design of the experience explicitly sought to make students reflect on their community involvement and to learn about team work and collaboration.

Over two years, 48 primary school students, ranging from 10 to 12 years old, visited the allotted garden space and reviewed existing plans for the area. They were introduced to diverse professionals, and brainstormed both individually and in class groups on the range of possibilities to design the garden. Students wrote and drew how the garden could consider birdlife, the characteristics of the swing sets, signs, etc., and followed-up the plans and architectural models of the professionals. They held meetings with the professionals to find out about administrative procedures, documents and programs to execute the project, including participation in the city council session in which the plan was approved. Students regularly visited the garden to follow the evolution of the works. The final reflective process included written assignments and discussions about the building of the facility, using photos taken from the working yard, creating a diary of the work progress and organising the garden's inauguration.

8.4. Context

EL is the leading pedagogical approach in adult education, and has received continued and growing attention in higher education (e.g. community-based activities, internships, leadership programs) and K-12 education, nurtured by growing attention to student-centred and learning-by-doing pedagogical models (Corradi et al., 2006). Mature learners long removed from traditional classrooms have been found to benefit especially from EL and, more generally, those who need more personal experience to value a subject and be more motivated. EL enables personalised learning by means such as using scaffolding extensively and reducing the cognitive load (Hmelo-Silver et al., 2007), peer-interaction, and flexibility in achieving learning goals.

8.5. Content

Students acquire skills and values in EL as the result of their experience and active participation, meaning there is less mediation that in conventional learning. EL is well-suited for those subjects and themes that are anchored in experimental and real-based projects, such as the sciences and social studies, or in subjects that are inherently based in practice, such as the arts. However, EL allows for a variety of methodologies that can meet the whole curriculum, even the abstraction of mathematics (Davidovitch et al., 2014), or mother tongue use in ESL courses (Knutson, 2003), or the teaching of statistics in middle and high schools (Fawcett and Newman, 2016).

8.6. Change

Several authors confirm that EL is not an 'all-or-nothing' approach, and teachers should not be discouraged by the skills needed for and the workload implied by whole-school approaches. As with the other pedagogical approaches in this compilation, the implementation of EL is a matter of scale; simple designs such as using manipulatives in mathematics or allowing for more reflection and peer experimentation can lead to the incorporation of EL-based activities. EL has been around in education for a long time and already permeates teaching practices in significant ways, even when they are not seen as explicitly incorporating EL principles. Implementing EL may start by making these EL-related characteristics present in the current learning designs more visible and explicit, and by moving from planning content-focused activities to activities drawing on learners' experience and cross-cutting skills.

It is not the activity which makes learning experiential, but rather the way it is framed. A general condition for engaging in EL is to decide which areas can be more effectively learnt and taught using EL principles, and to identify potential EL activities that fit course objectives, including complementary activities. A second stage is to frame activities and lessons as problems to be solved, or make them revolve around challenges, rather than as information to be understood, memorised and linearly applied. A critical point in the design of EL is the role of scaffolding and structure: EL should become a platform for students to engage in active and reflective experiences, but this platform needs to be built, and the reflective process properly and explicitly encouraged.

8.7. In summary

- EL is an approach that starts from the careful design of meaningful experiences and includes reflection to stretch students' existing knowledge.
- EL works as a stand-alone approach but is also often combined with at least three other pedagogical approaches: project-based learning, service-based learning and the teaching of uncertainty competences.
- Guidance and scaffolding are key elements to ensure room for experimentation and collaboration while avoiding that the task is either too challenging or too abstract.

References

Billig, S. (2000), "Research on K-12 school-based service-learning: The evidence builds", *School K-12, Paper 3*, http://digitalcommons.unomaha.edu/slcek12/3.

Camps, A. (2006), "Let's make a Garden, a cooperative programme between a school and a council to urbanize a public space in Granollers', in X. Martin and L. Rubio, *Experiences of Service Learning*, pp. 46-63, www.fbofill.cat/publicacions/experiencies-daprenentatge-servei.

Celio, C.I., J. Durlak and A. Dymnicki (2011), "A meta-analysis of the impact of service-learning on students", *Journal of Experiential Education*, Vol. 34/2, pp. 164-181.

Chapman, S., P. McPhee and P. Proudman (1995), "What is experiential education?", in K. Warren, (ed.), *The Theory of Experiential Education*, pp. 235-248, Kendall/Hunt Publishing Company, Dubuque.

Davidovitch, N., R. Yavich, and N. Keller (2014), "Mathematics and experiential learning: Are they compatible?", *Journal of College Teaching and Learning*, Vol. 11/3, pp. 135-148.edsawcett, L. and K. Newman (2016), "The storm of the century! Promoting student enthusiasm for applied statistics", *Teaching Statistics Trust*, Vol. 39/1, pp. 2-13.

Fiennes et al, (2015), *The Existing Evidence Base about the Effectiveness of Outdoor Learning*, Commissioned by the Blagrave Trust, www.outdoor-learning-research.org/Portals/0/Research%20Documents/Research%20Reports/outdoor-learning-giving-evidence-revised-final-report-nov-2015-etc-v21.pdf?ver=2017-06-26-110330-480 (accessed 12 Apr 2017).

Harris, M.J. (2015), *The Challenges of Implementing Project-Based Learning in Middle Schools*, University of Pittsburgh, PhD Dissertation, http://d-scholarship.pitt.edu/23533/.

Hmelo-Silver, C.E., R.G. Duncan and C.A. Chinn (2007), "Scaffolding and achievement in problem-based and inquiry learning: A response to Kirschner, Sweller, and Clark (2006)", *Educational Psychologist*, Vol. 42/2, pp. 99-107.

Knutson, S. (2003), "Experiential learning in second-language classrooms", *TESL Canada Journal*, Vol. 20/3, pp. 52-64.

Kolb, D.A. (1984), *Experiential Learning: Experience as the Source of Learning and Development*, Prentice-Hall, Englewood Cliffs, New Jersey.

Kolb, A.Y. and D.A. Kolb (2005), "Learning styles and learning spaces: Enhancing experiential learning in higher education", *Academy of Management Learning & Education*, Vol. 4/2, pp. 193-212.

National Youth Leadership Council (2008), *K-12 Service-Learning Standards for Quality Practice*, https://nylcweb.files.wordpress.com/2015/10/standards_document_mar2015upd ate.pdf.

Scogin, S.C., et al. (2017), "Learning by experience in a standardized testing culture: Investigation of a middle school experiential learning program", *Journal of Experiential Education*, Vol. 40/1, pp. 39-57.

Tauritz, R.L. (2016), "A pedagogy for uncertain times", in W. Lambrechts and J. Hindson, *Research and Innovation in Education for Sustainable Development*, pp. 90-105, Environment and School Initiatives – ENSI, Vienna, Austria.

Warren, K. (1995), "The student-directed classroom: A model for teaching experiential education theory", in K. Warren (ed.), *The Theory of Experiential Education*, pp. 249-258, Kendall/Hunt Publishing Company, Dubuque.

Wurdinger, S.D. (2005), *Using Experiential Learning in the Classroom*, Scarecrow Education, Lanham.

Chapter 9. Embodied learning

Embodied learning refers to pedagogical approaches that focus on the non-mental factors involved in learning, and that signal the importance of the body and feelings. The chapter includes a wide conceptualisation of embodied learning, including arts and design-based learning, new approaches to physical education and the maker culture movement. Then the discussion focuses on key elements in the effective implementation of embodied learning pedagogies, including the identification of particular challenges that need to be addressed. One area of special interest is the need to re-think the way physical education and arts are taught in schools, and to use these domains as platforms for introducing new pedagogies and fostering non-cognitive skills in the whole curriculum. The chapter ends with two dimensions that are key for planning and integrating embodied learning in the school: the scale of the implementation, and the level of expertise required.

9.1. Definition

In embodied learning, the main idea is that students who consciously use their bodies to learn are more engaged than those who are at a desk or a computer. The brain, while important, is not the only source of behaviour and cognition (Stolz, 2015): situated cognition highlights the need to include the physical, the emotional and the social in the learning environment. 'Embodiment' connects with 'lived experience' as the outcome of sensory engagement with the environment – cognition is situated in the constant feedback between the person and the environment. For example, young children in play-based activities do not compute and think through everything to provide correct responses; instead, they continuously provide perceptual and emotional responses which will often be unintentional and unconscious. Indeed, a significant part of the power of play as a learning tool comes from the many ways in which children, by engaging in joyful activity with a sense of wonder, learn through embodiment. Box 9.1 summarises some of the pedagogical principles involved in approaching learning as a process of embodiment.

Box 9.1. Pedagogical principles of embodied learning

- Body and mind work together in learning.
- Movement and concepts are connected.
- Action and thinking take place simultaneously.
- Science and art influence and support each other.
- The physical and the ideal are in dialogue with each other.
- Reality and imagination are intertwined.
- The living body and the lived body are united in forming human consciousness.

Source: Svendler, C. et al. (2013), "Young people's embodied voices: Experiences and learning in dance education practices across the world", in S.W. Stinson, C. Svendler Nielsen & S-Y. Liu, *Dance, young people and change: Proceedings of the daCi and WDA Global Dance Summit,* Taipei National University of the Arts, http://ausdance.org.au/uploads/content/publications/2012-global-summit/dance-learning-rp/young-peoples-embodied-voices-experiences-and-learning-in-dance-education-practices.pdf.

These principles are important for pedagogy, for they make sense of two natural learning inclinations of children: creativity and expression (Figure 9.1). First, action and the impulse to create are among the most basic of human drives; people achieve contextual knowledge by tinkering, and making and experimenting with tangible tools (Bullock, 2016). Second, creative activities based on the primacy of self-expression and aesthetics are more likely to engage learners than academic activities. When learning environments are coupled with the arts, schools become places of discovery where personal experiences are more easily channelled. They offer challenge, which is the lever for motivation and learning (Bradley et al., 2013). In combining these two driving forces – creating and expressing – in terms of skills, embodied learning can be understood as the conscious use of creative experiences and the active involvement of students to champion the acquisition of knowledge.

Figure 9.1. Situated cognition as the outcome of creation, expression and experience

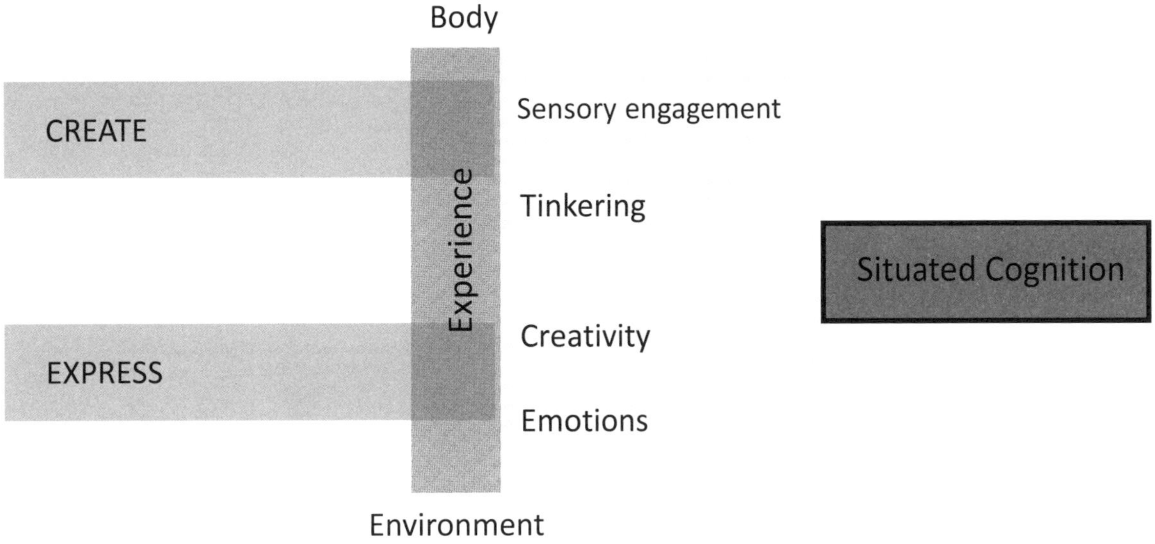

Body

CREATE

Experience

Sensory engagement

Tinkering

Creativity

EXPRESS

Emotions

Situated Cognition

Environment

9.2. Combinations

Embodied learning is closely connected with the idea of learning-by-doing and by engaging with the environment, which are significant aspects of experiential learning. Although both approaches share the importance of interaction, experimentation, and the ambition to offer students a comprehensive learning experience, in embodied learning the focus shifts from the cognitive to the emotional, physical and creative aspects. Activities revolving around the active role of students where the emotions play an important role (e.g. simulations and role-playing) are also forms of embodied learning.

Depending on whether the focus is put on the body, the emotions or creating things, it is possible to identify three main strands of approaches within embodied learning:

School-Based Physical Culture focuses on enhancing learners' shared experiences of physical engagement to contribute to school aims (Thorburn and Stolz, 2015). Better Movers and Thinkers (BMT), a pedagogical approach launched by Education Scotland, builds on embodied learning in addressing the improvement of executive functions to enhance personal qualities, thinking skills, physical literacy and physical fitness (Figure 9.2). Executive functions are those mental tools that develop self-regulation, such as attention, working memory, inhibition control, cognitive flexibility, planning and goal-directed behaviour. BMT also pays attention to scaffolding and connecting classroom learning and skill development through sports.

Figure 9.2. Significant aspects of learning in physical education

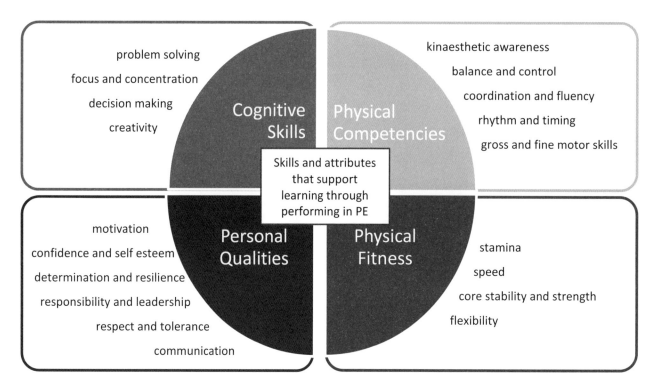

Source: Education Scotland (2014), *Better Movers and Thinkers Resource Pack*, https://education.gov.scot/improvement/hwb09-better-movers-and-thinkers (accessed 17 May 2018).

Arts education and arts-integrated learning: Arts education and arts integration have been consistently linked to increased student engagement, motivation and persistence, thereby promoting creativity, fine motor skills, confidence, higher-order thinking skills and critical thinking (e.g. Chand O'Neal, 2014). Arts integration focuses on creative processes connecting an art form and another subject area so meeting objectives in both (Silverstein and Layne, 2010). The range of art forms is wide, although they typically involve theatre, music, dance, visual and the plastic arts. Some of these have long traditions in school curricula, such as music and art, whereas others have tended to be part of other subjects (such as dance in physical education) or have more recently been seen as a way to enhance the curriculum (e.g. theatre). In some cases, such as natural drawing in sciences or drama/role-play in the social sciences or literature, schools have integrated art within the curriculum.

Maker Culture revolves around tinkering and the construction of physical objects. It takes place in labs – makerspaces – where learners can use, explore, and experiment with diverse materials and tools to build up engines, more complex tools or artefacts. Given appropriate scaffolding, collaboration and interaction, the process of tinkering can embrace deep student learning, making learners interested in and capable of doing science (Bevan et al., 2015). Within the maker culture, tinkering is a good deal more than simple fabrication because it focuses on creative, improvised problem-solving. Although *Maker Culture* is strongly connected with STEM subjects and design thinking, much of its potential comes from the way tinkering is linked with the principles of embodied learning, and in particular from how the physical acts of doing and creativity are both intertwined in makerspaces (Box 9.2).

9.3. Connoisseurship

Box 9.2. Marketspaces

A marketspace can be a work space inside a school, or a separate facility for making, collaborating, experimenting, learning and sharing. Ideally it is provided with the necessary tools - digital and analogic - and raw materials for students to play with open-ended exploration. The underpinning idea is that students are immersed into projects where art, technology, learning and collaboration – formal and informal - collide, with the ultimate goal of building something together. Although these spaces are designed to promote self-directed learning, marketspaces can be incorporated in learning environments, aiming to foster design thinking, engineering, multidisciplinary and more generally communities of practice.

Source: Sheridan K. M. et al. (2014), "Learning in the Making: A Comparative Case Study of Three Makerspaces", *Harvard Educational Review*, Vol.84/4, pp. 505-531.

There is limited research around the impact of arts or the training of executive functions on achievement, and still less evaluating the maker culture approach. For promoting 21st century skills, well-being and engagement, however, these approaches have been frequently reported as having a strong influence. One of the challenges in estimating the impact of embodied learning is the difficulty of encapsulating its principles in discrete teaching practices. For example, Flynn (2016) notes how many of the positive aspects associated to BMT experiences, such as pupil enjoyment of physical education, are simply the result of effective pedagogical practices. A similar argument can be made around arts integration in the curriculum, as a precondition for the successful integration of the arts is the presence of quality pedagogical tools.

One of the potentials of embodied learning is in opening a window for innovation and the development of new teaching approaches. Take dance and the growing attention it receives as an art form as well as the way it encompasses the physical (movement), the emotional (expression), and creativity (producing dance, choreography). It is also notable in its strong relationship with the visual, music, and theatre and because of the importance of interaction and collaboration with peers (Bradley et al., 2013). Dance education can take different forms in schools, depending on whether it is strongly connected with other subjects or a stand-alone subject, whether it is connected with PE or whether more oriented to the arts and creating meaning through movement. For mainstream teachers, it is a challenge to incorporate dance education into regular classrooms outside PE, dance or art lessons. Although robust evaluations are lacking, there is a growing number of reports describing good practice that offer a starting point. For example, there are particular areas, such as maths, that are being increasingly merged with dance through the development of specific programmes (e.g. Maths Dance or SHINE for Girls) that can be implemented by mainstream teachers, while others have made available lesson plans for creative dance integration into all school areas (e.g. Cravath, 2011; Annenberg Learner, 2015).

Box 9.3. Tips for teaching dance

- Say 'when' before 'what', highlighting the moments when students will do something and providing appropriate cues to guide them.
- Allow a little chaos, allowing students to express their own ideas before worrying too much about the correct/incorrect way to interpret creative prompts. The research suggests that in dance students need to make their own choices.
- Challenge students - creative movements should be accompanied of scaffolding to enable learners to improve their technical and expressive skills. These guidelines should be clear and concise, and distributed over time, thus not concentrated exclusively in the period before the activity starts.
- Dance with the students, as their commitment to the movement increases, instead of giving instruction and witness the task performance - participate with learners rather than demonstrate.
- Make rules for dance, so that children don't feel that in dance classroom rules no longer apply.

Source: Cravath, E. (2011), Creative Dance Integration Lesson Plan, BYU Arts Partnership, https://education.byu.edu/sites/default/files/ARTS/documents/educational_movement.pdf.

9.3.1. Example of practice: Dance to deepen the understanding of Geometry

Moore and Linder (2012) describe the collaborative project between a dance specialist and four 3rd grade classroom teachers at an arts magnet school. In their design, they addressed the challenge of how to assess through a rubric an integrated unit built on national geometry and dance standards (Table 9.1).

Table 9.1. Rubric used by the teachers to assess maths and dance components

Maths components	Points earned
Right angle	/8
Acute angle	/8
Obtuse angle	/8
Triangle	/8
Square	/8
Closed figure with more than 4 sides	/8
Line of symmetry	/8
Dance components	
Dance phrase that has a beginning, middle and end	/8
Smooth transitions	/8
Repeated phrase	/8
Low, medium and high levels	/8
Maintain concentration and focus throughout performance	/12
Total maths and dance components score	**/100**

Source: Adapted from Moore, C. and S. M. Linder (2012), "Using Dance to Deepen Student Understanding of Geometry", *Journal of Dance Education*, Vol. 12, 3, pp. 104-108.

The 3rd grade project lasted four weeks. The task introduced by the teacher was to create dances incorporating geometric concepts while including dance concepts and skills.

Students worked in groups of four to six and discussed and planned how to incorporate all the elements as displayed in the rubric presented by their teacher. Mathematics concepts were:

- identifying objects as circles, squares, triangles, or rectangles;
- classifying lines and line segments, angles, and triangles;
- exemplifying points, lines, line segments, rays, and angles;
- classifying polygons according to the number of sides.

In relation to dance, concepts that were addressed included:

- demonstrating a dance phrase that has a beginning, middle, and end;
- including smooth transitions, including a repeated phrase;
- representing low, medium, and high levels;
- maintaining concentration and focus throughout the performance.

During the lessons, students explored ways to illustrate scalene, isosceles and right-angled triangles with their arms, used their bodies to shape different figures and were given 15 minutes at the end of the class to plan and practice their dances. Practice included performing in front of their peers to receive feedback and further reflection.

The assessment of the dance activity occurred throughout the project and in diverse forms. Self-assessment, assessment by peers, and assessment by teachers took place informally by constantly using the rubric, which was displayed on a digital blackboard. Different points were awarded depending on the way targeted components were incorporated and represented (e.g. if they were clearly performed or if all the members of the group performed the dance in the same way). At the end of the project, students also provided written reflections of the experience with explicit references of the ways in which integrating dance and geometry had contributed to their understanding.

9.4. Content

There is a fruitful connection between the principles of embodied learning and the pedagogical relevance of physical and arts education in schools. On the one hand, growing research on the positive impact on learning of physical and arts education (e.g. Hanna, 2008) suggests ways in which cognition, emotion and the body are connected. On the other, embodied learning can be a foundational pedagogical cornerstone in which physical education and dance are integrated into academic tasks and core subject areas. The natural context of maker culture means that makerspaces can become conducive settings for STEM subjects to promote skills and content that cut across these areas.

Embodied learning is particularly suited to address creative skills such as curiosity, sensitivity, multiple perspective taking, risk-taking, and metaphorical thinking, among others (Treffinger et al., 2002), as well as other metacognitive and executive skills which foster learner achievement. Arts-based forms of embodied learning are especially suited to develop socio-emotional skills. Dance can help learners recognise and manage their emotions, cope successfully with conflict, navigate interpersonal problem-solving, show empathy for other and help develop positive relationships (Andreu and Moles, 2014). Through collaboration in the arts, other fundamental, cross-cutting content (e.g. gender issues, diversity) and important dimensions of classroom management (positive leaders, affinity groups) can be addressed.

9.5. Context

Embodied learning can introduce a range of alternative practices which can be particularly useful for disengaged and/or students with low confidence. This is achieved through addressing personal qualities, as well as accommodating active learning, collaboration and physical interaction. Physical activity and the arts have been frequently reported as having a positive impact for the emotional well-being of students (e.g. Lu and Buchanan, 2014; Bradley et al., 2013) and for making learning more engaging (Yoo and Loch, 2016). By incorporating the emotional and favouring moments when students can experience sensory immersion, embodied learning can help teachers to shift the onus from abstract thinking and declarative knowledge to a more integrated learning environment, one that offers opportunities for students to experience, reflect and share.

9.6. Change

Embodied learning can be elusive as it entails a significant shift in the understanding of human cognition, towards a strong connection with emotions, the physical and creativity. Since learning environments have traditionally favoured abstract thinking, individual dynamics and passive content attainment, embodied learning can appear particularly challenging. However, it is useful to explore the diverse ways in which the main principles of embodied learning can be fulfilled rather than necessarily address all its components at once or envisage it as something that only specialists and professional artists can develop.

For one thing, an activity or design can focus more on one component than another, say, the physical rather than the expressive or creative elements of embodied learning. The embodied learning principles may also underpin a particular lesson or content only to a certain degree or instead they may channel a whole subject area. Plus, teachers may engage in simple maker or artistic activities with the necessary confidence and skills and, if needed, progress to more complex activities or ways to integrate embodied learning in the curriculum.

Figure 9.3. Ways of integrating embodied learning according to discretion and expertise

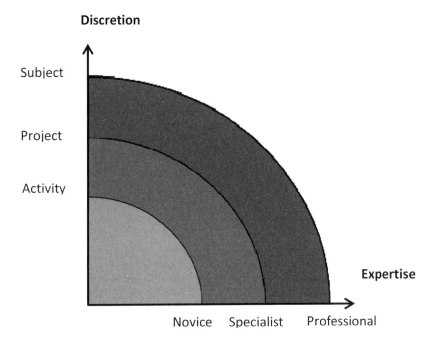

Using the variables 'discretion' and 'expertise', Figure 9.3 describes three levels in which embodied learning can be implemented in schools:

- *Activities/experiences,* in which physical and arts classes occasionally address other content areas or vice versa. Robelen (2010) describes a science class in which the explanation of photosynthesis is mixed with dance to help students learn this process. In conveying the elements involved in the photosynthesis, learners explore the whole body and use new movements to express water, sunlight or carbon dioxide. Embodiment already takes place in parts of lessons that engage learners in interactive, experimental activities, so teachers might just need to be more conscious of these moments and explore ways to scale up these activities.

- *Workshops/projects.* By creating partnerships with outside professionals and artists, workshops can be venues for re-thinking how lessons and content can be approached using embodied learning. For example, HighlySprung in the UK provides schools with projects such as theatre workshops specially designed for children; the interactive science project, Commotion, combines dance, drama and physics to explore theories of sound, light and electricity. Specialised teachers work in collaboration with mainstream staff to create and implement projects as workshops.

- *Integrating physicality, creativity and the emotional in the school and in core subjects.* Although the full integration of physical culture, arts and maker culture in subjects and schools is still recent, there is a growing number of schools, initiatives and specialised centres that offer guidelines and even toolsets of integrated embodied learning activities, such as the California County Arts Initiative, The Kennedy Centre, Better Movers and Thinkers initiative or Education Closet.

9.7. In summary

- Embodied learning is closely connected with the idea of learning-by-doing and by engaging with the environment in a comprehensive way, including through emotions and interaction.
- Although the core concepts of embodied learning are commonly present in any experiential or expressive activity, arts, physical education and maker culture are key platforms to build embodied experiences.
- There are three main pathways to implement embodied learning in the school: starting with single experiences based on core subjects or physical education and art lessons; introducing and expanding workshops/projects led by professionals or specialised teachers; and by integrating physical education and art throughout entire subjects and schools.

References

Andreu, J. and R. Moles (2014), *Five Days to Dance*, SUICAfilms, www.suicafilms.com/five-days-to-dance/.

Bevan, B., et al. (2015), "Learning through STEM-rich tinkering: Findings from a jointly negotiated research project taken up in practice", *Science Education*, Vol. 99/1, pp. 98–120.

Bradley, K., J. Bonbright and S. Dooling (2013), "Evidence: A Report on the impact of dance in the K-12 setting", National Dance Education Organization, www.ndeo.clubexpress.com/content.aspx?page_id=22&club_id=893257&module_id=153248.

Bullock, S.M. (2016), "Digital technologies in teacher education: From mythologies to making", in C. Kosnik, S. White, C. Beck, B. Marshall, A. L. Goodwin and J. Murray, *Building Bridges: Re-thinking Literacy Teacher Education in a Digital Era*, pp. 3–16, Sense Publishers, Rotterdam.

California Country Superintendents Arts Initiative (2018), http://ccsesaarts.org/ (accessed 12 Mar 2018).

Chand O'Neal, I. (2014), *Selected Findings from the John F. Kennedy Centre's Arts in Education Research Study: An Impact Evaluation of Arts-Integrated Instruction through the Changing Education through the Arts (CETA) Program*, The John F. Kennedy Centre for the Performing Arts, Washington, DC, https://artshealthnetwork.ca/ahnc/kc-ae-selected_findings_ceta_v16.pdf.

Cravath, E. (2011), *Creative Dance Integration Lesson Plan,* BYU Arts Partnership, https://education.byu.edu/sites/default/files/ARTS/documents/educational_movement.pdf

EducationCloset (2018), https://educationcloset.com/ (accessed 12 Mar 2018).

Education Scotland (2014), *Better Movers and Thinkers Resource Pack*, https://education.gov.scot/improvement/hwb09-better-movers-and-thinkers.

Flynn, J.J. (2016), "Better Movers and Thinkers in the primary school context: innovation or good practice?", *Physical Education Research Digest*, www.blogs.hss.ed.ac.uk/peresearch/better-movers-thinkers-primary-school-context-innovation-good-practice-jordan-john-flynn/.

Hanna, J.L. (2008), "A nonverbal language for imagining and learning: Dance education in K–12 curriculum", *Educational Researcher*, Vol. 37/8, pp. 491-506.

Highlysprung (2018), www.highlysprungperformance.co.uk/ (accessed 12 Mar 2018).

Lu, C. and A. Buchanan (2014), "Developing students' emotional well-being in physical education", *Journal of Physical Education, Recreation & Dance*, Vol. 85/4, pp. 28-33.

Moore, C. and S. M. Linder (2012), "Using Dance to Deepen Student Understanding of Geometry", Journal of Dance Education, Vol. 12, 3, pp. 104-108.

Sheridan K. M. et al. (2014), "Learning in the Making: A Comparative Case Study of Three Makerspaces", Harvard Educational Review, Vol.84/4, pp. 505-531.

Stolz, S.A. (2015), "Embodied learning", *Educational Philosophy and Theory*, Vol. 47/5, pp. 474-487.

Svendler, C., et al. (2013), "Young people's embodied voices: Experiences and learning in dance education practices across the world", in S.W. Stinson, C. Svendler Nielsen & S-Y. Liu, *Dance, young people and change: Proceedings of the daCi and WDA Global Dance Summit*, Taipei National University of the Arts, http://ausdance.org.au/uploads/content/publications/2012-global-summit/dance-learning-rp/young-peoples-embodied-voices-experiences-and-learning-in-dance-education-practices.pdf.

The Kennedy Centre (2018), www.kennedy-center.org/ (accessed 12 Mar 2018).

Thorburn, M. and S. Stolz (2015), "Embodied learning and school-based physical culture: Implications for professionalism and practice in physical education", *Sport, Education and Society*, Vol. 22/6, pp. 721-731.

Treffinger, D.J., et al. (2002), "Assessing Creativity: A Guide for Educators", *Centre for Creative Learning*, www.creativelearning.com/images/freePDFs/AssessCreatReport.pdf.

Yoo, J. and S. Loch (2016), "Learning bodies: What do teachers learn from embodied practice?", *Issues in Educational Research*, Vol. 26/3, pp. 528-542.

Chapter 10. Multiliteracies and discussion-based teaching

This chapter describes a pedagogical cluster that combines two inter-related main approaches: multiliteracies and discussion-based teaching. While multiliteracies focuses on the multiplicity and diversity of platforms and languages that learners require to become literate, discussion-based teaching revolves on the critical and cultural variables through which learners actively construct the meaning of texts. The chapter opens with the importance of an active, reflective and cultural understanding of literacy and the need to foster critical thinking skills. Then the discussion focuses on key elements for the effective implementation of these pedagogies, including the identification of particular challenges that need to be addressed. The chapter then explores the suitability of this approach for young learners and its potential impact on those students most at risk. It is highlighted how this approach can prepare learners to negotiate and interchange interpretations and ideas, as well as the need for teachers to adopt a less authoritative role and improve their awareness of students' lives and experiences.

10.1. Definition

Literacy lies at the heart of student learning, for it is the interface where knowledge is communicated, formulated, negotiated and applied. The idea of 'multiliteracies', first coined by the New London Group in 1996 (Cazden et al., 1996), looks beyond literacy as decoding written text and instead focuses on literacy in multiple forms in a context of cultural diversity and of ubiquitous technology and multimedia in communication.

Box 10.1. Pedagogical principles of multiliteracies

- *Situated Practice.* Use students' life experiences to create meaningful classroom activities within a community of learners; pedagogy must consider the affective and socio-cultural needs and identities of all learners.
- *Overt Instruction.* Active teacher interventions to scaffold learning activities, as collaborative efforts between teachers and learners in complex tasks, by offering knowledge and drawing attention to critical aspects of literacy learning.
- *Critical Framing.* Allow learners to gain the necessary personal and theoretical distance from what they have learnt, constructively critique it and then creatively extend and apply it with their own ideas and problem-solving skills.
- *Transformed Practice.* Encourage students to connect their learning experiences with their daily classroom tasks, thus making it work in other situations and cultural contexts.

Source: Cazden, C., et al. (New London Group) (1996), "A Pedagogy of Multiliteracies: Designing Social Futures", *Harvard Educational Review*, Vol. 66/1, pp. 60-92.

Critical literacies, approaching text as ideological artefact, are inherently related to the concept of Multiliteracies (Breidbach et al., 2014). Highlighting their mutual dependence also brings into focus the importance of discussion-based teaching underpinning both approaches to literacy. Class discussions not only represent a valuable pedagogical technique *per se*, but become central with the questioning of a predominant semiotic system which dislocates the centrality of the written language, any dominant language – lingua franca – and indeed the apparent ideological neutrality of any given text (Burke and Hardware, 2015).

Figure 10.1. Power, diversity and personal experiences framing literacies

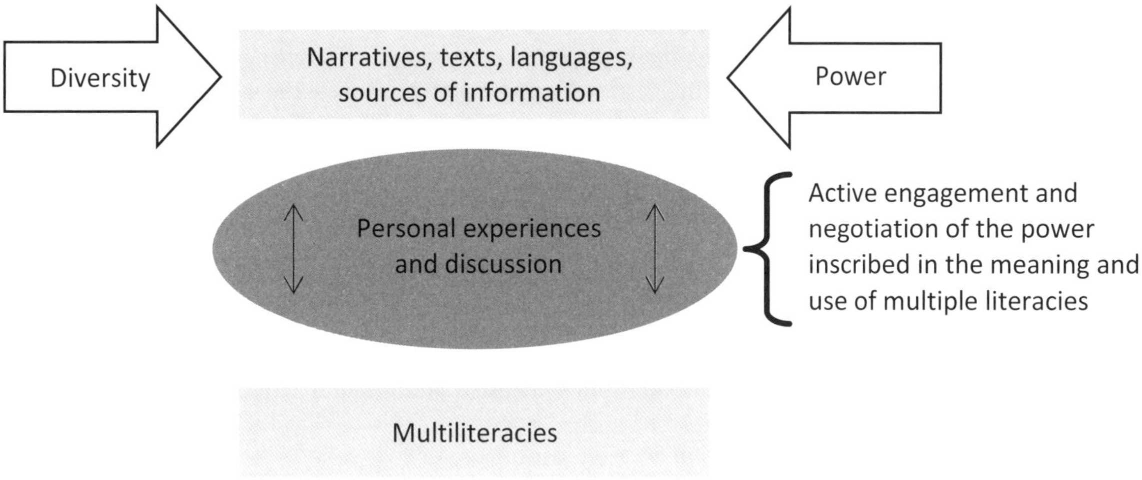

Diversity and power frame the narratives and languages that learners experience and acquire (Figure 10.1). By focusing on active engagement and the multiplicity of texts, discussion-based teaching becomes the interface to allow students to share, discuss and give sense to the implicit power relations and become aware of and value multiple modes of literacy. Discussion-based teaching works as a pedagogical lever to teach rational thinking, affective judgements, and higher-order thinking skills. This is particularly relevant given how the Internet shapes the way people get informed and make sense of the world, and in challenging the 'backfire effect', the psychological defence mechanism to avoid cognitive dissonance when supposed facts do not fit with one's beliefs.

10.2. Combinations

In given prominence to learners' experiences and identities, multiliteracies and discussion-based teaching are related with 'culturally responsive' pedagogical approaches, as both aim at making the curriculum more relevant. These approaches aim at addressing the lack of connection between teachers and students, leading to the emergence of conflict and unresponsiveness to students' needs (Mildner and Tenore, 2010). Cultural responsiveness helps teachers strengthen relationships with their students by stepping into their worlds, and facilitates critical reflections by students about themselves and the tensions both inside and outside the classroom.

The focus on critical framing and reasoning is also connected with the premises of experiential and embodied learning, and builds on the importance of designing meaningful experiences that challenge students' beliefs and facilitate collaboration, experimentation and the negotiation of meaning. Dialogue and discussion are central to problem-based learning and the teaching of uncertainty competences, which in turn can be used as the starting point for addressing controversies and promoting debates. Regarding arts-based learning, performing a play includes interpretation, negotiation and 'reading between the lines'; this way, learners grasp the play's meaning and produce a revised, idiosyncratic form through transformative practice. Further, this approach also shares goals and techniques with bilingual education and with the introduction of philosophy programmes in K-12.

10.3. Connoisseurship

Burke and Hardware (2015) have reviewed the effectiveness of multiliteracies in urban schools and particularly among non-dominant groups, discussing how this approach acknowledges cultural and linguistic diversity and improves the acquisition of second languages. Kalantzis and Cope (2008) propose that the four principles of multiliteracies pedagogy, as showed in Box 10.1, do not need to be followed in a rigid or sequential way, as the key to their successful implementation lies in the interaction between these elements. For example, critical framing combined with situated learning becomes more grounded. They present five questions to guide teachers when designing activities to take on board multimodal literacies (Box 10.2).

Box 10.2. Five questions to design multi-modal activities

- Representational: What do the meanings refer to?
- Social: How do the meanings connect the persons they involve?
- Organisational: How do the meanings hang together?
- Contextual: How do the meanings fit into the larger world of meaning?
- Ideological: Whose interests are the meanings skewed to serve?

Source: Kalantzis, M. and B. Cope (2008), "Language Education and Multiliteracies", in S. May and N.H. Hornberger, *Encyclopedia of Language and Education, 2nd Edition, Volume 1: Language Policy and Political Issues in Education*, pp. 195-211, Springer Science, New York, NY.

A particularly challenging issue is how to ensure that overt instruction does not become direct instruction. Overt instruction provides scaffolding to students as they write, discuss or analyse (Ranker, 2009); it aims to maintain the right balance between providing too much information too early (direct instruction) or too late (high academic demands). Overt instruction should be strategically coupled with situated practice so that it becomes a resource for learners to draw on as learning experiences are attuned to students' interests and competences.

Multiliteracies and critical literacy are not just related but inherent in all literacy engagements (Silvers et al., 2010): multimodal resources and analysis lead to critical reflection and connection with everyday experiences and vice versa; critical engagement with literacy always involves a multiplicity of communication forms. Reflection around controversial questions provides a route to enhancing critical reasoning and promoting discussion. Simpson (1996) offers guidelines and techniques for teaching critical literacy.

> **Box 10.3. Insights for enhancing the critical understandings of a story**
>
> - Stories and characters are not seen to reflect reality but are selective versions of it, told from a particular point of view.
> - The author leaves gaps in the text that the reader must fill, which are filled differently by different readers.
> - The author positions the reader to respond in particular ways through use of language, point of view, etc. and this preferred or dominant reading may be challenged.
> - Authors write for particular audiences which they assume to possess specific cultural knowledge and values, which may be privileged in the context where they are located.
> - Disrupting and juxtaposing texts, making insertions, additions and deletions, and providing alternative endings are creative mechanisms to challenge the meaning of texts and stories.
> - Role playing/reversal, parody and examining the social context are fundamental for analysis and reflection to unmask assumptions and hidden ideologies.
>
> *Source:* Adapted from Simpson, A. (1996), "Critical questions: Whose questions?", *The Reading Teacher*, Vol. 50/2, pp. 118-127.

Gonzalez (2015) describes 15 strategies to facilitate discussion. These are grouped into "higher-prep" (calling for advanced planning), "low-prep" (stand-alone activities which can be used in any lesson), along with other strategies to combine with other activities that not revolve around discussion. For Hess (2004), effective discussion revolves around seven variables:

1. Focus on interpretable text, issue or idea.
2. Students and teachers have prepared the discussion beforehand.
3. Most of the talk comes from the participants, not the facilitator.
4. Enough time and flexibility is provided to explore ideas in full.
5. There is a right balance of comfort and argument among participants.
6. Many people talk.
7. The ongoing conversation refers to previous points made before – avoiding erratic discussions.

Box 10.4. Fostering participation in discussions

- Make explicit and challenge student ideas emerging from discussion, such as "knowledge is just an opinion", "personal experience is the only real source of knowledge" or that "we should never be made to feel uncomfortable".
- Guide students to seek the most robust arguments instead of trying to convince others about the validity of their points of view, and to keep an open mind when listening to divergent arguments.
- Avoid looking only at who is talking and monitor the reactions of all the participants.
- Control excessive talkers and ask for examples and illustrations to attract as many interventions as possible.
- Allow for pauses to give the more introverted students an opportunity to talk, or to give others a chance to seek clarifications.
- Be sensitive to feelings and emotional reactions and recognise student's contributions.

Source: Adapted from Cashin, WE. (2011), "Effective classroom discussions", *Idea Paper #49*, pp. 1-5, www.ideaedu.org/Portals/0/Uploads/Documents/IDEA%20Papers/IDEA%20Papers/IDEA_Paper_49.pdf.

10.3.1. Example of practice: transliteration and bilingual children

It is critical for bilingual children to have the opportunity to learn their mother tongue through mainstream schooling in order to use and master it (Cummins, 2010). Proficiency in these languages benefits the children in many ways. It improves intergenerational relationships, allowing students to communicate better with parents and grandparents, and enriches their identities as learners. It deepens the understanding of a language and cultural knowledge, and it helps students improve their proficiency in the dominant language (OECD, 2010). Proficiency in written language opens reflective activity with words and concepts. In communities whose language does not have script at all or it differs from Roman script (if that is used for the dominant language), children who may have a good command of the dominant language find it difficult to write in their mother tongue. This in turn challenges the communication between learners and their parents, especially those parents without a good command of the dominant language.

In these case examples, taken from Al-Azami et al. (2010), researchers in collaboration with teachers from primary schools with diverse students proposed transliteration as a strategy to allow children to write in Bengali or Sylheti and engage in activities with their parents. The process of transliteration transforms one script to another through mapping the sounds of one language into the writing system of another, usually choosing the letter with the most similar pronunciation (see Example 1). Transliteration in classrooms offers a richful illustration of multiliteracies, for it shows the malleability of written language and the importance of discussion in the construction of meaning.

Example 1.

Shingho ow idhur ('the lion and the mouse' in Standard Bengali, transliterated).

Shingho ow oondur ('the lion and the mouse' in Sylheti, transliterated).

The activity was designed so that teachers, children and their parents could communicate ideas about a story to each other (see Example 2): the teachers asked students to prepare questions for their parents using transliteration, with free code-switch between Bangla (and Sylheti) and English. Parents were asked to describe pictures about the story with their children. The basic instruction to children was 'use Bangla, but with English letters to sound it out'.

Example 2.

Cene Bangla beshi important? ('Why is Bangla very important?').

Through a series of discussions, transliteration helps children to grasp sound-symbol relationships, fosters awareness of grammatical issues (such as the use of suffixes or ambiguity in grammar), and generates discussion about word meanings. Transliteration allows children to be authors in the way that they interpret and recompose words, phrases and texts that are heavily subjective. In doing so, they also learn how to build on their full linguistic repertoire in communication, involving code mixing and code switching, thus becoming more confident as bilingual speakers and writers. It facilitated the move to Bengali script that before had proved to be very challenging for these students.

Table 10.1. Multiliteracies and transliteration

Pedagogical principles	Transliteration
Situated practice	Written and oral English, oral Bangla and Sylheti. 'Story Shared' approach. Home.
Overt instruction	Scaffolding practices for doing transliteration.
Critical framing	Group discussion and reflection of English grammar, phonetics and meanings.
Transformed practice	Rewriting of the story, use of the 'new' language at home. Improving parent-child relationships.

10.4. Content

Multiliteracies and discussion-based teaching are most closely connected to three core subjects: language, foreign languages and social sciences. The teaching of foreign languages has proved to be a fruitful area where multiliteracies has taken root (Breidbach et al., 2014), while discussion-based teaching has addressed social issues and science controversies (Cashing, 2011; VanDeWeghe, 2005). In emphasising the practice of skills such as critical thinking and the creative use of communication, this approach can also be useful in the arts (e.g. creative writing, theatre, multimedia), civic education, philosophy, sciences (e.g. design and debate around experiments), and mathematics.

10.5. Context

The complexity inherent in multiliteracies and the prominence of discussions around controversial topics might suggest that it is more suitable for higher education - or at least that it is challenging to implement in K-12. While it is suitable for higher education, research has shown that it has been rewardingly applied in primary and secondary schools, and in the early years (Sandretto and Tilson, 2013; Applebee et al., 2003). Multiliteracies and discussion-based teaching are well-suited for culturally, socially and linguistically diverse children. In engaging learners by connecting strongly to their own lives, this approach helps to make visible and connect the diverse ways in which learners communicate in their homes and how literacy is taught in the classroom. Similarly, in locating texts and narratives within the broader political, socio-cultural and economic context and addressing controversial topics, this approach can also bring the diverse life experiences of all children to the forefront in classrooms.

10.5. Change

Multiliteracies and discussion-based teaching refers to a range of practices and principles rather than an overarching pedagogical approach. It does not seek to discredit conventional forms of literacy, but to nuance them with additional complexity and context (Burke and Hardware, 2015). It is, at the same time, a way to learn literacy and a way to use literacy more efficiently everywhere. There are three basic practices:

1. Situating literacies in a political, cultural and authorial context.
2. Interpreting/deconstructing narratives and their relationship with experience.
3. Interchange and collaboration as important resources for constructing meaning.

There are challenges to introducing this approach into classrooms and schools:

- *Knowledge of students' lives and experiences.* Teachers need to get to know the lives and interests of their students and establish concrete connections with their experiences outside the classroom. Of particular importance is their knowledge about the whole community where the students live and the historical forces impacting on these communities and the larger society.
- *Flexibility regarding teachers' authority and role.* Overt instruction is commonly misunderstood as direct instruction when instead it means that the teacher must ensure proper scaffolding to let learners build on their existing skills to address complex tasks and reflection. In allowing other languages and interpretations into the classroom and into the subject, some teachers might feel threatened by competing views and use of language.
- *Expertise in multimodal literacies.* Insufficient competence in learner communication and language can be an important barrier to implement this approach. Teacher collaboration with specialists (e.g. ESL teachers or families) can help address this challenge. Lack of teacher competence and confidence in the use of technology and audio-visuals to design and analyse narratives other than the written text can also be barriers.
- *Awareness of political and social issues and discussion techniques.* To establish connections with the wider political and social context teachers need to be trained regarding power issues involved in any mode of communication and narrative. The explicit addressing of controversial topics can appear as particularly challenging given the active student role, the need to address potential conflicts and to be confident and skilled in discussion techniques. Like any other content area, if the teacher is not well-versed in the use of these techniques, this practice can lead to unexpected and sometimes unwanted results.

10.6. In summary

- The idea of Multiliteracies looks beyond literacy in written language and focuses on the multimodal ways in which language is used and shared.
- This approach fundamentally questions the prominence of a single semiotic system and thus dislocates the centrality of the written language, any dominant language, and the apparent ideological neutrality of any given text.

- Multiliteracies and discussion-based teaching do not aim to discredit conventional forms of literacy, but to nuance them by adding more complexity and context.

References

Al-Azami, S., et al. (2010), "Transliteration as a bridge to learning for bilingual children", *International Journal of Bilingual Education and Bilingualism*, Vol. 13/6, pp. 683-700.

Applebee, A.N., et al. (2003), "Discussion-based approaches to developing understanding: Classroom instruction and student performance in middle and high school English", *American Educational Research Journal*, Vol. 40/3, pp. 685-730.

Breidbach, S., J. Medina and A. Mihan (2014), *Critical Literacies, Multiliteracies and Foreign Language Education*, Vol. 43/2, pp. 91-106.

Burke, A. and S. Hardware (2015), "Honouring ESL students' lived experiences in school learning with multiliteracies pedagogy", *Language, Culture and Curriculum*, Vol. 28/2, pp. 143-157.

Cashin, WE. (2011), "Effective classroom discussions", *Idea Paper #49*, pp. 1-5, www.ideaedu.org/Portals/0/Uploads/Documents/IDEA%20Papers/IDEA%20Papers/IDEA_Paper_49.pdf.

Cazden, C., et al. (New London Group) (1996), "A Pedagogy of Multiliteracies: Designing Social Futures", *Harvard Educational Review*, Vol. 66/1, pp. 60-92.

Gonzalez, J. (2015), "The Big List of Class Discussion Strategies", *Cult of Pedagogy*, www.cultofpedagogy.com/speaking-listening-techniques/.

Hess, D.E. (2004), "Discussion in social studies: is it worth the trouble?", *Social Education*, Vol. 68/2, pp. 151-155.

Kalantzis, M. and B. Cope (2008), "Language Education and Multiliteracies", in S. May and N.H. Hornberger, *Encyclopedia of Language and Education, 2nd Edition, Volume 1: Language Policy and Political Issues in Education*, pp. 195-211, Springer Science, New York, NY.

OECD (2010), *Closing the Gap for Immigrant Students: Policies, Practice and Performance*, OECD Publishing, Paris, http://dx.doi.org/10.1787/9789264075788-en.

Sandretto, S. and J. Tilson (2013), "Reconceptualising literacy: Critical multiliteracies for "new times", *Teaching and Learning Research Initiative*, www.tlri.org.nz/sites/default/files/projects/Sandretto_Summary_final_1.pdf.

Silvers, P., M. Shorey and L. Crafton (2010), "Critical literacy in a primary multiliteracies classroom: The hurricane group", *Journal of Early Childhood Literacy*, Vol. 10/4, pp. 379-409.

Simpson, A. (1996), "Critical questions: Whose questions?", *The Reading Teacher*, Vol. 50/2, pp. 118-127.

VanDeWeghe, R. (2005), "Discussion-based approaches, student understanding, and student achievement", *Research Matters*, Vol. 94/5, pp. 99-102.

Part III. The networks of innovative schools

Chapter 11. The Innovative Pedagogies for Powerful Learning networks

This chapter provides an overview of the features of a large set of networks working on innovative pedagogies. The networks are classified into three categories: "Pedagogical Approach Networks", which includes networks implementing the same innovations and defined by common pedagogical principles; "Innovation Promotion Networks", which features those networks that share their different innovative pedagogies; and "Professional Learning Networks", which are focused on providing professional development to schools and teachers. Using the responses to a questionnaire completed by 68 different network members, including practitioners and main organisers, the chapter links lessons from classrooms with the views of those leading and managing the network according to their mission and principles. The chapter concludes by discussing the factors describing why many networks have grown and continue to do so, while others are deliberately maintaining stable membership. It additionally discusses those elements which hinder growth.

11.1. Introduction

To understand better the nature of innovative pedagogies, the project combined desk-research and responses from innovators and practitioners on the ground. As well as the elaboration of the *Compilation* of pedagogies presented in Part II, innovative networks of schools were identified and these are discussed in this section of the report. The networks contacted are all deeply engaged with pedagogy and its innovation. They are primarily focused on schools and children, but some are working closely with different partners and/or seeking to facilitate the transition to post-school life through different models of teaching, learning and institutional arrangements. Some of the clusters of pedagogies discussed in the previous Compilation section were identified through the networks advancing such practices (e.g. experiential or blended learning); in other cases, it was the interest in an innovative approach (e.g. embodied learning), which directed attention towards networks and initiatives revolving around the arts or physical education.

The double focus on pedagogies and networks made selection for this project universe more complex. It involved ascertaining the nature of the network activity; it meant clarifying and targeting the role of pedagogies in each network; and it meant assessing the coherence of the pedagogical practices among schools participating in the network. Another related challenge was to secure practices that are related with innovation. All this had to be done in advance of the network completing the questionnaire, rather than for any to be excluded on the basis of the information contained in the completed questionnaire(s).

The search for cases from different continents was deliberate, and the project succeeded in identifying important cases outside the often-cited Anglo-Saxon systems. In fact, it was more challenging to persuade networks in the USA to submit questionnaires, whom the project hoped would have taken part. There is a trade-off to be made between setting the boundaries as widely as the project has, so eliciting a rich range of insights and information, and insisting on tight selection criteria which enhances comparability but risks to reduce numbers significantly.

It has been noted how the nature of the networks varies, and these have been classified them into three groups: "Pedagogical Approach Networks", which includes networks implementing the same innovations and defined by common pedagogical principles; "Innovation Promotion Networks", which features those networks that share their different innovative pedagogies; and "Professional Learning Networks", which are focused on providing professional development to schools and teachers. Although the analysis did identify different elements that support these three groups, these labels are neither definitive nor aim to simplify the rich nature of these networks, as some would come within two or even the three labels. For example, although OPEDUCA works as a network for promoting innovative pedagogies, they have a strong commitment to developing a common pedagogical approach. Another example could be the International Step by Step association, which might be seen either as a network promoting innovative pedagogies according to their quality framework, or as a group of organisations supporting teaching learning and continuous professional development.

Beyond these broad labels, they vary in other key ways, too. Certain of them are international in scope (Escuela Nueva, New Pedagogies for Deep Learning, ISSA); some operate within a particular national system (e.g. Komplex Instrukciós Program in Hungary, ECOLOG in Austria or Innova Schools in Peru). Some are related to educational reform in a specific country but with an aim of becoming an international platform (Innovative Schools Network in Japan), some are more regional in focus (such as Galileo in Alberta, Canada or OPEDUCA in the Rhine-Meuse region of the Netherlands), right down to relatively small groups of schools, such as the Amara Berri in Spain, Amico Robot in Italy or the Art of Learning in Scotland. Some of the networks have developed strong international connections despite being strongly anchored in a particular system – Whole Education in England and NOII in British Columbia being good examples. There are corresponding wide variations in scale – from the 000s of schools in Escuela Nueva or ISSA to the small groups of 10-20 schools. Such variety means also different forms of organisation and funding. Certain of them have emerged from policy initiatives or have the strong involvement of the education authorities while others have been established precisely to offer alternatives to mainstream policy. Trusts, foundations and partnerships are prominent in certain cases (e.g. Studio Schools, Lumiar Institute, OPEDUCA, and Whole Education).

This chapter presents short vignettes of those who took up the invitation to complete the questionnaire. In all, 38 networks were approached, from which 27 completed the questionnaire, with 68 replies altogether adding in the different network members and practitioners as well as the main organisers (see the full questionnaire in Annex A.2.) It includes discussion of the different responses given by the networks about whether or not they had grown over recent years.

11.2. The "Pedagogical Approach Networks"

11.2.1. Amara Berri (Spain)

This is a network of around 20 schools sharing a pedagogical approach developed by teachers in the Amara Berri School in the late 1970s, putting the learner in the centre and stressing creativity, active pedagogy, socialisation, play, freedom and globalism. Children are organised according to their interests and needs rather than age, and teachers often work together in the same group. The Amara Berri School is located in the Basque region of Spain, with other network schools in the region plus several in other parts of the country. In 1990, the regional authority declared Amara Berri to be an "innovative school" - since then professionals work to support schools interested in implementing the approach.

11.2.2. Amico Robot (Italy)

The network "Amico Robot" was created on the back of the Educational Robotics Festival in Lombardy in 2007, after a decade when several schools had tried different experiments using robotics. The network started with a pedagogical approach based on learning-by-doing through the building and programming of robots. The network is active in projects involving diverse academic and cultural organisations. Since 2014, it has organised seminars to share and reflect on experiences, with the participation of teachers, university students and researchers. Currently, 12 middle and high schools take part and Amico Robot is working with the Ministry of Education in drafting curricula that include robotics.

11.2.3. Art of Learning (Scotland)

The Art of Learning project brings together 11 primary schools in southern Scotland, working in the shared belief in the benefits of an arts-rich, creative learning programme, delivered intensively in schools over a number of months. The hypothesis is that this can have a positive impact on the development of creativity skills, executive functions and attainment in children, particularly those living in poverty. The project works through a partnership involving 11 primary schools and 11 professionals, and different agencies and organisations - Education Scotland, Creative Scotland, and Creativity, Culture and Education. It aims at developing in teachers a deeper understanding of creativity skills and executive functions and how they support learning; for learners, it offers opportunities to develop creativity and executive functions through arts activities.

11.2.4. Better Movers and Thinkers - BMT (Scotland)

The Better Movers and Thinkers (BMT) approach is designed to develop the ability of all children and young people to move and think, with a specific focus on developing Executive Function (EF) skills. EF provides essential tools that support learners' cognitive processes. BMT is a pedagogical approach incorporating physical education, physical activity and sport (PEPAS). The information collected refers to Fife authority, which has adopted BMT as a core pedagogical approach in the context of the Scottish Attainment Challenge (SAC). SAC targets young people in areas of highest deprivation, focusing on literacy, numeracy, health and well-being.

11.2.5. Escuela Nueva (Colombia/International)

Escuela Nueva is an educational model designed in the mid-1970s to improve the quality, relevance and effectiveness of Colombian schools. It revolves around four core principles: collaborative learning, personalised teaching, a comprehensive and systemic approach, and constructivism. This model grew to become a wider model of school innovation for more than 24 000 rural schools. A foundation was created to ensure the integrity and implementation of the approach, and to further innovate it including for urban areas and other countries, and it has developed programmes targeting vulnerable populations. The Federation of Escuela Nueva also gives advice on a national and international level. To date, the model has inspired many educational reforms worldwide, reaching more than 16 countries and impacting more than 5 million children.

11.2.6. Innova Schools (Peru)

Innova Schools is a private school network founded in 2004, with at present 41 schools and 32,000 students. The approach revolves around four areas: putting students at the centre; 21st century skills; early childhood education; and reshaping student-teacher interactions. The networks mission is to create an intelligent, ethical and inspired generation of students, within an affordable and scalable schooling model for the emerging middle-class. Their guiding learning principles include: students are able to build their own learning; learning is a social construction; learning starts with demands that come from students' real context; learning should be meaningful; students should be highly engaged; learning is both intellectual and ethical; learning should include discovery. It identifies a key role for technology and it has established pedagogies built around group learning, solo learning, and flipped instruction. Innova Schools sees itself more as a set of interlocking systems than as a network.

11.2.7. KIP - Komplex Instrukciós Program (Hungary)

KIP began in a single school in 2000, using the Complex Instruction (CI) program originally developed at Stanford University to boost learning and improve behaviour and motivation, and then adapted to the Hungarian context. It took three years to create the

KIP. The basic ideas of CI and KIP are the same but with certain differences, especially in the technology. The teachers ascribe significant improvements specifically to this instructional system. In 2009, the dissemination of KIP began and by early 2017, the network consisted of 71 schools, 15 000 pupils and 1400 teachers.

11.2.8. Lumiar Institute (International)

The pedagogical approach of the Lumiar Institute embodies six main principles: multi-age grouping, distinct roles for tutors and "masters" (expert from the community), the Mosaic competency-based curriculum, formative evaluation, project-based learning, and learner agency with participative management. The first Lumiar school was set up in Sao Paulo in 2002 by the Semco Foundation (now renamed Ralston-Semler), promoting innovative educational, cultural, and environmental projects in Brazil. The distinctive idea of a Mosaic Curriculum was created by the Lumiar Institute, and a partnership between Lumiar and Anima Educação allowed the Digital Mosaic to progress and expanded the school network. There are now eight Lumiar Schools (five in Brazil, two in the UK, and one in Holland) for children from ages 2 to 15, with a number of schools in additional countries lined up for 2018.

11.2.9. Networks of Inquiry and Innovation (British Columbia, Canada)

In 2000, educators from 34 schools came together, with a provincial grant at the beginning, with a shared interest in learning progressions in literacy, social responsibility and numeracy to deepen learner agency. It became a province-wide network of schools that agreed on five big ideas:

1. Learner metacognition: A key goal is deep learning in which learners are able to coach themselves for improvement.
2. Nimble and responsive teaching: Educators need to use evidence of learning constantly to adapt teaching and learning to meet student needs.
3. Assessment for and as learning are key to shifting ownership of learning from the teacher to the student.
4. An inquiry mind-set is a necessity for learners, teachers and leaders, using thoughtful strategies and then looking for evidence of deeper learning.
5. Teamwork is essential - the isolated efforts of individual educators, no matter how well intentioned, will not suffice.

The original network has now evolved into a small number of innovation networks all using a disciplined, evidence-informed approach to collaborative inquiry (the "spiral of inquiry"). One network is intensely focused on improving the learning outcomes of Indigenous young people. Another is about creating better learner health outcomes, while another is focused on engaging young people in a sense of community and place through filmmaking and digital forms of learning.

11.2.10. New Pedagogies for Deep Learning (International)

New Pedagogies for Deep Learning (NPDL) is a global partnership dedicated to new pedagogies to foster deep learning competencies, and to establishing new measures of student progress and success. The initiative began in 2013 and its approach is currently put into practice in seven countries and some 900 schools. The aim is to engage students in meaningful, real-life learning experiences and to facilitate deep learning as mastery of academic content, the creation of new knowledge, and acquisition of deep learning competencies. NPDL works with the following core elements:

- learning partnerships between and among students, teachers, families and the wider environment;
- trusting learning environments operating 24/7 with students responsible for their learning;
- pedagogical practices to design, implement, monitor and assess learning;
- leveraging digital to accelerate access to knowledge beyond the classroom and generate deep learning.

11.2.11. Senza Zaino (Italy)

"Senza Zaino. Per una Scuola Comunità" (Without Backpack for a Community School) came from a school principal in Lucca, Tuscany. The principal invited other teachers and experts in the project, beginning in 2002, to create classrooms as innovative environments. The project revolves around two closely interacting dimensions: the hardware of physical spaces and materials, and the software of pedagogical strategies and methods. Senza Zaino substitutes a small bag for the heavy school backpack, where all the classrooms are provided with functional furniture and tools to implement innovative approaches. Every classroom is multipurpose, with different work areas with large tables, where students can work individually, in pairs, in groups or with the teacher depending on the learning aims.

11.2.12. Studio Schools (England)

The Studio Schools Trust developed its Studio School model based on its own CREATE skills framework. This covers academic excellence, employability and enterprise skills; CREATE stands for Communication, Relating to people, Enterprise, Applied skills, Thinking skills and Emotional intelligence. The wider model embraces personalised curriculum; project-based learning and work with employers in the classroom; regular work placements for all students; small schools; and catering for diverse abilities. CREATE skills underpin all activities and are used by coaches to encourage and track students' development. The Studio Schools Trust is a facilitating and developing organisation enabling the sharing of best practice as well as providing advice and curriculum support. After being established in 2009, there were 36 Studio Schools in England by 2017, with more foreseen.

11.3. The "Innovation Promotion Networks"

11.3.1. AND (A New Direction) (England)

A New Direction (AND) was formed around a decade ago from the four regional London delivery organisations for Creative Partnerships (CP). AND's mission is to introduce all children and young people in London to high quality arts and culture. It became the Arts Council's 'Bridge' organisation for London in 2011. It works with a wide range of teachers and schools, the cultural sector, employers, young people, and in local areas, focusing on:

- understanding of and commitment to the value of arts, culture and creativity in education;
- cross-curricular learning, project-based learning and using the arts beyond arts subjects;
- trying new things and taking risks;
- continually developing and improving practice and the offer to students.

11.3.2. Creative Partnerships (England/international)

Creative Partnerships (CP) was launched in 2002 by the Creativity, Culture and Education (CCE) international learning foundation. It supports teachers to create high-functioning learning environments within which pupils develop their creative skills and are physically, socially, emotionally and intellectually engaged. It has supported numerous innovative, long-term partnerships between schools, artists and other creative professionals. It grew quickly until, by 2008, it was operating in 2 500 schools across England each year. The programme ended in England in 2011 and CCE now works elsewhere - in Chile, Czech Republic, Hungary, Norway, Pakistan, Scotland, Slovakia and Wales.

11.3.3. ECOLOG (Austria)

ECOLOG is an action programme and network for the greening of schools and promoting education for sustainability. It was developed in the mid-1990s by a team of Austrian teachers in the international project "Environment and School Initiatives" (ENSI). It is a national support system for individual schools and promotes this sustainability approach through regional networks and regional governments. Key practices include:

- project-oriented teaching and learning;
- focal topics and school development plans;
- student involvement;
- aligning teaching development and school development;
- systematic reporting and evaluation;
- inquiry-based learning on real-life issues apparent at the school and local levels.

Overall coordination is ensured by the University of Klagenfurt in partnership with the Federal Ministry for Education.

11.3.4. ESCXEL Project – School Network for excellence (Portugal)

The ESCXEL Project is a network based on a partnership between public schools of eight municipalities, the correspondent 32 school clusters, and CICS.NOVA, an interdisciplinary Social Sciences research centre at Faculty of Social Sciences and Humanities of Universidade Nova de Lisboa (FCSH-UNL). Its main goal is to promote reflection about pedagogical practices and their results in a collaborative learning process through means such as good practice dissemination, results analysis, and discussions in schools. In 2017, there were 32 clusters in the network, covering 166 schools and nearly 60,000 students.

11.3.5. Innovative Schools Network (Japan)

The Japan Innovative Schools Network (ISN) applies deep active learning to global concerns, including through project- and inquiry-based learning, and promotes 21st century skills. ISN aims to develop and disseminate new educational approaches through research activities (its "Think-tank") and operational field practices ("Do-tank"). Schools from eight countries, as well as ISN in Japan, belong to six "core clusters" in which they collaborate in common projects as well as some "voluntary clusters" of innovative schools. Each school/cluster addresses regional and global issues through student-led projects with global collaboration aimed at regional revitalisation. There are three themes underpinning ISN: Think Green (environmental issues); Skills Supply and Demand (creating new jobs, innovating local industries), and Go Global (diversity, migration, globalisation). ISN originated with the "OECD Tohoku School" project seeking renewal after the devastation of Fukushima. It is a public-private consortium located in the University of Tokyo, with the support of OECD and the Ministry of Education, Culture, Sports, Science and Technology.

11.3.6. International Step by Step Association (ISSA) (International)

The Association builds on the early childhood education reform project 'Step by Step' (SBS) launched in the mid-1990s by the Open Society Foundations in 15 countries in Central Europe and Eurasia. The programme introduced social inclusion, child-centred practices, and community and family-based approaches through a series of pilots in public kindergartens and primary schools. It supported preschool and school networks implementing innovative approaches and practices, regarded in some cases as "alternative", in each country. It sought to influence decision-makers to:

- provide high quality care and educational services for all children from birth through primary school, with a focus on the most disadvantaged;
- promote child-centred, individualised teaching and learning, combining high-level instruction with support for the needs of each child;
- promote diversity, social justice, inclusive practices, and culturally appropriate learning environments;
- recognise educators as facilitators, guides, and role models and their need for autonomy, self-improvement and professional development;
- ensure family and community involvement in children's development and education;
- promote social education and community engagement in public education.

Over the years, ISSA has grown its membership and functions as a network of organisations co-constructing knowledge, peer learning across countries, adopting innovative approaches, and bridging policy, research and practice.

11.3.7. The Lighthouse (Finland)

The Lighthouse began when the Finnish National Agency for Education (EDUFI) invited the education directors from the ten biggest municipalities in Finland to form a school development network to introduce new pedagogies, working cultures and learning environments in schools as part of the basic education core curriculum published in 2014. The response was very positive. Other network goals were to improve cooperation between national and the local education strategies and to implement more research-based initiatives. At first, about 100 schools were involved; the message was (and still is) that any municipality or schools that are interested may join. There is no money on the table; the sustainability of the network is based on the benefits gained from cooperation and mutual support. In 2017, numbers had grown to 50 municipalities and more than 260 schools.

11.3.8. OPEDUCA Project (Netherlands/International)

The 'OPEDUCA Project' integrates a wide range of pedagogical practices such as inquiry-, problem- and community-based learning into a coherent, impactful approach. It develops skills in entrepreneurship, environmental education, technology and citizenship. It aims to create active, real-life learning that matches the ways of living and learning of today's pupils and students. OPEDUCA operates as regional alliances of schools, industry, regional government and science organisations. It bases schooling on education for sustainable development, focusing on the empowerment of both teachers and students and is innovative in enabling AAAA-Learning; Anytime, Anyplace, with Anybody, through Any device.

11.3.9. Red Escuelas Líderes (Chile)

This is a network of "leading schools" that have developed and adopted different pedagogical approaches, with the network aim of sharing and implementing new practices. It works especially in deprived contexts, aiming both to achieve excellence and the full development of the students. It started in 2007 with publications on educational innovation in situations of complexity and an initiative to make visible schools leading in innovative practice. The aim has been to fuel the interchange and cooperative work among network members and to promote similar developments in other schools. Now, 100 schools belong to the network.

11.3.10. Second Chance Schools (E2C/E2O) (France/Spain)

In the context of implementing the White Paper "Teaching and Learning: towards the learning society" (1995), the European Commission launched the "Second Chance Schools (E2C)" pilot projects in 1997. The main aim was to offer education and training to young people who lack the skills and qualifications necessary to find a job, or wholly benefit from conventional training. In France, the first project started in Marseille and then the network expanded to other regions. In 2004, they created an association "The Network of Second Chance Schools in France", and published a charter of the principles emerging from their experiences to promote the concept, advance the pedagogical principles, and offer technical support to new E2C schools. The French network has 49 schools, and their students show a 62% success rate in finding jobs or further training. The national network in Spain, ESO, created in 2016 by six founder organisations, consists of 28 members representing around 7 000 youths and 400 professionals. As in France, the Spanish ESC schools base their approach strongly on individualisation, motivation and the acquisition of useful skills and competences.

11.3.11. Whole Education (United Kingdom)

In late 2009, the Royal Society of Arts, Manufactures and Commerce (RSA) developed a Charter for 21st Century Education. This originated in response to a growing concern around the pressure to create "exam factories", at the expense of preparing young people for the modern world out of which Whole Education emerged in 2010. Its core tenet is that all children deserve an engaging, rounded education which supports academic achievement, while developing the skills, knowledge and qualities to flourish in life, learning and work. It is an independent, not-for-profit organisation, with lead Partner Schools, Pathfinder Schools, and a larger group of associated network schools, supporting and learning from each other. Schools work in networks, engage in leadership programmes and joint innovation projects, peer review each other's practice, share professional exchange events, and come together in a highly visible annual conference.

11.4. The "Professional Learning Networks"

11.4.1. Computing at Schools (CAS) (United Kingdom)

Computing at School (CAS) is a grassroots organisation that supports computer science teaching in schools. CAS was born out of a serious concern that many students are losing interest in computing - due to the perception that it is dull and pedestrian. The goal is to put excitement into computing at school. CAS supports teachers in both primary and secondary schools, primarily in England but also across the U.K. Much of the support provided through CAS focuses on computer science subject knowledge, but pedagogy also plays a part and arises out of the activity or learning tool being used by the teacher. Main projects include Teach London Computing, and physical computing and programming using such tools as Scratch and Python. Membership is very broad, including teachers, parents, governors, examination boards, industry, professional societies, and universities.

11.4.2. E-Norssi (Finland)

e-Norssi in Finnish stands for the network of Finnish Teacher Training Schools. It was founded in 2000 to encourage cooperation within teacher education but then expanded its mission to become a resource centre for all Finnish schools. The close relationship between theory and practice forms the basis for teacher education, ensuring that educational theory can be applied in practice. Strengthening the connections between the teacher training schools, departments of teacher education and other university departments allows student teachers to apply theoretical knowledge from early in their studies.

11.4.3. Galileo Educational Network (Alberta, Canada)

The Galileo Educational Network was created in 1999 following the success of the Galileo Centre founded three years earlier in an Alberta school in establishing new images of teaching and learning. The network began with provincial seed funding and the engagement of the University of Calgary. At first, the network focused on technology and supported leadership in the Alberta K-12 sector. Since 2000, the mandate has expanded so now the Galileo Educational Network creates, promotes, and disseminates innovative teaching and learning practices through research, professional learning, and networking, locally and internationally. Network influence is extended through: leading and learning; building capacity of district and school leaders, teacher leaders, and teachers; focusing on improvement and innovation, and collaborating with educators in participatory forms of research and design-based professional learning. Currently, the Galileo Educational Network is part of the Werklund School of Education at the University of Calgary.

Box 11.1. Experience of Hannah Blades, Galileo Learning Leader

"For the past three years, as a teacher and learning leader for the Calgary Board of Education (CBE), I have attended Galileo's Learning Leader Sessions where teams of Galileo consultants have facilitated highly effective training sessions for large groups of teacher/leaders around teaching, learning and leading for increased intellectual engagement. As a learning leader at first a community elementary school and the next year a junior high, it was my role to attend the sessions and bring the learning back to teachers at our school in the form of professional development."

11.4.4. Network of Innovation Schools (Estonia)

This network was established in cooperation between the University of Tartu and leading schools and kindergartens in Estonia. It shares the results of educational research, develops and tests innovative methods of teaching and learning, assessment, and professional learning. The network aims to bridge theory and practice through communities in which schools and the university are equals. They benefit from each other's strengths: the university colleagues gain experience addressing practice-related problems and solutions while the school colleagues improve their scientific thinking and become involved in collaborative research.

11.5. Diverse experiences of growth

There are widely varying experiences of change in numbers and membership among the networks responding to the questionnaire (Table 11.1). For some, growth is part of the *raison d'être* of the network – spreading numbers, spreading influence, growing viability. For others, stability is valued over growth: the network may well be tight and lacking the infrastructure and incentive to grow. Both experiences characterise the networks covered here.

Table 11.1. Networks experiencing overall growth

Network	Increase	Period of time
Amara Berri	From 1 to 21	1979-2017 (38 years)
Innova Schools	From 3 to 49	2010-2018 (8 years)
KIP	From 1 to 71	2000-2017 (17 years)
Lumiar Institute	From 1 to 8	2002-2018 (16 years)
NOII	From 34 to 250 in British Columbia	2000-2017 (17 years)
NPDL	Up to 1000 schools in 10 countries	2013-2018 (5 years)
Senza Zaino	From 80 to 270	2013-2017 (4 years)
ECOLOG	From 21 to 500	2001-2016 (15 years)
ESCXEL	Up to 166 schools	2008-2017 (9 years)
ISSA	From 30 to 80 organisations	2012-2017 (5 years)
Lighthouse	From 100 to 260	2014-2017 (3 years)
Red Escuelas Líderes	From 20 to 110	2007-2017 (10 years)
E2C France	From 9 to 116	2003-2016 (13 years)
ESO Spain	From 6 to 23	2016-2018 (2 years)
Whole Education	From 30 to 200	2012-2017 (5 years)
Galileo	From 3 schools in 3 schools districts to teachers and leaders across Canada	2000-2017 (17 years)

Box 11.2. NOII practitioner on network growth

"The network and leadership have nurtured and supported educators moving from a handful of amazing educators in the province to hundreds of strong educators equally committed to the promise of every student graduating with dignity, choice and purpose. The Network is a force upon itself and members have pride in the differences that they make; it is about purpose The Network and number of inquiry-based schools has constantly grown. Network members support each other and there is powerful network leadership, embedding expectations of high performance for both adult and student learners. The network and leadership have nurtured and supported educators moving from a handful of amazing educators in the province to hundreds of strong educators equally committed to the promise of every student graduating with dignity, choice and purpose."

Other examples show stable membership with no growth foreseen. These seem to be where growth is not seen as inherently desirable and where maintenance of established membership relationships is sought over the long term to provide stability and predictability into network development. This is the case of the Innovative School Network, local clusters of the international Step by Step association (e.g. Slovenia), E-Norssi, the Art of Learning network, Amico Robot, Better Movers and Thinkers and A New Direction.

There are other interesting examples, revealing of aims and dynamics. One comes from the Estonian network of innovative schools, which wishes to grow because of unmet demand but aware that this will require restructuring to move into a more ambitious phase.

- *"The network has not grown, but there is a need to restructure it soon, because many schools that are currently not the members of the network are interested in cooperation and have innovative ideas to share and bring into the network. The network of innovative schools should not be exclusive"* (Estonian Network).

In other cases, networks have followed different phases. For example, the Studio Schools, after growing significantly between 2010 and 2015 as a result of a government drive to support their schools, they stabilised the number of schools in networks, with some closing and new ones being opened. In the case of Escuela Nueva, it started in the mid-1970s in a small number of rural schools, but then their model was assumed by the Ministry of Education and scaled up to 8 000 schools. By the 1990s, 20 000 in Colombia – the host country of this international network – were using Escuela Nueva's model as the result of being part of the national policy. A fourth stage consisted on their model being adopted in 16 countries of Latin America, reaching more than 5 million children in total.

Box 11.3. OPEDUCA

"There have been quite 'explosive' stages of growth going from local, to regional, to national try-outs throughout the country, to European scale and sometimes with schools in other continents. Each time we decided to reduce the growth since we never strived for 'numbers' but for creating a truly working approach as we envision it, then to be disseminated as far as it goes when the concept, practical application and time are ready for it. We changed (brought back and rebuilt) our organisation three times. A reason for 'holding back' has been to prevent 'half-baked' implementations that would obscure the purer concept and transition process. This has resulted in serious 'shake outs' of the network. It was a strategic decision to remain 'small and beautiful' as long as possible. We wanted to wait out the wave (especially in Western Europe) of over-funded 'nice projects' that were thrown into the system. Many of these worn out, and returned to old habits after our initial shake-out. We now go for a full-scale all-inclusive invitation to schools to join, aiming at the development of 20 OPEDUCA-regions throughout Europe and 20 more worldwide as strong bases to stand on."

Source: OPEDUCA network leader.

The examples of OPEDUCA (Box 11.3), Computer at Schools and Creative Partnerships are different from all these. For OPEDUCA, there has been a desire to maintain 'purity' of network aims, undiluted by participation that is not actively promoting those aims. They deliberately engaged in a process of pruning ('shaking out'), in order to ensure healthier growth in pursuit of those aims. But having engaged in this pruning, not once but several times, the strategic aim is now very different and to go for very ambitious international growth.

It will be interesting to see how far this can be achieved without running into the dilution that had resulted in previous membership reductions. Computer at Schools, being a grass-root organisation, is based on the energy coming from its members, and these Lead Schools spearheading diverse clusters of schools across the country. That means that whereas the network has strengthened its structure – through the creation of hubs, regional centres, master teachers and strategic partnership with universities -, in some areas the network can diminish its presence, mostly because of the role played by the volunteer workforce. Finally, Creative Partnership was working in the UK from 2002 to 2011, reaching a peak of schools involved in 2008 (2 500 schools). Then the programme ended in England in 2011 and shifted its role by supporting the implementation of creative learning programmes internationally.

11.5.1. Factors seen to facilitate or hinder network growth

Facilitating factors

A key factor identified by several networks is *organisational effectiveness*: unless the network itself is well organised and appropriate for the context and circumstances it is unlikely to be sustained, especially when it is promoting practice that challenges traditional routines.

- *Innova Schools:* The growth is explained by the financial model: financially, the network has to reach scale to be self-sustainable and profitable. Visibility and an attractive value proposition facilitate this growth.

- *Step by Step Benevolent Foundation - ISSA member in Armenia:* In recent years SBS BF's role has increased dramatically and it has become a key player in the sector. Being in ISSA means benefiting from conferences and other professional development events as well as having access to ISSA materials. It allows connection with innovative educational organisations/experts from around the world, bringing new ideas to local needs.

- *Lumiar Institute:* Recent growth has been facilitated by the further development of the Digital Mosaic as a tool that supports individual learner competency development in a flexible learning environment. There have been many requests from around the world to open Lumiar Schools, in large part due to the innovative methodology used at Lumiar and because of their Mosaic digital platform - capable of supporting schools moving to competency-based learning even if they are not using the Lumiar methodology.

- Whole Education network leader: *"First, the network focused mostly on conferences and events bringing schools together to share practices and learn from lead practitioners. This has changed immensely, bringing best practice from around the world to the schools by leading, mentoring and supporting innovative educational projects. We also increased our support and training to all levels of school leadership."*

Effectiveness is thus seen to embrace both viability and success in bringing messages and new knowledge to practitioners. These particular networks clearly value bringing global experts and experience to local practice. They have been ready to embrace even quite marked change in their organisation. One aspect of the effectiveness is visibility, and several other networks refer to *success in dissemination* as an integral factor to network growth:

- Amico Robot network leader: *"Levers for growth include the partnership with cultural institutions and universities, and the organisation of the festival, as well as the enthusiasm of teachers and students once they know more about robotics."*

- *Creative Partnerships:* Even after the programme started in England, the growing international interest in developing creative skills and the sheer scale and impact of the initial programme meant that CCE was frequently invited to support creative learning programmes across the globe; in 2017, this included Chile, Czech Republic, Hungary, Norway, Pakistan, Scotland, the Slovak Republic and Wales.

- *ESCXEL*: The main factor has been the dissemination of the work done within the network, mostly by our partner schools.

- Issa Slovenia network leader and practitioner: *"We are actively working on spreading the idea of Network - we have 'open days' and organise Network presentations in some preschools to which preschools from neighbouring locations are invited."*

- *NOII:* Factors facilitating the growth include reputation and word of mouth, levels of district support, a strong cadre of network leaders and the relative simplicity of the format.

As several of the above passages have already suggested, effectiveness and dissemination are not just organisational matters but depend critically on the *core mission* of the network and how it is perceived - the value proposition and how well it meets pressing needs.

- Amara Barri network leaders: *"The model is viewed as truly alternative, and with the renewed interest of innovation in education the model has been the focus of different reports and news items; this has helped to expand the network outside the Basque region, as well as to maintain existing members."*
- *ISSA:* The main reason for success are the values, the cross-national learning supported in the network (transfer of innovations, peer support and learning among members, member driven initiatives), the co-creation of knowledge that it is forged with and among members, as well as the annual conferences which are learning platforms for the members and organisations around the world.
- *Lumiar Tutor: "Yes, there are new schools in recent years, and this is a result of growing interest in alternative/innovative education."*
- *Senza Zaino:* The new organisation of the classroom and the didactics: i) improve the quality of effectiveness of the teaching and learning; ii) creates a climate of well-being for teachers and students; and iii) makes students protagonists of their own learning. These all motivate teachers to get into the model and make it happen, with passion and openness towards innovation.
- *Whole Education:* Among the factors that facilitated network development, the main one is a strong and clear moral purpose, amongst school staff and leadership, to provide pupils with an education that equips them with the skills needed to thrive in life and to reduce the gaps between them. The need for support, partnership and exposure to best practice has led the schools and organisations to join.

An interesting aspect of these replies regarding network growth is the perception that the general climate is becoming more accepting of innovation, as innovation is increasingly seen as the way to tackle the urgent educational issues that have not been addressed through traditional methods.

This momentum favourable to innovation itself is powerfully shaped by *policy*. For innovation to move from being the exceptional practice of a few enlightened leaders and to become mainstream, the general tenor of debate and the governance and accountability systems need to be aligned to make it acceptable. Several responses stress the role of policy in stimulating and sustaining the network's aims and practice.

- *Escuela Nueva:* Four key areas explain success and growth: 1) the existence of demo schools; 2) the role of research and evaluation; 3) technical, political and financial feasibility of the model, and 4) public-private partnerships plus the important role of civil society. The network benefits from having leaders in strategic institutional positions in a time when rural education and widening access to quality education has been a national priority and of other international organisations.
- *KIP:* There has been a state initiative to introduce playful learning in which school staffs could learn how board games can raise motivation, help the talented, as well as to develop logic and social competences. KIP methodology is about to be rolled out within the framework of a 5-year, EU-funded project, named *Complex Basic Program,* aimed at addressing early school leaving through teacher education in at-risk schools. All teacher training centres, the central Education Office and the Hungarian Institute for Educational Research and Development are involved.

- *Second Chance, France:* The growth is explained partly through political awareness of the need to reduce youth unemployment, combined with institutional support through the regions, enterprises, and the financial support of the state, together with the promising results of E2C.

Box 11.4. Factors supporting ECOLOG

- The network is in place, and is commissioned, financed and co-coordinated by the Ministry of Education together with the University of Klagenfurt.
- A support structure in each of the nine Austrian provinces (teams of the school board, teacher education universities, regional governments, teachers, NGOs, and universities).
- The regional teams are nationally coordinated, with a national steering body.
- The website serving as a central information tool.
- Incentives of certificates and recognised teacher hours and project funds provided by the educational authorities.
- ECOLOG is aligned with current educational reforms, especially those for improvement and evaluation, including tools of whole-school development plans.
- The long-term nature of involvement for schools, not ephemeral projects.
- Spaces for experiences and developing routines as well as inviting new innovations.
- ECOLOG schools are active in other initiatives and networks.
- Societal relevance in helping to implement Environmental education (EE), ESD, SDG and related cross-curricular decrees.

One of the problems with reliance on policy initiatives and funding, however, is that it may disappear as readily as it appears. The full engagement of the Austrian authorities in ECOLOG (Box 11.4) is an example where the policy engagement goes well beyond funding to include administration and certification and this has allowed it to become long term rather than a temporary project. Such levels of government support may be less positive, however, when the agenda run counter to innovation, including support for innovative pedagogies.

Hindering factors

There are diverse factors identified as hindering network growth, which are closely inter-related: lack of funds and lack of commitment, for instance, can amount to the same thing when finance is short and difficult choices need to be made. As might be expected, financial barriers are identified by several networks as inhibiting growth, but these are not the only reasons given.

- *ECOLOG:* The main hindering factors are: i) financial and time constraints; ii) different levels of support in the nine provinces.
- *Step by Step Benevolent Foundation - ISSA member in Armenia: "Currently financial difficulties limit the realisation of some interesting ideas that might be very important for further improvement of education quality in our country."*
- *Issa Slovenia:* Some of the preschools withdraw from Network for financial reasons (the fee).

- *Lighthouse School:* The possibilities to collaborate have been restricted by financial constraints.
- *Senza Zaino*: The main negative points are the lack of appropriate financial means and the mobility of teachers of recent years.

The issue is not simply a lack of finance but also the uncertainty and termination of project funds. So often, innovations that have been launched through funded project initiatives do not survive long beyond the end date of the funding.

- *Amico Robot:* Lack of financial resources, and that those teachers participating in the network do it in a voluntary basis. Project closure is always a serious threat, and participants tend to give up making efforts when financial and professional help ceases.
- Creative Partnerships network leader: *"In 2010, the government announced that it was withdrawing funding from Creative Partnerships in schools in England (so that the network became increasingly focused on international work)."*
- *KIP network leader and practitioner: "When the project ends and subsidies cease, schools find themselves without help and resources; consequently, most of them will lose their motivation."*
- *NOII:* Factors inhibiting growth are related to funding levels being uncertain from one year to the next and the resulting challenges in building on-going capacity.
- *Studio Schools*: Grew significantly between 2010 and 2015; however, in many cases once approved, schools found their funding drop in real terms. This lack of funding has had an impact on what individual schools are able to do and in some cases, has led to schools being closed. In many cases the more innovative aspects of the curriculum are cut first.

The barrier that gets frequently bracketed with money is *time*. Several of the networks refer to a lack of time as a hindering factor, and a lack of sufficient incentives to make the effort that the outlays of resources and time require.

- *AND:* The networks have grown but only slightly and slowly. The main barriers are lack of teacher time and lack of school budgets to support teachers to be out of the classroom (as well as lack of emphasis on arts subjects in many schools due to government policy).
- *KIP*: Project mechanisms in general are unsuitable for sustained development, mostly because the preparation period always needs more time than planned (Box 11.5), real activities in the field are always late and there is too little time until the end of the project to achieve genuine results which need at least eight years. Planning resources for the time after the project tends to be missing at all levels. Some of the most interesting responses regarding hindering factors are the perceptions from some that there is insufficient dynamism and adaptability to sustain the ambitions of the network and the pedagogical approach.

Three different examples follow. In the first, the problem is identified in a form of complacency - being part of the network but without sufficient commitment to change and improvement. In the second, the problem is seen to reside in an accountability system that is too rigid and limiting to foster innovation.

- *Issa Slovenia network leader and practitioner: "A quarter of the preschools have been in the network from the very beginning. They are very loyal to the idea, but some have difficulties in understanding that the Centre is not merely implementing an approach but working on professionalism and quality."*

- *Studio Schools network leader: "Growth has also been hindered by the UK accountability system, which is essentially 'one-size-fits-all' and has difficulty assessing the impact of innovative approaches which may not have the same goals as mainstream schools. Accountability is still very much focused on raw exam outcomes."*

Box 11.5. Komplex Instrukciós Program (KIP): 'The first step is the hardest'

"It is relatively easy to learn the technology, but the vision, beliefs, pedagogical concepts, culture, and attitudes are much harder to change, do so slowly and only with continuous reinforcement. Teachers say that the very first step is the hardest: to recognise the need and the possibility to change and to take up the burden of learning and working even much more than usual, being already overloaded. They say that success is the most potent motivator, which comes right from the beginning."

Source: KIP network leader.

The third example identifies part of the problem to lie in a market approach but also in a phenomenon more rarely discussed: the misplaced or superficial innovations or 'modernisations' that can flourish in the market conditions. It is a reminder that innovation is not simply change for its own sake (which can often result in superficial faddism) but instead needs to be grounded in genuine endeavours with the potential for positive change.

- *OPEDUCA network leader: "A hindering factor has been the too-generously funded 'modernisations' flooding the educational system, often driven by smooth-talking consultants, seeing schools as a market. As OPEDUCA is open source, it may even be felt as a threat to the commercial side of the educational market. This hindering factor has been exacerbated by political efforts to push systems and schools to achieve ever higher ranking, often at 'whatever the cost'. Neither the commercial nor the political influence has done schools much good."*

Even more basic than a lack of dynamism is a lack of commitment and buy-in from the beginning. Like dependence on temporary project funding, this is a challenge facing many innovations and especially when the aim is to erode traditional, well-established practices.

- *Amara Barri network leaders: "There are cases of schools that have tried to implement their model but have failed, due to lack of commitment and cohesion among teachers."*
- *Escuela Nueva network leader: "The microcentres, or teachers' learning circles, where teachers get together to share experiences, require, at least, political support to take off; nevertheless, the high turnover of teachers is a serious problem for it weakens the microcentres' work and sustainability."*
- *KIP network leader and practitioner: "Not all teacher training centres are convinced that this is the methodology worth promoting. There is country-wide roll-out of the methodology. However, the innovation should be changing the culture of pedagogy and it is in changing the mind-set that new methods can be sustained, but this is the hardest to achieve."*

- *CAS network leader: "Originally there were supposed to be hubs in all Local Authorities in Scotland, but it was difficult to get 'buy-in' from all of them."*

The final bullet point recognises the multi-layered factors at work in both facilitating and hindering growth. In this case, they are categorised as external and internal factors as perceived by *Innova Schools*:

- *External*:

    1. (lack of) availability of strategically located lands for new schools;
    2. national and local regulations, bureaucracy and inefficient public administration;
    3. low average teacher effectiveness in the country.

- *Internal:*

    4. (lack of) availability of experienced professionals for leadership positions at both the school and the system level;
    5. ineffective administration to support the scale and growth of the network.

One feature that deserves a particular attention is the key role played by individual schools in driving the establishment of the networks, especially at the beginning. There are examples where universities are closely involved, and play a key role of research support and professional development, but less of originating the innovation. Sometimes that has come through policy initiatives and programmes. However, what stands out is the key role of individual educators or innovation teams launching and implementing an idea to change the nature of teaching and learning.

11.6. In summary

- The questionnaire identified three different kinds of networks of schools that are scaling up and out innovative pedagogies. A first group that share a common approach, "The Pedagogical Approach Network", another group of hubs for sharing and discussing innovative practices, "The Innovation Promotion Network", and a third group of networks providing continuous professional development, the "Professional Learning Network".
- The networks highlight key factors lying behind growth – network effectiveness, powerful dissemination, a clear and valued mission, and a positive policy climate are among the most frequently-cited. Reasons forwarded as inhibiting growth are problematic funding, lack of time, as well as insufficient dynamism, commitment and buy-in.
- Scale and sustainability often requires complex network infrastructures but this should not detract from the key role played in this universe of cases by particular schools and innovative educators on the ground.

Chapter 12. Approaches to innovative pedagogy, teaching and learning

This chapter focuses on the main approaches to teaching and pedagogy, according to the various networks. The analysis in this chapter draws particularly on the "Pedagogical Approach Networks", for their experiences revolve on common approaches that have already expanded. It follows the structure of the questionnaire, which was designed to engage the different networks. First, it describes the networks main pedagogical approaches and their relation to some fundamentals of learning (as described in previous OECD/CERI work). It also includes how the networks secure learners' voice and agency. After, the analysis moves to how these pedagogical approaches are suited for specific learners or subjects. Towards the end of the chapter there is discussion on how these identified key practices support the effective implementation of their pedagogical approaches. This discussion is particularly relevant to address one of the dimensions of the conceptual framework of the project, connoisseurship.

12.1. Introduction

This chapter first explores the main factors that characterise the pedagogical approaches used by the networks, the extent of their match with the OECD learning principles, and describing the role of assessment, learners' voice and agency. Then the discussion moves to questions of context and content, including explicit commitment to the teaching of 21st century skills. Third, the question as to how central technology is for these networks is introduced. Finally, the chapter concludes with an analysis of key practices that best explain the successful implementation and sustainability of their innovative approaches.

12.2. The key elements of the Pedagogical Approach Networks

This section summarises the key pedagogical practices that underpins the pedagogical approaches of each network (for reference, the full questionnaire is described in Annex 2.A). The "Pedagogical Approach Networks" are all able, therefore, to summarise a complex set of elements that together make up the overall approach. These diverse elements embrace pedagogy and include a philosophy of what is important to address in learning and how to rectify certain shortcomings apparent in much of the mainstream schooling on offer in their systems. That they are networks encourages this feature of coherence and an explicit approach, needing to develop a set of cornerstones that can be shared with others. These emerge again when the networks explain how their approach adheres to the OECD learning design principles.

12.2.1. Amara Berri

This network espouses the immersion of real life into classroom activities and through interdisciplinary and project-based designs. The pedagogical approach revolves around gaming activities and student interests. Further, the classroom should facilitate children to acquire and practice the competences central to their well-being.

Box 12.1. Amara Berri practitioner

"There is a globalism to the approach, seeking to develop skills and competences for life. The main pedagogical ideas are: start with the interests and motivations of children; respect the learning pace of students; adopt a comprehensive approach to learning; follow a clear methodology for every activity so that students are aware of it and self-regulate their own learning; focus on inquiry as a leading learning principle; the teacher is guide and supporter of learners; and cooperative work."

12.2.2. Amico Robot

Robotics is used by the schools involved to meet three different goals: 1) the implementation of alternative pedagogies around constructivism and metacognition; 2) the innovative use of ICTs; and 3) the development of 21st century skills. Amico Robot also seeks to emphasise lab work so as to promote learner participation and peer collaboration and true, deep learning – compared with "the traditional learning sequence" seen as superficial ("in the end these learning experiences rather slip down like raindrops on window glass, and do not transform into deep learning.")

12.2.3. Art of Learning

The key pedagogy behind the project is active learning, with a range of strategies to promote:

- Creativity skills: inquisitive; open minded; imagination; problem-solving.
- Higher-order thinking skills, in particular: analyse; create; apply; evaluate.
- Active collaboration through peer learning / review and self-assessment.
- Group evaluations.

These are deployed together through different arts activities which promote the executive brain function - self-control, working memory and cognitive flexibility.

12.2.4. Better Movers and Thinkers

BMT is an approach to learning and teaching in physical education designed to develop the ability of all children and young people to move and think in a more cohesive way, with a specific focus on developing, enhancing and fostering Executive Function (EF) skills. EF provides essential tools that accurately and consistently guide the cognitive processes towards the intended outcome. The six Executive Functions are: Focus of Attention, Working Memory, Inhibition Control, Cognitive Flexibility, Planning, and Goal-Directed Behaviour. Planning for the development of the six EF skills is intrinsic to the BMT approach. There is a distinctive approach to 'scaffolding practices', which focus on the development of the Significant Aspects of Learning. In turn, these support the development of discipline specific skills. These scaffolding practices involve both physical and cognitive processes.

Some of the key features of the pedagogical approach are:

- Lessons must contain moderate to vigorous levels of physical activity throughout.
- Lessons must include scaffolding practices that help develop the Significant Aspects of Learning by consistently increasing the complexity of the cognitive tasks, and the refinement of the physical ones.
- Lessons must include the development of targeted Executive Function skills.

12.2.5. Escuela Nueva

Escuela Nueva promotes a reflexive, active, collaborative and participative learning, centred on the student, emphasising the role of the community and assessment. Key practices are: working through learning guidelines, for students to use individually or in groups; learning corners for projects in which students can experiment and interact; the classroom library; and the student government, which works through students' committees and various classroom instruments such as suggestions and friendship mail and self-monitored attendance, among others. Using the words from a network leader:

> "We transform the conventional school teacher-centred school based on memorisation, authoritarianism and the transmission of knowledge in a school that promotes the cooperative learning, participation and the active involvement of the student, and a strong relationship with the community."

12.2.6. Innova Schools, Peru

Innova Schools use a standardised approach aiming for the same quality standard throughout the network because of so many new and relatively young teachers. Teachers access learning units through the digital Teacher Resource Centre (TRC), through which they can interact and share with each other. Main principles are:

- *Put students at the centre of the learning process and of the system.* Students inherently have the ability of building their own learning through discovery and collaboration with teachers and their peers.
- *Develop 21st century skills.* The curriculum should develop seven key competences: (1) effective communication, (2) mathematical competence, (3) scientific thinking, (4) digital literacy, (5) innovation, (6) ethics and leadership, and (7) citizenship.
- *Address early childhood education*, in which children are viewed as competent and come to discover the world with the classroom environment as the "third teacher", within strong family/teacher partnerships.
- *Reshape student/teacher interactions.* Teachers as learning facilitators, who need professional learning for their new role, and to support students to build their own knowledge. Student autonomy becomes a pivotal factor for learning and well-being from early childhood throughout secondary education.
- *Learning through collaboration.* Teaching and learning are social and collaborative, activities promote discussion and the co-creation of solutions, and classroom layout enhances collaboration.
- *Adopt real world and complex learning tasks.* Predesigned learning units are used as guidance by every teacher built around specific, real world and complex tasks (problems, projects, questions, situations). Classroom activities are scaffolds to support students as is regular feedback.
- *Use technology to transform learning.* Technology is embedded in the learning process, and students have access to a wide range of digital tools. There is blended learning from 4th to 11th grade in Math, Spanish, English and Science.
- *Prioritise students' well-being.* The school environment embraces diversity, with students feeling safe, valued and respected. They build positive relationships with peers, with teachers and with other adults. Teachers and leaders receive professional learning to support students and eliminate negative behaviour.

12.2.7. KIP

The KIP is a teaching programme, practised in the United States and worldwide. It aims to create equitable classrooms, appreciate and evaluate a variety of intelligence forms and capacities, and make children active in their own learning. It builds on three pillars:

- *Multiple ability assignments*: Assigned tasks are open-ended and require different approaches and skills to be completed successfully.
- *Group-work*: Most assignments are undertaken in groups of four or five pupils, changing the classroom atmosphere from competitive to collaborative while altering power relations.
- *Status treatment:* A principal goal is to lessen status differences and allow all children to experience success in the classroom, primarily through the inclusion of lower-status children in group work, appreciating their contributions, and enhancing their self-confidence.

12.2.8. Lumiar Institute

There are six tenets underpinning the specific pedagogical practices:

1. Multi-age groups organised in six "cycles" compressing to two years each, from 1 to 14 years old.
2. Tutors and masters: The tutor follows the group through the whole cycle, is the key reference of the group, and manages the curriculum. The master can be anyone from inside or outside the school interested in developing a project/workshop with the group.
3. Mosaic Curriculum shaped specifically to each group using "the competencies matrix", "the skills matrix" and "matrices of content of knowledge" (one for each area of knowledge). In a project/workshop, the tutor and the master choose which competencies, skills and knowledge are being developed and students are assessed on these.
4. Formative evaluation: There are two qualitative evaluations: the student self-evaluation and the "tutor&master" evaluation. The results are registered in the individual folder of the Digital Mosaic, to which parents also have access.
5. Inquiry-based learning: Time and the activities are organised around inquiry using different modalities such as the "World Reading", "Individual Research", "Projects" and "Workshops".
6. Participative management: The students, parents, educators and staff decide on the most important issues, especially through the weekly "circle" in which every participant has equal rights to listen and to be heard.

Box 12.2. The view of a Lumiar tutor

"The students and educators have different roles from the conventional schools. Students are invited to participate in decisions, to question, elaborate hypotheses, debate, and to choose, collectively and individually, what and how they are going to study, learn and investigate.

The educators are two: the tutor, a figure of reference to each group, and the master, a specialist who comes in once or twice a week on a project or other learning modality. The master does not have to be a licenced educator and could be, for example, an architect. The tutor helps the master and the group, and deals with all kinds of demands, from pedagogical issues to conflicts and other questions that arise. The schools work as a direct democracy, in which students and staff discuss decisions and needs of the community."

12.2.9. NOII

Network schools engaging in spirals of inquiry are asked to regularly pose four key questions to their learners:

- Can you name two people who believe you will be a success in life?
- What are you learning and why is it important?
- How is it going with your learning?
- What are your next steps?

Box 12.3. The view of an NOII practitioner

"I believe the Spiral of Inquiry is used constantly in the myriad of teaching decisions made daily. The Spiral has become the framework to embed wise practice in the classroom and has become itself a pedagogical practice. Teachers in the classroom are constantly scanning students, refocusing themselves based on how the students interpreted the learning opportunity. Teachers immediately develop a hunch about what needs to be redirected, learning immediately that they unknowingly have not supported the learning in the desired way, pull students back into directed learning and then check to ensure the problem is solved."

Practices shift, sometimes dramatically, towards increasing connections, decreasing anxiety, and building resilience, directly teaching the development of growth mind-sets and learning how to incorporate mindfulness strategies into the everyday life in schools.

As well as the OECD learning principles, Network schools are actively applying holistic indigenous learning principles, focused on connectedness, reciprocal relationships and a sense of place. Learning includes recognising the consequences of one's actions, it values patience, and requires the exploration of personal identity. Teachers create greater connections to the broader community and to elders, and make explicit how what is being learnt influences the self, the family, the community and the land.

12.2.10. New Pedagogies for Deep Learning (NPDL)

NPDL has identified four key pedagogical elements which combine to mobilise deep learning:

- *Learning Partnerships:* Cultivated between and among students, teachers, families and the wider environment. Teachers are activators, while students become active in the design, implementation and measurement of learning experiences. Partnerships enjoy high partner equity, transparency, mutual benefit and accountability.
- *Learning Environments:* Fostering continuous interaction in trusting environments, where students take responsibility for their own learning in a culture of engagement and motivation to learn with anyone, anytime and anywhere. Learning design needs to adapt flexibly to new areas, learning experiences build on earlier successes, and include both authentic and virtual learning environments.
- *Pedagogical Practices:* Combining research-proven models with emerging pedagogies, scaffolding thinking and levels of complexity, and personalising learning to the knowledge, interests and needs of individual learners. The pedagogies engage students in a range of assessment approaches with rapid cycles of self- and peer-feedback, using a broad mix of qualitative and quantitative assessment evidence.
- *Leveraging Digital:* Accelerating access to knowledge beyond the classroom, cultivating student-driven deep learning, and facilitating partnerships with students, families and the community members regardless of geographical location. Technology is an accelerator of deep learning, while the new pedagogies it enables are the drivers of deep learning outcomes.

NPDL has identified six competencies ("6Cs" – *Character, Citizenship, Collaboration, Communication, Creativity* and *Critical Thinking*) as the foundation of what is important for learners today.

12.2.11. Senza Zaino

The Global Curriculum Approach is fundamental, with a strong connection between hardware and software. Its key pedagogical practices follow five steps:

- *Organising space* into work areas and enriching them with didactic tools.
- *Classroom management and differentiated instruction*. Students and teachers negotiate activities that enable students to work autonomously.
- *Designing and assessment*. Teachers and students share the learning targets - writing them down with attention to graphics and design. The students engage in self-evaluation and have the feedback so they can improve.
- *Promoting the community school*. This means viewing both teachers and the learners as communities. Student participation is encouraged throughout their school life. There is tutoring, peer education, and reciprocal teaching, with ample opportunities for teachers to exchange ideas and practices.
- *Sharing visions with parents and opening to the world*. Parents are involved in school activities and vision, and develop collaboration and cooperation.

12.2.12. The Studio Schools

The essential elements of the Studio School model are: Academic excellence in the national curriculum and recognised qualifications; employability and enterprise skills within the CREATE skills framework; personalised curriculum in which students have access to a personal coach to help plan their studies and life beyond school; practical learning through projects and classroom work with employers; real Work, through regular work placements for all students; small Schools (up to 300 14-19-year-old students); and students of all abilities included.

12.3. Adherence to the OECD learning principles

The questionnaire asked networks to select the 2-3 of the OECD/ILE learning principles (see Box 1.1) that apply especially to their approach. Table 12.1 summarises the answers given by the different networks, while some of the detailed comments on how they are implemented are presented afterwards. It is important to note that in some cases networks found it difficult just to emphasise 2 or 3 principles, while in others the table reflects the collective response given by networks and schools. This is the reason behind the variation in the number of principles they selected.

Table 12.1. Networks and correspondence to OECD learning principles

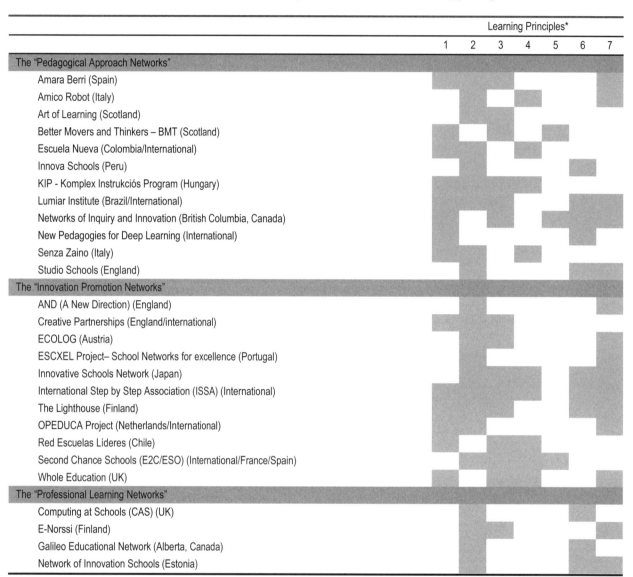

* Note: The Learning Principles refer to: 1) learner centredness and engagement; 2) learning as social; 3) recognising emotions; 4) recognising individual differences; 5) stretching all students; 6) appropriate and formative assessment; and 7) horizontal connectedness.
Source: OECD (2017), *The OECD Handbook for Innovative Learning Environments*, OECD Publishing, Paris, http://dx.doi.org/10.1787/9789264277274-en.

Although the networks are not a random sample and so not representative of a larger population, the pattern of responses it still interesting. The importance of enhancing engagement and putting learning at the centre stands out, as does emphasising the social aspects of teaching and learning. There is a prominent focus on formative assessment. Certain of the networks emphasise emotions, and the need for holistic approaches to individual development. There is also attachment to horizontal connectedness, which defines Principle 7. Somewhat less apparent is the personalisation inherent in Principles 4 and 5, whether because it is viewed as less important or because they are understood as subsumed by the other learning principles.

12.3.1. Insights from the Pedagogical Approach Networks on the OECD learning principles

Matching their approach to the OECD learning principles was an exercise that the networks found appropriate and useful. In fact, some emphasised how difficult it was to select amongst them as all apply to their approach in one way or another, as showed in the following excerpts:

> *"All the principles are connected with Lumiar's teaching practices."*

> *"All seven learning principles from the OECD are having a significant influence in shifting practice [in NOII]."*

1) Make learning central, and encourage engagement and awareness in students of their own learning strategies.

- The *BMT* approach puts quality learning and teaching at the heart of learners' experiences and classroom performance. BMT facilitates higher levels of engagement amongst participants through layering refinement and complexity onto the physical tasks.
- *Escuela Nueva*: The tools and strategies deployed in the classroom are central to allow students to reflect about their roles and contributions to the learning taking place.
- *Lumiar Schools*: The Mosaic Curriculum projects the learning outcomes and comes to life only by mobilising the student's interest, needs and engagement. This mobilisation occurs mainly through projects, workshops and other organisational modalities with final products built by the students.
- *NPDL network leader: "Deep learning involves continuous awareness, development of and reflection on the process of learning and its outcomes. Students begin to experience a 'seamless ecology of life and learning in which learning, doing, knowing, adapting, inventing and living meld together."*
- *Senza Zaino network leader and practitioner: "The ownership of learning is fundamental. Students are partakers of cognitive aims that await them, involved in the design of activities, and monitor their progress step by step. Strong feedback and formative assessment encourages student awareness about their own learning strategies."*

These responses align with the discussion of student voice and agency, which is the focus of a subsequent section of this chapter: the extent to which the learners are made central and are fully engaged and at the same time acquire significant control and understanding of their own learning.

Box 12.4. Practitioner illustration from a NOII rural secondary school

Teachers have developed information around a local issue; connected to Social Studies outcomes, social justice issues and literacy outcomes. Students have been 'frontloaded' with content and several research strategies and an inquiry focus developed on a topic of personal interest.

During sharing circle, students exchange names of people they are connecting with…people in media, authors and other community members. Students share their learning activities, while charts around the room display overarching learning targets and big ideas and they connect their learning activities to these. The teacher introduces new books and websites and she reviews the strategy charts, refocusing students on useful strategies for the day's learning.

Learning projects are on-going, and students work in small groups, pairs, individually, or in the large class group for information sharing. They access exemplars, and self-assess and peer assess using co-constructed criteria. The teacher constantly scans the learners and students approach the teacher frequently, suggesting adaptations that they have incorporated in their work and ways that they think others will benefit. The teacher gives oral and written feedback, connects learners with similar ideas together and scaffolds the learning for others. Students are encouraged to think creatively as well as critically. They bring their life experiences and personal interests to the task.

Work pauses as a sharing circle is called, and everyone shares where they are at with their learning. During circle-sharing some students may display 'information overload' so they work separately with the teacher to help them prioritise. Students know where they are with their learning, and strategy charts posted around the room advise them on possible next steps. Students use iPads or tablets to take pictures of their work, and post feedback, inviting feedback from the teacher or parents or from other students who are working on a similar issue with another network teacher.

2) Ensure that learning is social and often collaborative

- Throughout the *Art of Learning* project, creative practices and higher-order thinking skills are at the core, with activities including the presentation of work to the broader group so making learning highly visible and each learner individually and collectively responsible.
- *Escuela Nueva*: The collaborative work is paramount and is a way to foster critical thinking.
- *Lumiar Schools*: Social relations, pedagogical practices and the organisation of the school routine are managed in a participative way. All projects and workshops seek to overcome traditional individualistic competitive methods.
- *NPDL*: The ability to collaborate deeply is still only emerging globally. Proficient collaboration encompasses students' ability to manage team dynamics and challenges, make substantive group decisions, and learn from and contribute to the learning of others. Strong interpersonal and team-related skills benefit learners throughout their lives.
- *Senza Zaino*: It is important to build a collaborative environment both by the hardware (the setting of spaces) and the software (coherent strategies and methods).

- *Studio Schools*: Students are often tasked with working together in teams to produce learning outcomes that would not be possible if they were working alone. Small class sizes and student numbers mean that students often have closer relationships with their peers and staff than they would in a larger school.

What comes out of these interpretations of the 'social' learning principle No. 2 is that it extends much further than the need for students to learn together in groups, important though collaborative learning may be. It includes collaboration in producing outputs (Studio Schools), developing critical thinking (Escuela Nueva), collaboration and decision-making (NPDL), and overcoming excessive individualism (Lumiar).

3) Be highly attuned to motivations and the emotions involved in learning

- *Art of Learning:* Typically, learners work together in groups where they have to recognise and acknowledge differing levels of motivation within the group.
- *BMT practitioner: "You need to build positive relationships with the community and people of each of the targeted schools."*
- *NOII:* One of the four key questions for learners in Network schools is: "Can you name two adults in this learning setting who believe you will be a success in life?"

What stands out from these comments is the connection between sensitivity to emotions and the wider community. Rather than interpret this principle as what takes place within each person's mind, the connection is built between the broad understanding of the aims of learning and the connectivity that the learner makes to those who matter in her/his environment, in school or more widely. A good example is the NOII focus on learner perceptions of adults supporting their success as key to motivation.

4) Be acutely sensitive to individual differences, including in prior knowledge

- *Escuela Nueva:* In order to respect the needs of students, teachers, along with their families, must be aware of their progress.
- *Senza Zaino:* The differentiated instruction gives space and attention to individual differences. Teachers investigate each student's interests, needs, prior knowledge and motivations and take into account the differences in gender, culture, ethnics, personal history and multiple intelligences.

These comments serve as a reminder of how interconnected the different principles are. For schools and teachers to be highly sensitive to individual differences, they need relevant, accurate and punctual information about each individual student, which further connects this principle with Learning Principle 6 - assessment.

5) Be demanding for each learner but without excessive overload

BMT facilitates differentiate by focusing on the work of the individual. Each learner is motivated to engage purposefully in practical activity at their own level, acquiring and establishing key Executive Function skills which can be transferred to the wider school curriculum. Yet one of the BMT schools also reported that demands on learners could seem excessive, at the beginning at least:

"Initially it was a huge demand on learners, and many children didn't cope with it and were quite resistant to the approach. As they got used to it the demand wasn't excessive. The children are not comfortable with a high challenge

> *environment where they are able to take risks, due to their home environments. As the learners got used to the approach their resilience to challenge improved noticeably and they were more likely to take risks in their learning.*"

At the outset, the BMT approach appeared to contradict this OECD Learning Principle through excessive overload. With embedding and practice, however, the balance shifted positively so that the learning remained highly challenging, but the degree of anxiety and overload was reduced.

6) Use assessments consistent with the main goals for learning, with a strong emphasis on formative feedback

- In *Lumiar Schools*, educators build an intentional process of learning and focused assessment, collect data to inform next steps, and give constant feedback. The Digital Mosaic platform records the evaluation of each student and group.
- *Studio Schools*: Project-based learning encourages Principle 6 and students receive a significant amount of formative feedback.
- NPDL network leader: *"Rather than identifying ready-made measures and constructing the teaching and learning process around them, it is necessary to look first at what learners truly need for success so as to measure what they and their learning partners actually value."*

The network comments serve as a reminder that certain pedagogies (in this case, project-based learning) promote this particular principle, but also that the principle can be so demanding as it requires re-examination of the learning goals that matter. So, assessment is not a technical matter separate from the core aims and objectives of the network or the school but must provide accurate, meaningful information to inform analysis of how well those aims are being achieved.

7) Promote horizontal connection across learning activities, across subjects, and across in- and out-of-school learning

- *Studio Schools'* strong connections with local employers ensures that Principle 7 is applied, what happens in the classroom is made applicable to the 'real world', and students have regular work placements.
- *Lumiar Schools:* Projects and workshops deal with real themes and issues, as they happen in the world using a multi-disciplinary approach. Students expand their understanding of how to think about complex situations and learn to make connections across different fields of knowledge.
- *NOII:* Increasingly, network schools are developing stronger community connections, exploring the outdoors as an extension of the learning environment, becoming full nature schools, creating multi-disciplinary units of study, and strengthening cross-generational learning.

The broader community for learning is again emphasised, and the extent to which the networks are eager to bring schooling closer to the real lives of young people. Instead of wishing to "protect" young people from their wider environment, including the workplace – as some progressive education has sometimes been tempted to do – the intention is actively to embrace it, while giving young people the tools, knowledge and capacities to live autonomously and responsibly within that environment.

12.4. The role of assessment in teaching and pedagogy

As might well be expected, formative assessment features heavily in the responses of the Pedagogical Approach Networks about the role of assessment in overall teaching strategies and pedagogy. Given the endorsement, as shown in the learning principles of making learning central, giving close attention to individual learners, and the power of feedback, it is scarcely surprising that formative assessment should feature so prominently in the replies, and many examples could be given. These include such powerful endorsements as:

- *Amara Berri:* There is a strong emphasis on the role of formative assessment, both for students and teachers, as the main tool to guide the reflection and design of activities.
- *Art of Learning*: The project has formative assessment practices at the centre.
- *BMT:* The principle "Assessment is for Learning strategies (AifL)" is applied to all aspects of the learner's processes, (physical, cognitive and personal) with teachers using observation and professional judgement.
- *NPDL:* All evidence of performance, after informing understanding of students' levels of development, is used formatively to support students' but also teachers' and leaders' efforts in deepening learning outcomes.
- Formative assessment is the *Senza Zaino* Lighthouse.

A number of other issues arise that extend beyond the belief in and practice of formative assessment and the power of feedback. Certain networks emphasise that the assessment information is gathered for design purposes, as well as for providing feedback to students to improve their learning. This raises the question of who receives the feedback as well as the students, and how often.

- *NOII:* Reporting to parents has become much more of an on-going communication rather than a once-a-term event. Further, a practitioner states that *"teachers and learners communicate student learning to parents, the school community and the community at large."*
- *Senza Zaino:* The assessment information is used to re-design our actions during the learning process together with students; if necessary these change, adapt or improve strategies or activities so that the target can be assured. This information is also shared with the parents too, to inform them how learning is going and how it could be improved for everyone.

In general, the networks indicate that they engage in summative assessments – experiencing no particular conflict between this and their strong focus on formative assessment.

- *Escuela Nueva – school*: Teachers mostly use continuous assessments, along with the self-assessment and co-evaluation students do. There are also the external assessments of the Ministry of Education.
- *Innova Schools*: By national regulation, assessment is used by teachers summatively. At the end of each term and school year, students receive certification that they have shown proficiency in the expected learning.
- *Senza Zaino*: The assessment information certifies also the grade at the end of the year.

In line with the innovative nature of the networks and schools involved, naturally many are seeking learning that extends beyond the measures that might be covered by the summative assessments and certification. This applies especially but not only to emotional capacities and engagement in learning, as well as measured cognitive outcomes.

- *Escuela Nueva:* There is a formative evaluation in each learning guide and at the end of each unit, students go through a reflective evaluation, mediated by an interchange with the teacher, and including other elements such as the emotional.
- *Innova Schools*: Assessment is also used to get at such aspects as family satisfaction, school environment, and student engagement. Internal studies measure the impact and success of the innovations that are put in place at the classroom.
- *Amara Berri*: They use a comprehensive and continuous assessment, including socio-emotional and relational dimensions. In the words of one network leader, *"We evaluate the 'essence' of the activity, the previous stages of learning, like motivation, interests."*
- *BMT School*: Assessment includes how quickly children settle in class and their engagement with learning. There is also assessment of improvements in resilience and learner willingness to take risks in other curricular areas.
- *KIP network leader and practitioner*: *"This gives space to applaud students for different and multiple skills they have (e.g. constructing, drawing, managing teams, being empathic and kind, presenting). Special appreciation is given to students that helped others during the group-work at the end of the class."*

The most detailed consideration in the replies to the OECD questionnaire about the nature of measures and the need for assessments that reflect the true range of learning aims is provided by the NPDL network. This is reported in detail (see Box 12.5).

Box 12.5. The NPDL approach to assessment

NPDL began from first understanding what really matters and then creating a comprehensive system of measurement designed to provide participants at all levels of the partnership with the capacity to measure, track and further their progress with deep learning. NPDL identified six deep learning competencies ("6Cs" – Character, Citizenship, Collaboration, Communication, Creativity and Critical Thinking) as the foundation of deep learning and at the heart of what is truly important for learners today. Measurement of students' deep learning competency development differs greatly from the types of assessment common in education systems globally.

It requires not only an understanding of the competencies themselves, but the capacity to connect that understanding with a wide range of learning evidence and to design learning that facilitates both the development and measurement of deep learning outcomes. This is referred to as "Authentic Mixed-Method Assessment", which involves analysis of all the pieces of available assessment evidence when measuring deep learning design, conditions and outcomes.

NPDL identified the following elements of deep learning as those requiring the development of new measures:

- deep learning competencies (New Measures: Deep Learning Progressions – one for each of the 6Cs);
- deep learning conditions (New Measures: Deep Learning Conditions Rubrics – one for conditions at the education system, school cluster, and individual school levels, respectively);
- deep learning design (New Measures: New Pedagogies Learning Design Protocol, New Pedagogies Learning Design Rubric, and Teacher Self-Assessment).

As for the use to which the assessment information is put, there is general agreement, with one clear exception i.e. the role of praise and the avoidance of negative messages. This disagreement is expressed most sharply in the following two extracts, the one emphasising the importance of praise, the other emphasising the need to avoid excessive praise.

- *"The assessment of students in a KIP class is only verbal and always positive. The important aspect of a KIP class is to encourage students and to praise the different skills held by the students, as an important and necessary part of the group"* (network leader and practitioner).
- *NOII – practitioner: "Formative assessment is deep learning and needs to be constantly revisited as we learn how to develop efficacy around this very multifaceted set of strategies. Changing teachers' language from praise to affirmation and feedback is an ongoing goal for many. Students in our system need support as their mind-set changes from performance evaluation to assessment for and as learning."*

12.5. Learner voice and agency

Learner voice and learner agency are concepts close to the heart of the approaches being followed by the networks covered in this chapter. This is summed by one KIP network leader, who locates learner voice and agency as the fundamental concept of the equitable classroom:

> *"An equitable classroom is where all students have access to a quality curriculum, intellectually challenging tasks, and equal status interaction with their peers and with the teachers; where students can see each other as competent, contributing, and learning, as colleagues and peers, while engaging in serious content. They solve problems similar to those in real-life, address dilemmas and have interesting topics to talk about. The aim is that they do that democratically and equitably."*

The responses below suggest a number of key dimensions underpinning learner voice and agency, including the engagement that feature so strongly in the network responses about the OECD Learner Principles. Unless learners are engaged, their voice and agency are bound to be seriously curtailed.

Both as a means to engagement and as an ingredient of learner voice, the networks identified another important dimension, viz. the relevance of the learning to student interests and lives.

- *Lumiar Schools*: Projects are based on student interests and on daily problems that require solutions.
- *NPDL*: Learning is deepest when it connects to students' lives – who they are, what they are interested in learning, and how they can use their learning to make a difference in their own lives, the lives of others, and the world.

Some referred to the classic forms of learner participation, in the form of councils and student bodies that formally give a voice as part of the overall decision-making:

- *Escuela Nueva*: The students' governing body is the strategy that allows them to take decisions and defend their rights in the school domain.
- The *Senza Zaino* model promotes student participation in school assembly to plan and to make decisions about school issues, in primary and middle school.

Beyond such formal expressions of participation, however, are the ways in which learner voice and agency are integral to the pedagogy. The pedagogies assume a prominent learner role and contribute to a school culture in which the responsibility for design and decisions not only rests with the teacher:

- *Amico Robot:* Teachers are an 'invisible presence' and students must 'learn-by-doing' and in the projects they share and discuss. The teacher leads rather than imposes the learning process, thus putting the students at the centre of the process.
- *Art of Learning*: Learners are actively involved in evaluating each of the activities, which informs planning for the next experience. Teachers and artists become facilitators of learning, providing appropriate support and challenge to groups as required. Learners too provide rich feedback to peers not only in their own group, but to other groups too, promoting dialogue about learning.
- *Escuela Nueva:* The participation of students is key to their own auto-regulation, along with the importance of maintain horizontal relationships between teachers and students, and among students.
- *Innova Schools network leader: "Our pedagogical approach considers learner voice as a pivotal factor to improve students' achievement and well-being. Learning is social and collaboration must be in place to develop all the skills students need for the 21st century. Students should have room to make decisions*

not only about their own learning, but also about the way they want to interact with their peers in both academic and social contexts."

- At *Lumiar Schools*, students have the chance to participate in the pedagogical decisions as well as in the collective rules and other issues that appear with such an intense and horizontal socialisation. In Lumiar pedagogy, the voice of the student is essential for designing the learning path.

- Within the *NPDL* model, pedagogy is no longer solely the concern of the teacher. At the deepest levels of learning, students seek out and form partnerships towards the direct development of ideas or solution of problems; take ownership of their learning both inside and outside classroom walls and directly contribute to the learning of others; partner in the design, implementation and measurement of their own and others' learning; and leverage and create powerful digital technologies that directly deepen every aspect of the teaching and learning process.

- *Senza Zaino*: the promotion of reciprocal teaching, peer review, tutorship (between novice and senior) ensures a high level of voice and a wide awareness in learning.

- *Studio Schools*: Learner voice and choice are vital components of project-based learning and take various forms depending on the nature of the project and the level of experience of students and staff involved. Learners have some say over the nature of their final product, if not the method by which they develop these. Learner voice is also emphasised by the use of Personal Coaches. Finally, learners find one-to-one conversations a valuable experience and often express that this makes the school feel more like a 'family' where their voices are listened to.

Box 12.6. "Circles" as venues for learners' voice

This is a pedagogical vehicle shared by diverse networks for making real the ambition of learner voice and agency, and creating horizontality.

- Lumiar Practitioner: *"One of the most unique moments is 'The Circle', a weekly meeting in which students, teachers and staff gather to discuss issues affecting the school and vote on key decisions. Each person has the same rights and obligations. They learn how to debate, how to express their opinions, and how to respect and value one another's contribution. Each group has its own "circle", a moment to listen to each other and to make collective reflections and decisions. This provides a sense of community, in helping each other to improve their relationships and attitudes towards the others."*

- NOII Practitioner: *"Many of the schools try to emulate the indigenous wisdoms embedded in sharing circles. Circles are safe places, where students and educators are equitable listeners and have equal responsibilities and rights. The circle protocols extend into the classroom environment. After learning some background information, students determine topics and strategies to take their learning deeper. Students are invited to talk about learning experiences in the classroom, ways that learning and the environment could be improved, and their ideas and thoughts are given equal weight as the teacher considers ways to move forward. Concerns are addressed, and restitutions are decided upon. Students give feedback to the teacher – teachers listen, and try to make changes."*

Though voice and agency overlap, the different networks recognise that the more demanding notion of "learner agency" goes beyond ensuring that students have a say in decisions relating to schools and classrooms. Rather, schools try to ensure that students are themselves empowered within school organisational cultures by contributing to decision-making about students learning.

- *NOII:* Learner voice means listening to the learners with the goal of understanding their experience within our learning settings – and then taking action based on their inputs. Four key questions applied consistently: Can you name two people in this setting who believe you will be a success in life? What are you learning and why is it important? How is it going with your learning? What are your next steps? These provide network educators with a coherent approach to learner voice. Learner agency implies that the learners are able to exercise discretion in what they are learning, how they are learning and where they are learning. This involves teachers giving up considerable control and making significant shifts in their pedagogical practices.

According to one network, there is a continuum that moves towards the more demanding and desirable:

- Lumiar practitioner: *"The agency of the students is gradually developed from autonomy, going through interdependence and finally reaching a sense of social responsibility."*

The development of agency may also mean that learners gain a more explicit understanding of the pedagogical approach and its benefits. One example of this comes from the BMT network, where two schools, in collaboration with the BMT staff tutors, have gathered samples of qualitative data around learner's voice with feedback obtained from cohorts of pupils who have engaged in the Direct Intervention Model. This feedback shows that learners have a profound understanding of the benefits of engaging in a BMT approach, and how it can impact positively on their learning across the curriculum.

However, the responses from the networks also suggest how the possibilities for the exercise of learner voice and agency, even if all in the school community agree on this direction, may be facilitated or inhibited by the structures and requirements of the surrounding system. Contrast one response arguing that curriculum reform has given room for more study in depth with fewer topics/subjects thereby enhancing learner agency, with another response making the same point but noting the constraining role of system requirements.

- *NOII:* The recent revisions to the British Columbia curriculum have reduced the number of learning outcomes, have emphasised core competencies and are providing the space for teachers to explore fewer topics in greater depth. This recent change, coupled with the persistent focus across the Networks on learner ownership, is leading to more innovative approaches to learner agency.
- *Studio Schools*: Learner voice and agency are constrained by the demands of the examination system, with GCSE subject choices largely mandated by government. Studio Schools have made efforts to introduce greater choice within subjects and by offering different pathways through the qualifications they offer.

12.6. The curricular and learner foci of the networks

The questionnaire asked a series of questions about focus – had the network's approach been targeted at particular groups of students or communities? Had it proved especially relevant for particular domains (e.g. STEM) rather than others? The questionnaire also asked how well the approaches aligned with the so-called 21st century competences such as creativity, collaboration, responsibility and digital literacy.

As opposed to the previous sections where it has been necessary to capture the detailed essence of particular approaches, the responses on these questions can be much more readily and succinctly summarised. The different networks provided very similar answers, albeit stressing that sometimes a particular focus had been due to demand or context rather than to any intrinsic property of the pedagogy. That is:

- Most respond that there are no particular students or communities for which their approach is best suited because the principles involved can be widely applied. The networks tend to stress, however, the inclusivity of the approach and that less privileged students especially are able to benefit.
- Again, most of the networks emphasise the coherence between their approach and broad curriculum requirements across the board, though they also mention those domains that have featured most in practice. Sometimes, indeed, the approach had emerged as a more effective educational vehicle for the contemporary curriculum than more established pedagogies.
- The alignment of the approaches with the so-called 21st century competences is striking to the extent that such competences often underpin the pedagogies and curricula reported. This refers not only to skill or domain areas but also to the importance of "deep" learning and understanding as a prerequisite of the commonly enumerated lists of 21st century competences.

12.6.1. Particular groups of learners or communities

The networks tend to underline the universality of their pedagogical approaches. Some simply answered the questionnaire 'no' when interrogated whether the pedagogies were more suitable or appropriate for some groups of students than others. But, others were clear that their approach holds particular relevance for the less advantaged. This duality – appropriate for all but especially relevant for the disadvantaged – was a theme of several of the ISSA responses:

> *"Our approach is for all groups of learners with special focus on children coming from vulnerable groups (mainly Roma). There is no quality without equality and research shows that vulnerable children benefit the most from quality programs"* (ISSA Slovenia).

> *"When first implemented in Romania, our educational program was named Head Start, mainly for children from socio-economical disadvantaged families and had a clear social component. In time, it became open for all children"* (Step by Step Centre for Education and Professional Development - ISSA member in Romania).

> *"No. There is no particular group of learners or communities for which our approach has been mainly applied though the professional community, preschools and schools recognise that is very successful with children from vulnerability groups"* (Open Academy Step by Step – ISSA member in Croatia).

Three further points about equity can be made. First, in some cases (especially in Latin America) the urban/rural division is a key dimension. Some of the networks started out in rural communities but then spread more widely – like the case of Escuela Nueva or Red Escuela Líderes. As illustrated in the case of Lumiar schools, its schools are located in populous cities and rural areas. The first was the natural consequence of attending an existing demand and the second was a deliberate consequence of transforming Lumiar Schools into a model for any economic environment (if it works well in a deprived rural area it should work in most places).

Studio Schools and Innova Schools point out that their schools have been located mainly in urban communities, largely because this is where the social demand existed. Innova Schools in Peru is distinctive by identifying its target social group as the emerging middle class, eager for high quality, affordable schooling using innovative and more effective methods than the large majority of available schools.

Second, of the socio-demographic groups singled out among the networks, the clearest example is provided by NOII in British Columbia, Canada that has worked extensively with indigenous students, families and communities. In 2008, networks leaders welcomed the opportunity provided by the provincial Ministry of Education to develop an inquiry network focused on improving outcomes for Indigenous learners – and for developing deeper understanding and appreciation of indigenous history, culture and ways of knowing amongst all learners. Issues of racism and the soft bigotry of low expectations have been pervasive, and addressing this situation for indigenous learners is of paramount importance.

Several of the networks also mentioned the importance of reaching young children, not as an alternative to school-age children but as an important additional reach. In the case of the Second Chance Schools, the target, as the name might suggest, is young adults aged 16-25 years old who did not attain qualifications while in mainstream schooling first time round.

Third, the NPDL and Art of Learning responses suggest that while under-served groups may need more scaffolding and support, the pay-off of realising deep learning can be all the greater for them. For the NPDL, one of the most radical and powerful ideas is "the equity hypothesis," which proposes that, while deep learning is necessary for all, it is most essential for students alienated from regular schools. Inequity may be best attacked through the excellence of deep learning that incorporates knowledge of brain functioning, relationship building, and engaging pedagogies (NPDL). In the case of the Art of Learning network, the hypothesis is that an arts-rich, creative learning programme delivered intensively in schools over a number of months can have a positive impact on the development of creativity skills, executive functions and attainment in children, particularly those living in poverty; ultimately, it can contribute to closing the attainment gap.

Box 12.7. Creative partnerships and equity

Creative Culture Education (CEE) is an NGO which holds a central ethos to support programmes in areas with high levels of deprivation. The Creative Partnership approach focuses specifically on important wider skills which support learners to achieve their potential academically while providing them with the skills required in employment in the 21st century. This approach also aims at providing learners rich opportunities for social, emotional and physical development. CEE is currently running a Creative Partnerships programme in Lahore, Pakistan where they are working with local NGOs in schools serving communities with extreme levels of poverty and in Hungary they are working in schools serving significant number of Roma pupils. In all these cases, the evidenced improvement in the learning outcomes of pupils has been considerable. In addition, the Creative Partnerships process requires schools to identify their specific school development challenges, which mostly mean to focus on underachieving or disengaged learners or those struggling with core literacy or numeracy skills. CCE's research provides a strong body of evidence as to the positive impact Creative Partnerships has on disadvantaged learners.

12.6.2. Particular subjects, content areas or domains

The main answer provided by the networks is that their pedagogical approach is relevant across domains and subjects. As with the previous question about whether the approach has particular relevance to certain groups of learners, several networks answered the question about appropriateness for particular subjects with a single, categorical 'no'. Some of the networks develop the arguments further in stressing how they need to make their approach cross-curricular, by encouraging the development of broader competences that do not fit neatly into curriculum subject domains. These examples match closely the issues discussed in the next sub-section, viz. the development of 21st century competences by the networks.

- ISN Japan network leader: *"The common target of ISN is to do Project Based Learning, because we hope students acquire competences of 'to identify issues' and 'to tackle open-ended problems without answers'. Why we focus these competencies is that we think these competencies were not sufficiently learnt in conventional Japanese school education."*

- *Lighthouse:* The main content areas lie outside subjects, in developing working culture, pedagogies, and learning environments applicable in all the situations in schools, including teaching subjects. Also in developing the new curriculum area of multi-disciplinary learning modules.
- *OPEDUCA:* All subjects, content areas and domains are integrated. Each of these benefits from the approach, and it specifically brings value to Education for Sustainability Development, Entrepreneurship, Personal Development, and use of ICT - all aspects that schools struggled with before.
- *ECOLOG* is a programme and network to implement Environmental Education (EE) for sustainable development into school life, and teaching and learning practise. It does not focus on specific subjects as EE/ESD is cross-curricular.

Several stress the value of rounded holistic curricula and pedagogical approaches. This is clearly the message of *Whole Education*, including in its choice of name. *BMT*, which uses physical education, physical activity and sport as a wider educational strategy, has a strong focus on these aspects of the curriculum by definition, though it also stresses the perceived spill-over benefits right through the curriculum. ISSA's *Principles of Quality Pedagogy* are not applied to particular subjects or content areas, but rather it is an approach that uses the curriculum to support the child's holistic development. This is further illustrated in the Art of Learning programme which, when delivered intensively in schools over a number of months, can have a positive impact on the development of creativity skills, executive functions and attainment in children, particularly those living in poverty and ultimately, can contribute to closing the attainment gap.

Nevertheless, there are examples where the innovative pedagogy is applied especially in certain subjects and domains rather than others, either because of the intrinsic nature of the approach, like Computer at Schooling and its focus on Computing Science, or because of the priority nature of the subjects, calling out for pedagogical innovation. In the Whole Education network, maths and language (see Box 12.8) have been targeted areas receiving a great deal of innovation. At Sandringham School, teachers reported that:

> *"The mastery, problem-solving approach and use of reflections and journals has been used primarily in maths – this was following a visit to Singapore by the Head teacher and maths lead and a significant investment in 'maths no problem' training for staff. We are beginning to apply these approaches across the curriculum."*

Box 12.8. Whole Education – Language Futures

Language Futures combines digital resources and language-proficient volunteers with project-based learning, peer collaboration and the MFL teacher's language expertise, to provide highly personalised learning, supporting students to choose their own language to learn. Whole Education is developing the model to incorporate an online tutoring element into the existing 'Language Futures Mentor' role. This project supports schools who wish to adopt Language Futures by:

- offering specialist consultant support with recruiting volunteer mentors, and choosing how to implement this flexible approach;
- funded meetings to share resources and approaches with like-minded colleague;
- start-up cash to support with implementation and cover in first two years;
- resource creation for new classes.

Similarly, the *2nd Chance, France* network (aiming at disengaged young adults who missed out on schooling earlier on) reports how its pedagogical approach applies especially to the foundation knowledge domains of French, maths, and informatics. The choices may, to some degree, be imposed by policy pressure as well as by educational choice, as reported by Creative Partnerships:

"While schools generally have the freedom to select the specific area(s) of the curriculum on which to focus their project work, projects to improve attainment in literacy, numeracy and science are by far the most prevalent in all countries within which the programme operates. Literacy and numeracy are foundation subjects that support all other areas of the curriculum. Inspiring pupils to engage in science is often highly challenging. And, accountability measures mean that both individual schools and countries are generally measured in these three core curriculum areas."

These suggest limitations of scope for reasons of practicality, focus and the need to make choices. Innova Schools deliberately avoided subjects that are central to other network approaches reported in this volume, such as emphasising the arts, physical education and sport:

"Our approach has been mainly applied to five content areas and one stage of school education: Early Childhood Education, Math, Spanish, Science, English and Social Studies...We have not focused our attention on other subjects such as Physical Education or Arts. In our financial model, in order to keep tuitions affordable to emerging middle class families, school facilities are not suitable for those two subjects."

12.6.3. 21st century competences

The networks strongly endorse the 21st century competences, whether as describing them as core to their approach or mentioning the relevance of a group of key skills and competences. In some cases, these skills are pursued through their own framework, such as ISSA's Principles of Quality Pedagogy (which includes qualities like persistence, curiosity and initiative); Lumiar's Mosaic Curriculum; Studio Schools' CREATE

Framework; Amara Berri's systemic approach; Creative Partnerships' Creative Habits of Mind; or Galileo's Teacher Effectiveness Framework.

Box 12.9. Galileo, participating school

21st century competences (including creativity, problem-solving, critical thinking, collaboration and digital literacy) are all explicit in a discipline-based inquiry approach. Each competency is developed at different stages through a task, and is also dependent on the task itself. For example, when students design their solubility experiments, there is an emphasis on problem-solving and collaboration; when students engaged in creating their own podcast on a lesser-told story in Canadian history, the emphasis is on creativity and digital literacy. Critical thinking skills are an integral component of this particular approach to learning. Given the authenticity of each designed task, students are focusing on a big question or specific concept that requires critical thinking skills; whether the students are determining if a question is testable or discerning a reputable website for research, students are being asked to reflect, interpret, analyse, make inferences and explain their thinking. These all shape a student's critical thinking skills.

Particular interpretations of these skills extend their definition in ways that underline the network's distinctive approach. One is provided by the Hungarian network *KIP* which draws a clear line between preparation for living and innovation and preparation for the workplace: "We don't prepare them for the new workplace, but we educate individuals for innovation who are able to develop and adapt for the fast-changing world." In similar vein, *Escuela Nueva* agrees with its alignment with 21st century competences but stresses that it goes beyond that in pursuit of democracy and responsibility. This is a theme repeated by the *Armenian network of Step-by-Step* and their focus on ensuring the learning of democratic behaviours and skills through critical thinking cooperation, problem-solving, citizenship and the skills necessary for life and work.

Not all the 21st century competences are pursued with equal enthusiasm by the networks. For example, digital literacy was often portrayed as less important:

- *AND network leader: "We focus on all of these (less so on digital literacy) in our work with teachers."*
- *BMT:* Schools reported that the pedagogical approach addresses competences of creativity, critical thinking, problem-solving, and collaboration, though not of digital literacy.
- *ECOLOG network leader: "The 21st century competences, which we call "dynamic qualities", have been the basis of the programmes and networks. Digital literacy is less in the focus, but working with IT is part of many school projects within ECOLOG."*
- *Issa Slovenia network leader and practitioner: "These are key approaches: we are more focused on developing critical thinking, problem-solving and collaboration, and less on digital literacy."*

On the other hand, two of the schools in the networks refer directly to digital literacy so the above statements are by no means a universal expression of priorities:

- *CAS practitioner:* The majority of these competencies feature within Computational Thinking, often addressed within the primary school. Where possible, the competencies are also examined in other subjects, with digital literacy regularly taught through cross-curricular links.

- *Lighthouse practitioner:* These competences are all part of cross-disciplinary teaching and with a focus on ICT in teaching and using digital tools and digital sources, students become potentially more aware of the importance of critical thinking in a digitalised world.

So central are these competences to the work of certain networks that they have elaborated their own formulations, used to guide the work and pedagogy. For NPDL, this means its own set of Cs, described as "deep learning competencies" (Box 12.10).

Box 12.10. NPDL's deep learning competences

- Character – Learning to deep learn, armed with the essential character traits of grit, tenacity, perseverance, and resilience.
- Citizenship – Considering global issues based on diverse values and worldviews, and with a genuine interest and ability to solve ambiguous and complex real-world problems that impact sustainability.
- Collaboration – Working interdependently and synergistically in teams with strong interpersonal and team-related skills including management of team dynamics, making joint decisions, and learning from others and contributing to their learning.
- Communication – Communicating effectively with a variety of styles, modes, and tools (including digital tools) tailored for a range of audiences.
- Creativity – Having an "entrepreneurial eye" for economic and social opportunities, asking the right inquiry questions, and leadership to pursue those ideas and turn them into action.
- Critical Thinking – Critically evaluating information and arguments, seeing patterns and connections, constructing meaningful knowledge, and applying it in the real world.

Lighthouse in Finland has similarly come to its own definition of 21st century competences, revolving around the ability to apply knowledge and skills, and focusing on skills that cross boundaries and link different fields of knowledge and skills; these are seen as a precondition for personal growth, studying, work and civic activity. They highlight competences which must be part of subject teaching and taught in all situations in learning:

1. Thinking and learning to learn.
2. Cultural competences, interaction and self-expression.
3. Taking care of oneself and managing daily life.
4. Multi-literacy.
5. ICT competences.
6. Working life competences and entrepreneurship.
7. Participation, involvement and building a sustainable future.

12.7. How central is technology?

The questionnaire asked the networks about the role of technology in the pedagogical approach and how central it is. None of the networks states that technology is not important and there is widespread recognition of the dominance of the digital world in the lives of young people. Opinion is divided, however, about how central it is, with some according it a place among a range of other factors and with others seeing it as central within the pedagogical approach.

- *Creative Partnerships network leader:* "*Technology does not play a central role in our pedagogical approach, though more schools are choosing to combine the development of student digital competences with the more generic creative competences.*"
- *Escuela Nueva* schools consider ICTs as important tools, but they are not they priority and it is difficult to implement certain technology in some schools.
- *KIP* is a technology on the surface but more fundamentally it is a status-treating programme. KIP is helped by ICT - in the equitable classroom children have access to a quality curriculum through digital devices as well.
- *Lumiar tutor:* "*I wouldn't say it has a central role, although it's very present.*"
- *NOII:* Technology does not directly play a central role in the BC network strategy; rather schools explore a range of approaches in their inquiries, including new technologies.
- *Senza zaino network leader:* "*Technology isn't neutral, but also it isn't central, mostly in infant and primary school. So, in our schools, technology is an important tool in learning as are books and tactile and iconic and visual tools.*"
- *Studio Schools* are relatively technology-neutral in their set up but have benefited from the use of technology where they have a technological theme.

The ISSA responses are in general clear that technology *per se* is not central to their approach but that it does have a role to play and can be highly motivating. The reasons offered for this position in the Armenian response refer both to the philosophical belief that young children should be encouraged with physical and social activities and to the absence of technological infrastructure:

- *Step by Step Benevolent Foundation - ISSA member in Armenia:* "*Technology is not central in SBS pedagogical approach. When we started implementation, people had very limited access to computers and Internet. Our approach does not encourage a lot of computerised activities for young children as it is a time for their growth and active development, so we try to work more on their physical, social-emotional, and self-help development. However, the inclination of children towards technology is growing automatically and nobody can stop this process.*"
- *Step by Step Centre for Education and Professional Development - ISSA member in Romania:* "*Technology is included in Step by Step classrooms and in educational projects according with actuality, even if we encourage children more on the direction on social abilities and team work. So, technology does not have a central role.*"

A similar duality – recognition of the importance of technology but valuing human relations and development more highly – can also be found in the different responses of the Japanese ISN, for in this network technology is indispensable because clusters of schools are remote:

- *ISN Cluster leader: "Students use online platform "Classi" to communicate each other, and it enables them to share their ideas even when they are in different places. However, we do not think necessarily that technology plays a central role; we believe that establishing healthy relationships among the project members is crucial."*
- *Japan cluster 2 leader: "We use many IT tools like Skype, Facebook and Classi and have many TV meeting using such tools. We do not think, however, that they play central roles in our main pedagogical approach and appreciate much more face-to-face than technology-based education."*

Following the experience of the ISN in Japan, it may also be useful to distinguish between the role of technology in implementation and at the core of teaching and learning. For instance, in Escuela Nueva, ICTs have played an important role for the implementation of their model and to maintain the network and the interchange between schools and teachers. Moreover, in Lumiar Institute, the Digital Mosaic is a platform and an essential instrument to implement and manage the Lumiar Institutes' model which the tutor and master access to follow the student's learning development. The director of the school can follow all the project and records. All the assessments are made inside the platform, as the students also do their self-evaluations there. In this manner, the technology encourages and facilitates meta learning of the individual and the group. About technological literacy, in the Mosaic Curriculum there is a matrix of Robotics, Informatics and Coding.

NPDL further expresses this duality: that technology is only valuable when it is effectively leveraged to deepen teaching and learning, and yet it is regarded as a core element in the network's framework, as expressed in the words of NPDL's leaders:

"The leveraging of digital technologies is one of the four core elements of our pedagogical approach, and is included as a dimension in each of NPDL's Conditions, Rubrics and Learning Progressions. Technology is an accelerator and enhancer of pedagogical practice, as well as playing a role in facilitating learning partnerships and student-driven deep learning. Its value in education is not inherent – it's only valuable when effectively leveraged to deepen teaching and learning. NPDL participants measure levels of progression in leveraging digital technologies at the school, school cluster, and system levels, and measure student competency in leveraging digital to develop and further deep learning outcomes."

These different viewpoints are not necessarily in tension, as it is possible both to endorse the potential of technology while recognising that it is only one among a number of the relevant factors involved. Certain networks were very direct about the importance of technology in their design of teaching and learning approaches. In Innova Schools, the importance of technology comes from their Blended Learning model, whereas in Whole Education the use of ICTs revolves around staff development and assessment (Box 12.11). For Galileo, the key idea is that teaches think carefully about the ways in which the disciplines or subject areas draw upon and utilise digital technologies to extend knowledge within the discipline. They argue that with digital technologies, the general vector of theory-into-practice is challenged, and it can question some of education's most deep-seated assumptions about the nature of childhood, cognitive development and effective learning environments. Finally, for the Schools for Second Chance technology is paramount to guarantee the proficiency in those digital skills that are needed in the labour market.

Box 12.11. IRIS film club in Northfield school (Whole Education)

IRIS film club is used to improve teaching and learning through sharing good practice, facilitating self-reflection and coaching for individual staff. All staff are provided with an iPad, which features strongly in lesson planning, and a set of laptops are situated in curriculum areas, which can be accessed by students. Several curriculum areas use 'Showbie' which is an assessment app on the iPad to give feedback to students. Drama and ICT have adapted 'Showbie' to give effective feedback. The Learning Student Assistants (LSAs) are trained in supporting student by reviewing and previewing the content for lessons. All LSAs and teachers have an iPad which they use to share resources and planning. This has allowed them to support students learning in the lesson and act as the expert to advise staff on particular student needs. The school has also developed its Virtual Learning Environment (VLE), particularly FROG – a specific VLE solution - to ensure greater consistency of practice and greater opportunities for students to develop independent learning.

12.8. Key practices – what must be practised?

The questionnaire asked if there are specific aspects that must be practised for the approach to be effective. The intention was to use and discuss the C of *Connoisseurship*, to move beyond practices that might be done in the name of an approach to identify prerequisites of successful implementation. The replies underscored the core defining practices of the approach and reaffirmed that multiple conditions are needed, not single "magic bullets".

- The *BMT* approach puts quality learning and teaching at the heart of learners' experiences, and links physical education to improved performance in the classroom.
- *CAS practitioner: "These approaches are most effective when pupils are developing programs over an extended period of time. For example, a computing unplugged activity might be used to introduce a programming concept, followed by a collaborative activity to plan a solution to a real-world problem. Guidance may also be offered on a program language's syntax and pupils undertake the task, which includes assistance from their peers. Formative assessment will take place throughout the activity, with the final programs submitted online and shared with a wider audience."*
- *Escuela Nueva network leaders: "Learning guidelines and well-equipped classroom libraries; local partnerships with the community; teachers well-trained in the pedagogical approach, teacher microcentres, as well as trained facilitators and specialised teachers who guide its implementation, while avoiding distraction by other projects and programmes."*
- *Innova schools network leaders: "Classroom work has to shift, from closed tasks to opened-ended problems that students address with their teachers and peers. Also key are school leaders and high expectations, quality communication between schools and families, and shifting curriculum structure and scheduling towards more depth and less breadth."*
- *KIP network leader and practitioner: "The whole school team has to take part in the training. Adopting KIP requires a change of teaching perspective, attitude,*

culture and that can be done only when the training is shared and teachers learn their new role during the lessons."

- *Lumiar network leader: "There are several innovative practices that characterise our complete model: a) division of roles between master and tutors with their distinctive tasks, b) the "circle" assembly for dialogue and democratic decision-making; and c) problem-based learning on meaningful issues."*

- *NOII*: Teacher professional learning in high performing countries share five attributes: inquiry-driven, professionally led, collaborative, linked and coherent, and taking place over time. In the words of a teacher:

  "Introducing new research and theory and making a connection to how they will improve students' learning is hugely important."

- *NPDL network leaders: "It thrives as a result of the implementation and interconnectedness of deep learning design, conditions, and competences."*

- Studio Schools network leader: *"Most schools practice all aspects of the model to some extent, but employer engagement and the CREATE Skills Framework seem to have the most impact."*

- *Senza Zino network leader: "The first essential is the new organisation of the classroom; second, to practice differentiated activities; third is the different role of the teacher as a coach, a facilitator, a tutor. The student can become responsible in every part of school life and fully autonomous."*

Certain variables stand out in what, at first sight, might appear to be quite a varied set of prerequisites. The need to change classroom and professional culture and practice is one. There is the key role assigned to educators and educator learning. There is the focus on quality rather than quantity such as in emphasising the quality of teaching and learning experiences or of privileging depth over breadth or in emphasising democratic learner engagement. There is the importance of trust and partnerships with families, employers and the wider community. One theme running through these is the importance of the cultural and that teaching, learning and pedagogy are essentially relational rather than formulaic.

Another common theme is the need for a strong focus on implementation, and maintaining focus with all on board. In this context, practical tools and guidelines can prove to be very helpful, as mentioned by several of the networks, like NPDL:

"Teachers assemble and share Deep Learning that describe what deep learning looks like and that facilitate collective identification of the new pedagogies to accelerate deep learning outcomes."

12.9. In summary

- The networks endorsed OECD Principles of Learning and in particular the social nature of teaching and learning, emotions and the importance of horizontal connectedness and assessment.
- In general, networks report that they do not target particular students or communities, although they highlight the importance of inclusion of less privileged students. Similarly, the approach of networks revolved around 21st century skills and cross-subject competences rather than particular domains.
- Technology is generally acknowledged as important not only in the design of teaching and learning but it is also essential for maintaining the network.

- There is widespread agreement on the need to change classroom and professional culture and practice, and the role of teachers in achieving that transformation. Networks emphasise quality over quantity, the need for a strong focus on implementation and on balancing 'realistic' expectations with the idealism and ambition of their educational goals.

Chapter 13. Professional demands and professional learning – the role of the networks

This chapter focuses on the demands on teachers and schools which arise from a network approach, recognised widely as more demanding than traditional practice. The analysis aims at providing useful insights on ways in which innovative pedagogies can be successfully implemented in the daily life of classrooms. It details the central importance of professional learning, which often represents core business for the networks themselves. In fact, the very nature of, and need for, continuous professional development not only guarantees the implementation of the educational goals of teachers, but it is also paramount to understanding the importance of school networking and its relation to innovation. The chapter ends with a discussion on whether and how the networks and participating schools have been evaluated.

13.1. Introduction

Through their engagement with the questionnaire, very rich information was collected from the networks on the nature of the demands that their approaches make on teachers and on schools. The networks recognise that their approaches are demanding, in part because of its intrinsic requirements of expertise and collaboration (often at different levels at once), and in part because of the distance that needs to be travelled from traditional practice that the network is seeking to replace. All of them place central importance on professional learning; this, indeed, often represents core business for the networks themselves. Due to the answers received regarding professional learning being very closely aligned with those given about how the network itself operates, these are treated together in this chapter. Finally, the chapter discusses whether and how the work of the networks has been evaluated, where the information is available, and what the results of the evaluations show.

13.2. How demanding is the pedagogical approach on teachers?

For the most part, the networks and their participating schools and practitioners agreed that the approaches being promoted are more demanding than those conventionally found in mainstream schooling; they also highlighted how these demands can be met, including through the work of the network in providing professional development and support. Several argue that higher demand resides in the need to 'challenge classroom pedagogies' (Creative Partnerships), the complexity of inquiry and reflection processes (NOII), the ambition within the idea of developing fully comprehensive approaches (ISSA), or the need of making teachers work as mentors (Lumiar Institute).

The demanding nature of the pedagogical approach reinforces the emphasis placed on *connoisseurship* – expert application – which the networks agree is necessary for the approaches to work given how challenging they are seen to be for the existing teaching force.

Several networks make clear that not only is their approach demanding of the professionalism of teachers. but that one of the most challenging aspects is the gap it represents with the main body of traditional practice that has to be bridged, as teachers are often not well prepared or ready to review their inherited roles as professionals. This is particularly the case when the context and goals of the networks is targeting learners that have been traditionally excluded, such as Roma (KIP), or rural learners (Red Escuelas Libres, Escuela Nueva). Another challenge is to prepare teachers for a multi-cultural approach or ask teachers to associate their subjects with real-life issues (OPEDUCA). Teachers are professionals who are always in need of updating their skills and pedagogical tools. This is something which always entails a degree of difficulty, like adapting to new curricula that emphasise technologies or more student-centred approaches.

It is not that teachers need to get ever-closer to their students; it may be that the demanding professionalism lies in giving learners the room and agency to learn for themselves, as explained by an ISN leader:

> *"Japanese teachers as co-agents of students are ready to support them and keep them from losing their way or from suffering in learning. But this reduces the impact of Problem-Based Learning. Therefore, it is necessary to practice not immediately offering support, which is difficult in practice."*

The replies, while acknowledging how large the shift in teacher beliefs and practices that may be required, also frame this positively, for teachers can envisage these demands as a way to improve their professionalism.

- *BMT practitioner: "It is extra workload, but staff recognise the value of BMT pedagogy and were willing to take on the required change. This included using the online BMT resource pack in addition to the direct intervention model."*
- *Galileo Network leader: "The design approach is demanding but it also creates results and has far-reaching impact. It requires educators to think differently and represents a shift from the acquisition of "know that" knowledge to understanding knowledge as dynamic, organised in living, developing fields, and adapting to new circumstances, evidence and discoveries."*
- *NPDL network leaders: "We support teachers to become less the "keeper of knowledge" and more of a guide, activator and active learning partner alongside their students and others; a creator of rich authentic and virtual learning environments; co-designers with a deep knowledge of NPDL tools and processes; and digital facilitators able to leverage technology and allow their learners to do so."*
- *Studio Schools network leaders: "It is more demanding of teachers, while offering the opportunity to do things differently; it tends to attract the staff who are willing to engage in the demanding work of innovation."*

The responses provide additional insights into how the professional demands may be met, with some even suggesting that, once the initial reluctance is overcome, the demands may not necessarily be greater than the traditional methods and pedagogical practices. The more depending step, in a Galileo practitioner's opinion, is to tackle the emotional heavy lifting of admitting that one's practice needs improving, and then living with the experience of change. For others, their approach is seen as accessible, in which staff become very receptive as soon as they see the educational value. Even in those approaches with a strong focus on transforming teachers' role (Lumiar Institute, Box 13.1), the initial challenges become easier to overcome once educators are more familiar with the pedagogical model. In other words, it is possible to see this process of transformation as one consisting of clear phases, in which the first one might be the hardest to address. This is well illustrated in the words of a KIP leader:

"At the beginning, a third of teachers were enthusiastic, a third were waiting and seeing, and a third did not see the need. Eventually, the teachers talked to each other and began to realise the progress. It took about 3 years to get all the teachers on board."

Box 13.1. Lumiar schools: Learning to live with the demands

The roles of the tutor and the master are demanding but they can become easier if they learn how to flow with the pedagogical model. In a metaphorical way, it is possible to say that the students are the voyagers that dare to explore and pursue what they want: they bring the will to make the trip and reach the dream. The masters spark passion inspiring to make the trip: they know those dreams, the external challenges, the sea and the stars, bring experience and the compass. The tutors are designers of possible paths of learning: they know the learners and their dreams, the internal challenges, bring maps and goals and keep the track. Together they define day after day the individual journey. The Mosaic Curriculum will reflect the experiences, the achieved goals and it will also invite more journeys.

13.3. Organisational demands of the network approaches

Many of the networks were able to identify a set of factors in response to the question about the organisational demands of their pedagogical approach. Some of these responses focused on descriptions of the demands confronted by schools when they seek fully to implement the approach.

- *Art of Learning:* A number of factors impact widespread adoption. For example, staff in school (staff turnover/job share/promotion), particular local community demands, and perceptions regarding innovation overload. There needs to be a clear articulation of how these pedagogical approaches will facilitate the achievement of core learner outcomes – the link between research, practice and impact.

Other networks based their answers on the positive preconditions that had been identified and distilled from experience as being most effective in putting the approach into practice.

- *Whole Education, Sandringham School:* Successful implementation requires a well informed and motivated leadership team with clear vision, ethos, aims and values – achieved through regular meetings, adequate training, engagement with research, and networking with other schools and professionals.

Some added to these conditions those imposed – demanded – by the networks as a requirement of membership of the network or organisation.

- *OPEDUCA network leader: "The organisation will need: i) Strong leadership, persistent yet open to different arguments; ii) Genuine parental partnerships; iii) To bring say and budgets back to the teachers – 'flat', bottom-up organisations; iv) 'Open learning spaces' within the school equipped with (broadband) Internet access; and v) OPEDUCA MasterClass participation for at least 30% of the teachers, and of all those working in OPEDUCA. These can and are met, especially as OPEDUCA-based education is less costly than traditional schooling."*
- *Galileo School network leader: "There are several organisational demands including: schedule flexibility, collaborative teaching teams, planning templates using focusing questions, shared preparation and specific planning time,*

application of the Teaching Effectiveness Framework rubric, and PLC (Professional Learning Community) time to discuss student work."

KIP maintains (Box 13.2) that with two preconditions – teacher training and change in teacher cultures – the successful adoption of the approach is relatively neutral of organisational forms. Such preconditions are nevertheless significantly demanding of schools.

Box 13.2. Komplex Instrukciós Program (KIP)

One of the strongest assets of the programme is its transferability to different cultural and institutional contexts. This capacity to adapt the "know-how" while staying true to the programme's philosophy and principles makes it a powerful method applicable in a wide range of schools. KIP can be applied in any school without major changes in its organisational structure, funding or even teaching curricula.

The main two preconditions for the successful adaptation of KIP are:

1. Teacher training: The first part is a 30- to 60-hour training – mostly for larger groups of a single school, in which teachers get familiar with the KIP methodology. Participants start applying KIP in their daily routines. Mentoring is provided by KIP trainers for a whole academic year. Mentoring also means bilateral visits. At the end of the academic year, and if the school decides to continue, there is another four-year cycle with professional learning support.
2. Change in educators' understanding of their role as teachers, as well as a different approach to the assessment of their pupils' capacities and abilities. KIP calls for acknowledgement of multiple talents.

A demanding aspect of realising ambitious organisational preconditions such as these is highlighted by one of the Japanese clusters, namely that teachers and schools may well have to find the professional expertise within themselves rather than to be able to draw on separate expertise and support from specialist bodies:

"There are no universities, research bodies and board of education in the cluster. High school teachers have sometimes to be a researcher, negotiator, government administrator. Evidence can be useful for the pedagogical approach and for the entrance examination for universities. In Japan, good education is still often judged by results in entrance examinations for universities."

This is autonomy in a genuine educational sense, not understood as isolation (after all, the schools belong to the larger cluster) but as finding the expertise and efficacy within their own collective practice to realise the change.

Another critical demand for organisations is *collaboration*, something described in Box 13.3 as not seemingly new or startling and yet often demanding fundamental cultural shifts in education and schools.

Box 13.3. The importance of collaborative cultures – the Galileo network

Their collaborative approach builds the capacity of teachers, teacher leaders, and school and district leaders. Collaboration may not seem new or startling, yet it demands fundamental cultural shifts in education. Understanding ideas as public, improvable objects challenges common-sense understanding that learning new ideas is about getting different information into one's head, and the skills to implement this knowledge. The assumptions of the status quo are so much part of their everyday experience that it is taken to them as givens.

The change to an inquiry stance, or to knowledge building rather than knowledge transfer, demands rigorous engagement with matters that are not very easy or comfortable. Further, the constant improvement of ideas demands a commitment to getting smarter collectively, not to the competitive hoarding of knowledge that so characterises industrial structures.

Several other networks stress this aspect. This is the case of Amara Berri and the importance given to the 'structures' that make possible the adoption and sustainability of the approach. Some structures 'organise' (e.g. subject departments) and some are related to the human side (group work, projects), but both fuel the collegiality and distributed leadership to guarantee the implementation of the approach. In diverse schools of the Lighthouse network, teachers emphasise the need for a strong commitment to teamwork, as well as the structures that promote collaboration and allow different organisational cultures to join together.

Not surprisingly, an organisational demand that features widely in the above lists (which is discussed in the following sections) is the need for well organised *learning and training* for all involved in the community, especially schools. Different networks emphasised the need for an effective continuous professional development (Amico Robot), or the provision of quality training time – including sharing practice by observation and joint planning (Whole Education).

Among the demands identified for the full implementation of the approach is the *willingness to engage fully with the approach* itself, i.e. to remain true to the full requirements of the model and to be ready to make the organisational changes implied. The tools and methods are given, leaving a major organisational challenge to use and apply them in the schools. These are offered less as conditions or prerequisites, more as the organisational demands intrinsic to the models themselves.

- *Escuela Nueva:* The main variable is the willingness of the community of teachers and professionals to implement the approach. There are requirements such as hexagonal desks and classroom configurations that favour collaborative work. Commitment and leadership are fundamental to implementing the model. In addition, microcentres are key to scaling the innovative approach.
- *Step by Step Benevolent Foundation - ISSA member in Armenia:* The SBS Program enjoys popularity and high reputation and its pedagogical approach serves as the basis for developing the preschool and primary school curriculum in Armenia. The organisational demand of widespread adoption is quality implementation and respect for the pedagogical approach.

- *Lumiar Institute:* The personalised digital platform makes it is more feasible to manage the daily routine and the Mosaic Curriculum; the Digital Mosaic and the pedagogical materials are good for spreading the pedagogical model.

These are taken a step further when the organisational demands are understood as network requirements, as in the case of ISSA, NOII and Creative Partnerships (Box 13.4):

- *ISSA:* ISSA has introduced a licensing process for using the Principles: sound reputation as a professional organisation, expertise about early childhood development and pedagogies, and capacity to work with the resources in the Quality Resource Pack.
- *NOII:* School teams agree to use the spiral of inquiry as the framework for a year-long inquiry; attend up to three face-to-face regional meetings; submit a written case study at the completion of the year; and participate in local showcases of learning and if possible, in the annual provincial symposium.

Box 13.4. Creative partnerships

The organisational demands of Creative partnerships are extensive, well-established and are set out in detail to schools prior to them joining the programme. There is also a detailed handbook to support them throughout their creative learning journey which generally lasts a minimum of two years. The main organisational demand is teacher and school leadership time for in-depth planning, co-delivery with creative practitioners and reflection. Alongside this there is a need for time to be given over to support learners to have an active role. Unlocking curriculum time requires careful consideration and leadership support, particularly in secondary schools where timetables are less flexible than in primary/elementary schools. Effective school leadership support for the programme is a requirement of all participating schools, so that whole-school improvement gains are met. Within each school, the School Coordinator and the teachers directly involved are also required to establish 'teacher clubs'.

In these examples, the conditions are formalised and laid out in detail in handbooks and even licensing procedures. Similarly, with Innova Schools, the model is a required feature not just a desirable, thus giving schools little space to implement shifts in the model. As a consequence, given the rapid growth of the network, the demand for leaders with experience in a particular pedagogical approach becomes more important. This is partially addressed with the use of digital resources to ensure professional learning and leadership, along with partnerships with other organisations to deliver training programmes.

To sum up, a range of conditions and means of meeting the organisational demands are identified by the networks which include factors that one might expect to be on any list: leadership, teacher learning, collaboration, vision. They go further than these broad headings to illustrate what this means in concrete terms and to identify other factors. They place a significant emphasis on time and creating sufficient time within the organisation to meet the demands. They emphasise cultural change, by the organisation and individual teachers, and recognise that technology can liberate organisational resources. Furthermore, they emphasise the development of partnerships and using them strategically. As part of all this, some recognise the importance of being committed to full implementation, and this is supported in some cases by materials and methodologies offering guidelines on how this should be done.

13.4. The networks and professional learning

Already a great deal of the discussion has focused on professional learning – it is indivisible from change, innovation and the work of the networks. This section uses the replies of the networks to focus especially on professional and organisational learning, including the role of the networks in organising such learning. As proposed by Law in Chapter 3, change in general can be conceptualised as learning; little wonder, then, that learning features so prominently in the work of the networks studied in this report.

13.4.1. How the learning is organised

As networks, the 'meso' level groups covered in this study can organise professional learning at different levels – from school to cluster to system-wide and even international – and often at more than one level. Sometimes, this is within particular schools in order to develop the capacity to implement the demanding requirements of the approach; this may itself be demanding in terms of professional commitment and time (see Box 13.5). It may even, as described in the third example, be experienced as 'ground-shaking' by the teachers:

- *Creative Partnerships network leader: "Teachers are supported through an intensive initial two-day Continuous Professional Development (CPD) programme. Back in their school context they then have to make time to work with creative practitioners on the design, implementation, reflection and evaluation of a bespoke creative learning project."*

- *Issa Slovenia network leader and practitioner: "We offer teachers training on different topics connected to the child-centred approach. Training is interactive, done in small groups, and in recent years, we have put strong emphasis on follow-up activities. In our Network we work with coordinators and we also work with directors of the preschools."*

- *OPEDUCA network leader: "The approach is first generally introduced to the whole school staff, and from that a first group of 15-18 teachers are offered a 4-day Master Class. This is a 'ground-shaking' experience for many, not done by classical teacher trainers but from experts outside education, and later by teachers' peer-to-peer. Only after that follows step-by-step try-outs, further teachers in the MasterClass, etc."*

- *Senza Zaino network leader and practitioner: "The network organises training sessions for teachers in each school. The professional trainers teach them the five steps and the vision (the three values and the Global Curriculum Approach). It requires 40 hours of training a year to become a Senza Zaino school at the initial level. Our approach is demanding, but it is a choice for each school and its teachers."*

- *Studio Schools network leader: "Teachers are supported in their professional learning by a member of the school leadership team, one who takes the role of the School Coordinator for the Creative Partnerships programme who also supports the educator learning. Other organisations have provided CPD – colleagues from organisations in USA including High Tech High and the Buck Institute of Education."*

Box 13.5. Better Movers and Thinkers (BMT)

The introduction of the pedagogical approach begins with a whole-school practical session, followed by development meetings with the teachers who teach the target student group. The direct intervention approach, over a 6-9-month period, is undertaken by each of the BMT Staff Tutors, in each of the SAC primary schools.

In the first stage, the Staff Tutor delivers a series of physical education lessons, using the BMT approach, with the targeted classes. There are opportunities for class teachers to observe and to team-teach with support from the Staff Tutor. In the second stage, class teachers deliver parts of the BMT physical education lessons, with their own classes, alongside the BMT Staff Tutor. In the final stage of the intervention, the class teacher delivers a quality physical education session, with support from the BMT Staff Tutor. Opportunities to transfer the BMT approach to the classroom are identified and developed. Post-intervention, assessments are made of Executive Functions development; Pupil Engagement (Leuven's Scale); and Physical Literacy (Processes of Locomotion).

Most of the professional learning during the intervention happens in school, using interaction and dialogue with the Staff Tutors. There is also Education Scotland's online reference bank of scaffolding practices. There are additional in-service sessions on the BMT approach throughout the school year.

The nature of the direct intervention model ensures that there is very close collaboration between the BMT Staff Tutors and the teachers for consistent delivery of the BMT pedagogy. Opportunities to observe peers and provide on-going feedback around the pedagogy are embedded in the model.

The advantage of being able to operate at a more aggregate level than the individual school is a key feature of many networks, while having the influence and range to be able to organise programmes and events from across the system. Further, the promotion of sharing experiences between schools is a valuable resource that adds an extra value of the seminars and courses organised by networks at the local or regional level.

In the CAS network, the intention is to cascade change and scale by creating a cadre of lead teachers who might serve as the fulcrums of hubs in their own local authority. The case of NOII provides an interesting extension of reach by embracing most of the teacher training institutions as well as teachers and schools. The network may even facilitate or organise professional learning at all different levels simultaneously, as it is the case of NPDL, which includes the international and national cluster levels, school districts, and individual schools.

The focus of the professional learning

Naturally, the content of much of the professional learning reported by the networks is for building capacity and expertise in the approaches being promoted. Some are relatively specific, while others are more wide-ranging. The main goals of these professional learning programmes include:

- Developing particular skills such as how to facilitate discussion, how to develop pupils' programming ability effectively, self-assessment strategies, how to prepare educational projects and facilitating the transition from school to work.

- Providing specialised knowledge on subject areas and pedagogical approaches, including self-reflection on their own practices.
- Preparing teachers for cooperation in research and collaboration and networking with their colleagues, including the production of shared knowledge.
- Overcoming the shortcomings in initial teaching training, such as: the excess of theory without practice, contradictions between what is taught in universities and the realities of the classroom.

There is a mix between more formal courses and learning through and with colleagues. Again, an advantage of the network is that it can often pool experience and expertise from different schools rather than collaborating purely in-house.

13.4.2. Network operations

Many of the network operations have been described above, or in the following section describing how fidelity is ensured. This section focuses on aspects describing how the network works in practice. Much of it comes through providing learning leadership within systems and organising ideas, events and forums for shared professional work.

When a network is small, there is the possibility of very regular meetings and good face-to-face contact which promote the network as a cluster of like-minded schools and educators. Small size does not preclude enjoying a visibility and influence far beyond the immediate grouping of professionals. This is the case of Amara Berri, as its pedagogical approach has been reported by diverse media and publications, contributing to its visibility outside the Basque Country. A network is dynamic and spreading when the communication flourishes outside of the formal seminars and conferences as well as within them, as it is the case of NOII through their Spiral of Inquiry methodology. Forging partnerships, including with universities, is an important aspect of some networks. In KIP, wider institutional cooperation plays a major role, not just schools alone. The scholars and civic actors make the programme accessible for future teachers through the university courses, for current teachers through the training, but also for the other stakeholders through the dissemination and advocacy activities. The cooperation between schools, university and the non-governmental organisation is vital, creating a platform for spreading the approach. The ISSA example from Armenia also points to the value of making connections between practitioners in the different levels of the education system who might otherwise rarely come in contact.

> *"We connect educators from different educational levels to promote the child-centred pedagogy and its benefits for creating learning communities. Our members exchange through social media, the Educational Portal, and newsletters."*

The generation and strategic distribution of tools and materials by a central network core is an important function that is critical to its success; it may be providing intelligence and inspiration that otherwise may not be readily available in the system. Two good illustrations come from ISSA and NPDL networks. For ISSA, the *Quality Resource Pack* supports and guides teacher's professional development bridging theory and practice: a guide book for educators, professional development tools, an assessment instrument, a video library, a guidebook for training providers, and advocacy leaflets. On the other hand, NPDL's Exemplars of powerful pedagogical practices represent not only a valuable resource, but a way in which the processes of building these resources engages teachers, other school leaders, and NPDL leadership teams in professional dialogue; develop a shared language and understanding around deep learning; and provide teachers and all NPDL participants with examples of deep learning for their own leverage.

13.4.3. Ensuring fidelity to the approach

The networks emphasise control and guidance, shared design, and collaboration with regards to ensuring fidelity. Some have specific organisational arrangements. The following extracts give a flavour of this range, including those who do not regard it appropriate to enforce one interpretation to which fidelity might be sought. It might be expected some of the differences to be more of emphasis than substance as in reality a range of factors are in play to direct the work of schools towards a particular approach to teaching and learning.

Among the more formal means of ensuring shared direction are:

- *Creative Partnerships:* All schools in the programme work with a Planning and Evaluation Framework which supports schools to deliver their creative learning project(s). The Creative Agent ensures that the project aligns with the Creative Partnerships pedagogical framework as well as meeting school development needs, with a quality assurance process to support fidelity to the Creative Partnerships approach and identify professional learning needs.
- *E2C France:* The pedagogical practices are organised through seminars and the coordination of the pedagogical teams. There is also a national platform to foster the sharing of practices among the different schools from the network.
- *Innova Schools:* The network has built monitoring processes to ensure fidelity to the pedagogical approach, involving: a) Regional directors; b) the teacher observation platform, used by teacher coaches and school leaders which generate information to assess fidelity to the pedagogical approach; and c) research and reports.
- *ISSA* provides licenced members with training and resources on the Quality Principles, especially the Assessment Instrument. There is a team of expert Reliability Coordinators.

The nomination of a particular role – the reliability coordinator, the Creative Agent – is an interesting feature of the latter examples as a means of supporting fidelity. Rubrics may be used to generate information for the institution itself as well as for the network about how well the school is progressing in implementing the approach, backed up by professional learning.

- *ECOLOG:* Schools have to write annual reports. Schools exchange and present experiences at regional in-service workshops. Nine regional network teams support schools and there is the central coordination. Fidelity to the approach is supported by communication, frequent exchanges, meetings, and public presentations.
- *Issa Slovenia:* Fidelity to the approach is assured through regular activities organised within the network, through continuous professional support, building on ISSA pedagogical principles, through personal contacts with directors, coordinators, and teachers.
- *Senza Zaino:* Schools evaluate their fidelity using a self-evaluation chart, made by the SZ staff. The SZ staff also organise visits and auditing meetings on site. Both levels focus on the strong and weak points to plan consolidation or improvement actions.

Some of the networks described this in terms of shared design methodologies and active sharing and collaboration among network members.

- *Amara Barri:* Collegiality is the cornerstone for guaranteeing the implementation of the approach. There are several 'structures' for this: the different departments where teachers meet, leadership, and meetings in local areas of representatives of different schools. Visits to the core school, Amara Berri, alongside other visits to schools are the basic way to learn the model.
- *NOII:* Schools identify the specific focus for their inquiry and the learning strategies that they will explore. Fidelity is enhanced through a common submission form and template for case studies. In the words of a teacher:

  > *"The Network encourages the use of the Spiral of Inquiry to develop a focus for all levels of learning; all members are using the spiral to develop a pathway or framework."*

- *OPEDUCA:* Fidelity to the approach is supported by design work, on the request of the schools themselves, to realise the vision and concept, giving guidance and an implementation plan. As few have the dedication or habit to go for it all the way, OPEDUCA alters the energy and commitment to improve, supported by the cooperation in the network, sharing essentials, fears, and achievements.
- *Studio Schools:* The trust maintains the model by delivering CPD and training to staff at newly-joined and existing Studio Schools. There are regular visits to open schools, to evaluate their progress within the model and identify areas for further development. School principals are encouraged to work collaboratively to assist each other as peers. The Trust also helps establish schools in the first place, and have sought official approval of projects that promote the spirit of the model.
- *Galileo Educational Network*: Consistency with the model is ensured through the combination of professional learning, research and the continual gathering and synthesising of data. There is the feedback shared with design teams, videos to summarise learning, videos of teaching and leading, design-team meetings, research reports, knowledge dissemination at professional and peer-reviewed conferences, and publications. Galileo disseminates its approach and most of the professional learning sessions, videos, and publications are on the website.

The Escuela Nueva has formalised the communities of practitioners who take the lead in the design and implementation as 'microcentres'. These 'microcentres' consist of meetings of those teachers leading the implementation of the model in a school, group of schools or in localities who build up the network and are the core. There, teachers and schools share practices, experiences and help each other, while ensuring fidelity to the approach. One school from the networks reports how the collaborative work of the network of teachers sustains the principles of the model. They are connected through their participation in the 'microcentres', via email and WhatsApp and also through their visits to other schools. Further, the network plays a pivotal role for transferring important reflections, experiences and decisions to the 'microcentres', unifying the criteria and ensuring fidelity to the model.

In Whole Education, on the other hand, there is no attempt to identify and enforce an approach but instead to allow a variety of approaches within the encompassing broad aims of holistic education. Being a voluntary network joined only by schools and organisations that share their mission, members may choose from a wide variety of projects that all embody the core values rather than requiring fidelity. Being in the network includes a membership fee so that schools are incentivised to take part in what the network has to offer.

13.5. Evaluation of the networks and their membership schools

Most – though not all - of the networks report some form of evaluation, whether of themselves as a network or of their member schools or both. In some cases, the network itself functions to provide the methodology, means or requirement to undertake evaluation. A certain number also give an indication of what the evaluative evidence shows about learning, whereas a small number of the networks report that no evaluations have been undertaken. However, even in these cases there is the suggestion that this will be done soon or else that the lack of evaluative evidence is a problem to be rectified.

Where evaluations have been undertaken, the level of detail offered about the extent and robustness of the evaluations undertaken varies widely. In some cases, innovative evaluation methods have been adopted in tune with the innovative nature of the network's approach, but sometimes quite conventional achievement and attainment measures are used. The next table summarises the evaluation on learning that these networks have implemented so far, and outlines its main outcomes:

Table 13.1. Evaluations carried out by the networks

Network	Evaluation on learning*	Outcomes
Amara Berri	No formal evaluation to date.	
Amico Robot	No formal evaluation to date.	
Art of Learning	No formal evaluation to date.	
Better Movers and Thinkers	Assessments include engagement with learning, resilience, and learner willingness to take risks in other curricular areas, as well as Physical Literacy.	Improvements in executive functions development, engagement and Physical Literacy.
Escuela Nueva	Diverse reports carried out by external agencies.	Success in providing quality schooling in rural and under-served groups, and improvement in student cognitive and socio-emotional skills.
Innova Schools	There is an Education Quality Evaluation Office, running a standardised tests system to measure student achievement and studies assessing the results of innovations being tried. Innova Schools is also evaluated externally by the national ministry, which conducts national tests for 2nd and 8th grade students each year. They have also been involved in two external studies, conducted by GRADE, a Peruvian NGO.	Data shows that Innova Schools perform better than other public and private schools.
KIP	The lead school has been evaluated several times. Lack of formal evaluations in the network.	Results in the national competences tests are at the system average, despite the high numbers of socio-economically disadvantaged children and those with learning and behavioural difficulties. They achieve 10-15% higher scores than schools of the same socio-cultural background.
Lumiar Institute	No formal evaluation to date.	
NOII	In 2013 a research study was commissioned by the federal government in Canada to examine the impact of school participation in the Aboriginal Enhancement schools Network.	Positive observations about the impact on teachers, support workers and learners and also used the term 'catalytic affiliation' to describe the connection that educators experienced with the network.
NPDL	First report with 'emerging' findings published in 2016.	Emerging data about the growing implementation of the framework and the competences targeted by the approach.
Senza Zaino	The most important evaluation was in 2010 on 500 students, half from traditional schools and half from the network schools.	More autonomy and high levels of empathy and collaboration among Senza Zaino students.

Network	Evaluation on learning*	Outcomes
Studio Schools	Small-scale evaluations of aspects of the model have been done through the work with schools, in which external evaluators are involved. There has not yet been a full-scale national evaluation of the work that Studio Schools are doing.	Not provided.
A New Direction	No formal/external evaluation to date.	
Creative Partnerships	Extensive and long-term independent evaluation which has supported its evolution, helped to establish its pedagogy and theories of learning and provided a better understanding of its impact.	The evaluations have shown, for instance, that programme schools saw significant improvements in pupil attendance, behaviour and attainment, as well as in parental engagement.
ECOLOG	Several external evaluations have been performed with quantitative and qualitative methods.	Participation in ECOLOG improves understanding of EE/ESD issues, supports commitment and offers space for students in concrete activities.
ESCXEL Project	Statistical reports providing diagnosis for local planning and qualitative tools – e.g. analysis of school's documents or school-family relationships.	These schools with good results and affirmative leadership are improving their processes and results after appropriating network proposals.
ISN	No formal/external evaluation to date.	
ISSA	Different reports have been published about the implementation and impact of the framework in 2010 and 2017. Some local clusters also reported independent evaluations with national quality agencies.	Impact on the quality of individual practice, schools and communities (e.g. better partnerships with families, introduction of a 'culture' of quality), and on education policy and practice.
Lighthouse	In the process of being evaluated.	
OPEDUCA	Beside the almost constant evaluation of the schools' stakeholders in the local context, there has been an extensive EU-funded evaluation of OPEDUCA in 8 European countries.	Concludes that the approach is 'valid and applicable'.
Red Escuelas Líderes	No formal evaluation to date.	
E2C France	Each E2C cluster must undergo an audit on all its sites every four years, done by a third-party organisation, l'AFNOR, which leads to a report listing strong and weak points and pathways for progress; the pedagogical principles are also evaluated at this time.	Not provided.
Whole Education	No formal evaluation to date.	
CAS	The network has been evaluated and the results appear in both a final report and a journal article. In both cases, the evaluation mainly concerned the teachers themselves, their attitudes towards the network, and the change in their practice.	Positive outcomes in teachers' professional development and some improvement on the learning competences targeted in the approach.
E-norssi	Universities evaluate the schools at some level, but generally the network has not been evaluated.	Not provided.
Galileo	Various evaluations exist in the form of a book, a significant number of research publications in peer-reviewed and professional journals, and doctoral dissertations.	Proof of evidence that student learning was being impacted (high school completion rates, improvements in Provincial Achievement Test Results and numerous parent surveys, teacher surveys and student surveys).
Network of Innovation Schools	No formal evaluation to date.	

* Note: Here it is described those evaluations that explicitly or partially addressed the assessment of the impact on learning and, whenever possible, carried out by external or independent researchers. Hence, self-reports have been excluded, or evaluations too focused on the implementation of the approach itself or the experiences of teachers rather than students' learning.

A quick overview of Table 13.1 reveals that a large minority of the networks are still in the process of implementing an assessment focused on learning outcomes. Out of the networks that did carry out evaluations, 37% report moderate or some positive outcomes, while the remaining 23% describe positive outcomes in particular dimensions (such as teacher's positive feelings), but are not conclusive in relation to learning outcomes.

These results need to be read with caution, given the different nature of these networks, the contexts in which they operate, and the educational goals they are aiming at, among other variables. In the case of the "Innovation Promotion Networks" and the

"Professional Learning Networks", their main mission is the dissemination and sharing of innovative practices among teachers, and schools and are therefore particularly focused on evaluating the extent of reflective practices and the promotion of skills among teachers. Even in the "Pedagogical Approach Networks", a good deal of emphasis is put onto the teaching of new competences, skills and on establishing different relationships between teachers, learners and content, rather than on measuring learning outcomes *per se*. Therefore, it is not surprising that the evaluation of a number of the networks is self- and peer-review. Of note is the role that the networks themselves play in these knowledge-building exercises, including by facilitating peer review within the networks or by requiring the production of self-evaluation reports using standardised rubrics and methodologies, with the aim of sharing the results within the network.

Some of the evaluation outcomes are more specific and relate especially to the aims of the networks – i.e. the member schools are successful in achieving the priority objectives of the network. Furthermore, all of these networks are commonly 'tested' by national assessments and evaluations, which also explains why they have not developed in full their own measurement tools. Those who explicitly mention their results in system-wide assessments report average or better performance compared to other schools. In some cases, as when networks focus on vulnerable students – Escuela Nueva, Red Escuelas Líderes, KIP –, to achieve an average performance on national tests is a clear mark of success.

In other cases, such as Lighthouse, Art of Learning, Better Movers and Thinkers, OPEDUCA or NPDL, these approaches are very recent or relatively new, and are still in the process of being implemented in the schools that are part of the network. Further, to show a balanced picture as a whole of networks that are present at a national – or even international - level or that are operating in highly diverse contexts is inherently challenging.

Even when evaluation *per se* is not conducted, the network may facilitate peer observation of practice. These evaluations have been excluded in the previous chart, but it is clear that some schools reflect that positive change is happening, although the pace of change is gradual. The following passage from an ESCXEL teacher reveals, with refreshing frankness, that positive results in the terms of the network are closely related to the aims and approaches of the educators involved: when they have embraced the aims their results improve but when they are not so convinced the results may actually decline.

> *"The best schools, with good results and affirmative leadership are improving their processes and results after appropriating our proposals. Those more conservative and resistant tend to show a decline, mainly because principals and teachers do not embrace intensive changes."*

13.6. In summary

- The networks and their participating schools largely agreed that the approaches they promote are more demanding than the main body of traditional practice, thus requiring more expert knowledge and reflective practice, and allowing the room and time for its exercise.
- A range of conditions are identified by the networks to ensure the implementation of innovative approaches, and stress the importance of schools being wholly committed to addressing cultural/organisational change.

- Professional learning is given central importance by the networks, and is the core mission and activity of many of them. The networks provide learning leadership within systems, organising events and forums for shared professional work, aiming at building capacity and expertise in the approaches being promoted.
- Most of the networks report some form of evaluation, whether of themselves, as a network or of their member schools or both. In some cases, the network itself functions to provide the methodology, means or requirement to undertake evaluation. Where the evaluative evidence exists, it is generally positive about its impact.

ORGANISATION FOR ECONOMIC CO-OPERATION AND DEVELOPMENT

The OECD is a unique forum where governments work together to address the economic, social and environmental challenges of globalisation. The OECD is also at the forefront of efforts to understand and to help governments respond to new developments and concerns, such as corporate governance, the information economy and the challenges of an ageing population. The Organisation provides a setting where governments can compare policy experiences, seek answers to common problems, identify good practice and work to co-ordinate domestic and international policies.

The OECD member countries are: Australia, Austria, Belgium, Canada, Chile, the Czech Republic, Denmark, Estonia, Finland, France, Germany, Greece, Hungary, Iceland, Ireland, Israel, Italy, Japan, Korea, Latvia, Luxembourg, Mexico, the Netherlands, New Zealand, Norway, Poland, Portugal, the Slovak Republic, Slovenia, Spain, Sweden, Switzerland, Turkey, the United Kingdom and the United States. The European Union takes part in the work of the OECD.

OECD Publishing disseminates widely the results of the Organisation's statistics gathering and research on economic, social and environmental issues, as well as the conventions, guidelines and standards agreed by its members.

OECD PUBLISHING, 2, rue André-Pascal, 75775 PARIS CEDEX 16
(96 2018 01 1 P) ISBN 978-92-64-08536-7 – 2018